CW00687856

The Forbidden Game

The Forbidden Game

Mike Rylance

League Publications Ltd
2005

First published 1999
This revised edition 2005

Published in Great Britain
by League Publications Ltd
Wellington House, Briggate, Brighouse,
West Yorkshire. HD6 1DN

A CIP catalogue record for this book is available from the British Library
ISBN 1-901347-05-2

Designed and typeset by League Publications Ltd
Manufactured in the EU by L.P.P.S. Ltd, Wellingborough, Northants

Contents

Preface

François Récaborde was one of the first Frenchmen to play rugby league. Recruited by Jean Galia to take part in the pioneering tour of England in 1934, Récaborde lined up at loose forward in France's first international team before going on to play a crucial part in establishing the rugby league club at Pau, which figured among the ten professional sides in the opening 1934-35 season. Alongside Récaborde in Galia's touring team and then in the France side which faced England was stand-off Charles Mathon, who was to become a prime mover in setting up rugby league in France's second city, Lyon. With Mathon as captain, US Lyon-Villeurbanne won the inaugural Coupe de France.

When war broke out and Germany occupied France six years later, both Récaborde and Mathon were to be found playing important roles as resistance leaders. But when France was eventually liberated in 1944 neither was there to take part in the celebrations. Récaborde had been deported by the Germans to the concentration camp at Buchenwald for his work in securing safe passage for Allied pilots. Mathon, falsely accused of being a Gestapo agent, had been summarily shot by members of the *maquis* whom he himself had helped escape German clutches.

These are men of heroic stature and yet they have never received their due acclaim from the rugby league world at large. There are others like them. The achievement of Galia and his sixteen pioneers, who successfully launched rugby league in France with barely adequate financial backing and only the experience of a handful of matches, was extraordinary. Today, as the game still seeks to push back its boundaries, that feat appears simply incredible, impossible.

French rugby league's ability to survive, in the face of extreme adversity, is hardly less astonishing. Prejudice, spite and the refusal in some quarters to allow the game a fair deal, have continually dogged *le rugby à treize*, a victim of the war like a number of its players. Those officials, players and supporters who, down the years, have helped the game in France to endure all hazards consequently deserve our admiration as well as our support. This book is therefore dedicated to those *treizistes de la première heure* whose vision and courage allowed rugby league to enter a new dimension across the Channel; and to those who have since sustained the *treiziste* cause against all odds.

The official archives of the French Rugby League did not however survive the Vichy period, so that important aspects of that first era of rugby league in France have become less than transparent. Although the French have begun to examine their wartime past with some rigour, a reluctance to discuss its darker aspects is still evident among some of those who lived through that period. Equally the ever-decreasing number of eye-witnesses who are able to recall accurately the events of their youth are not easy to locate. Those who did come to my assistance are gratefully acknowledged below.

My task in writing this book would have been immeasurably harder without the helpfulness of certain individuals. In the absence of official archives or record-keeping body the work of Jean Larronde has been an immense boon: not only did he place his own research at my disposal but painstakingly and unfailingly answered my many queries over several years. I am indebted to my *Treize-magazine* colleagues for their assistance: to the late André Passamar, a colossus among rugby league writers, whose own *Encyclopédie* provided the initial spark, and who pointed me in the right direction many times; to Henri Andrieu, who, despite his own hectic schedule, ensured access to important material; to René Verdier, in whom the *treiziste* flame has burned brightly ever since he played as a young boy in the curtain-raiser to Villeneuve's first rugby league match, and who has been a fount of documentation; and to Jacques Cavezzan, who opened up new avenues in Lyon. I am grateful also to Jérôme Cavalli, who collaborated with me in the early stages of my research; to Jacques Jorda, who inimitably provided food for thought; to Noël Altèze, whose knowledge of rugby in Roussillon is unrivalled and who provided me with a great deal of invaluable information; to Louis Bonnery, Raymond Revert and Jean Roques, whose assistance on various matters was willingly offered; to Pierre Lafond, Georges Pastre and Jacqueline Pastorello, who fielded specific enquiries; and latterly to Robert Fassolette, whose comradeship and advice as we ploughed parallel furrows was greatly appreciated.

It was both pleasurable and enlightening to hear the views and reminiscences of the following ex-players, most of whom are sadly no longer with us: the late Antonin Barbazanges, Jean Barrès, René Barnoud, Sylvain Bès, Paul Déjean, Laurent Lambert and Augustin Saltraille. I also thank Madame Marcelle Galia Kaplan, the late Madame Marcelle Mathon and Madame Arlette Gironde for sharing memories of their husbands' careers and for providing photographs and other material. I am similarly indebted to the late tennis-player and government minister, Jean Borotra, for allowing me to interview him.

I wish to acknowledge the assistance given by the staff of the following institutions: the Archives Nationales, Bibliothèque Nationale and ARCPP; the departmental archives of the Gironde and the Haute-Garonne; the municipal archives of Villeneuve-sur-Lot, with particular thanks to the curator Hélène Bergon-Lagés, and those of Bordeaux, Pau, Perpignan, Toulouse and Vichy; and the archives of *La Dépêche* newspaper. I am also grateful to numerous writers, among them the journalists who reported on rugby league during the period covered by this book. Their work is acknowledged in either the bibliography or footnotes section, though sadly many journalists of the pre-war period, particularly in England, wrote without a byline. Wherever possible, sources have been indicated, although the provenance of some material, taken from cuttings and scrapbooks, has unfortunately not been possible to identify. I am similarly thankful for the work of various unknown photographers whose work has been passed on to me from private collections. I apologise to copyright holders for any infringement but hope they will understand that the main purpose of this book is not a commercial one.

On this side of the Channel, Robert Gate generously provided both source material and answered many questions, for which I am indebted, as did the RFL's archivist, Tony Collins. I am also grateful for the assistance of Neil Tunnicliffe; for the valuable suggestions made by Neal Rigby; for the encouragement of the late Tony Pocock and Harry Edgar; for the academic introductions provided by Professor Roderick Kedward of Sussex University and Jim Dolamore of Leeds University; and for the help of the staff of Wakefield Library. I also wish to thank colleagues at League Publications, particularly Tim Butcher and Tony Hannan, for bringing this project into production, and Danny Spencer for this second edition.

No less important has been the interest and patience of my wife, Judy, and daughter, Laura, both at home and in distant corners of France. For that I am grateful too.

Finally I should like to record my gratitude to my late father, Ron Rylance, who, at stand-off one May afternoon at the Parc des Princes, side-stepped France's full-back to touch down for an inspirational try.

Chapter One
THE FRENCH PERSPECTIVE

Salvador Dali called the railway station at Perpignan the centre of the universe. The civic authorities were so pleased by this flattering if unexpected description that they in turn commemorated the flamboyant artist by naming the square outside the station after him. It's not immediately clear, however, as you step off the train, what Dali had in mind. Unusually for a painter, there are no visual clues. Even as you walk out into the street, among the parked cars and loading bays, a significant vista fails to open up. The claim seems just surreal.

It depends perhaps on where you're coming from. For Dali, born on the Spanish side of the Pyrenees at Figueras, Perpignan was the first city on the route to wider horizons where his talent would find greater expression and recognition. From this point of view Perpignan offers new perspectives.

At the same time, it is a dark, brooding city that looks in on itself, even though open stretches of Mediterranean beach are a twenty-minute drive away and the heights of Canigou and the Pyrenees the same distance in another direction. Palm trees line the main thoroughfare and you can have dinner peacefully in the shade they cast over the restaurant *terrasse*, but there are sombre alleyways too, where even the fierce sun doesn't penetrate for long. Smart boutiques line the now-picturesque precincts which run parallel with streets of flaking buildings where washing is hung out and the pavement is never dry.

This is the capital of the French Catalans. It has none of the sedate, self-assured oneness of other regional *préfectures*. Too many influences are at play for that. There's something here of Spain, something of North Africa, both past and present. This is a city with an edge and its people have an intensity that contrasts with the openness of their nature.

In 1929 Dali painted one of his first surrealist compositions. In English it's known as *The Lugubrious Game* or, depending on the translation, *The Dismal Sport*. Now there's absolutely no evidence to suggest that Dali was interested in that other essential element of Catalan culture, the game of rugby. But it's the kind of coincidence that surrealists found so enlightening that makes us think of applying both titles to rugby union in France at that same time, before its partial metamorphosis into rugby league.

It was in 1934, the year of the birth of rugby league in France, that the Perpignan club, the Treize Catalan was founded. Until joining forces with neighbouring St Estève in 2000, it was one of only three French clubs to remain in continuous existence since then. Perpignan therefore throws open another door: to the game of *rugby à treize*. Beyond the Catalan region, with its own nucleus of important clubs, the world of French rugby league fans out before you. Toulouse, Villeneuve and Bordeaux lie in a direct line north-west of here, Albi and Carcassonne to the north, Carpentras, Avignon and then Lyon over in the east. These are some of the towns and cities where rugby league has survived for more than seventy years. But the present-day situation of rugby league in France has been shaped by the unique circumstances surrounding its birth and its first period of existence. Those were the seminal years in which the *treiziste* spirit developed, in contrast to, and often at odds with the older code of rugby.

Catalans played key roles during that period. None more so than Jean Galia, who brought the game to France, or, perhaps more precisely, brought the French to the game. It all started, they say, with a *coup de coeur*, a sudden attraction, a reaction in favour of something new and against the familiar. Since then the game here has always been played, followed and talked about with emotion. French rugby league was not made exactly in the image of the English game. It was and is shaped by the characteristics of the place and people.

In the foyer of the old Hôtel de France I met two great ex-players, Augustin "Tintin" Saltraille, XIII Catalan's stand-off before the war and an outstanding coach of junior teams, and Paul "Popaul" Déjean, who succeeded him in the same team after the war before going on to represent the national side and the Catalans de France.

The dual identity suggested by that last-named team is felt throughout this region and is replicated in other areas of the south of France where the people have a double allegiance.

"We're French, but we're also a race apart," says Déjean. "We are both Catalan and French and rugby is very much part of the Catalan mentality. Whenever we played, it was fixed in our minds that we were the heart of the region we were representing, we were defending our colours of blood and gold, with the passion of a proud country."[1]

As in the North of England rugby league was taken up here by men whose work was hard and physical. The miners of Yorkshire and Lancashire found their counterparts in the men who worked the land throughout the south-west of France. And, as in England, a philosophy of how the game should be played has evolved over the years, encapsulated in a number of golden rules. The relative value of these truisms varies according to the country in which the game is played. Tintin Saltraille, who, as an *éducateur*, was responsible for introducing generations of players to rugby league, strings out one pearl of wisdom after another.

"You don't receive the ball, you go and get it," he says, hands reaching forwards in illustration, as if running on to a pass. He follows it up with a related theory: "Without acceleration there's no penetration." You can't make a break from a standing start.

"You don't neglect defence," he continues, for this aspect of the game is less appreciated in France than the more spectacular attacking skills. "But the best attack is better than the best defence."[2]

"Rugby league is about entertaining the public," adds Déjean. "If you enjoy yourself, others will enjoy watching you."[3]

The French concept of rugby league contrasts strongly with the pragmatism and percentages of what they call the Anglo-Saxon approach. French organisation on the field of play has always relied more on individual decision-making than the game plan, on the quick thinking of star players rather than the set move, while in defence, tough as they may be, they have lacked the cohesiveness of the Australians and the British.

"We should not imitate the Australians," says Saltraille. "We are Latins. We thrive on artistry and inspiration."[4]

But as most of the rest of the rugby league world becomes increasingly professionalised, France is still trying to shed its role as the gifted amateur. Yet it remains a marvel - and a compliment to the game's origins - that a country with such a rich cultural heritage and whose people have characteristics we do not always share, should have taken so readily to this sport which emanates from a landscape so different from their own.

It is in France that the spirit of rugby league exists in its most concentrated form, for *treiziste* attitudes have been shaped by the game's struggle for existence there, which has never been less than turbulent. The scale of French rugby league's development in the years leading up to the war was one of the great sporting successes, its rise a triumph over the discrimination and hostility which beset the game at every turn. Its sudden demise, after only six seasons, was the result of one of sport's great injustices, which still finds echoes up to the present day.

It has often been said that in order to understand modern French attitudes you have to look back to the Second World War and the period leading up to it. The same is true of *le rugby à treize*, whose progress in those early years defied reason but not, ultimately, the sinister forces which were bent on its destruction.

Chapter Two

THE STATE OF THE UNION

Catalan rugby has always been punctuated with controversy and, true to character, Catalans played an important part in the tempestuous events which led to the establishment of rugby league in France. But although the Perpignan club was a founder member of the Ligue Française de Rugby à Treize, the land of *la race* was not destined to become the birthplace of the game in France.

Had it not been for the tendency of Catalan players to migrate to other parts of France, Perpignan might well have provided the setting. On the other hand one of the big provincial cities could equally well have become the cradle of rugby league: Bordeaux, for example, where one of France's oldest rugby clubs was established and which would be home to one of the strongest rugby league clubs; or its rival, Toulouse, another important centre which attracted the top players; or even Lyon, whose major rugby club had figured in three consecutive championship finals and which was to take to the new game with enthusiasm. But great events do not necessarily unfold in great cities.

Although it would have a role to play, Paris, the seat of the status quo, was an unlikely scene of revolution, despite its association with rugby from the earliest days. It was in the capital that the first important French rugby clubs had formed in the 1880s, after the game had been taken across the Channel by English enthusiasts, who were responsible for establishing the first club in France to play something resembling rugby at Le Havre in 1872. The membership of the Le Havre Athletic Club can be guessed at by their choice of colours - a combination of Oxford's dark blue and the light blue of Cambridge. The first club to be set up in the capital, Paris Football Club, founded in 1879, lasted only seven years but by then Racing Club de France and Stade Français, who remain a power in the land today, had been established, drawing their players from the same kind of background as in England, where the rugby-playing public schools provided the model. Pupils and former pupils of the great Paris *lycées*, university students, the middle and upper classes, professional men - these were the first French rugby players, often playing alongside or against expatriate Englishmen of similar standing. From the beginning the game carried an exclusive label. And since the purpose of these clubs was as much social as sporting, membership went hand in hand with privilege. Rugby was a sport favoured in this society for its snob value and was much more esteemed than association football which was already attracting the wrong sort of person. Although in fact both of those highly selective Parisian sports clubs, Racing and Stade Français, ran soccer sides, they did so without the enthusiasm which they reserved for rugby.[1] In more class-conscious times than our own the well-to-do did not, as a rule, waste their leisure time consorting with their social inferiors. They preferred to pack down with their peers.

Clubs were soon set up in other French cities such as Bordeaux, Grenoble, Lyon and Toulouse. But if the game began to take on a provincial aspect, it acquired little in terms of social diversity. University students and *lycée* pupils, who in those days tended to come from a much narrower social range than now, were largely responsible for taking rugby outside the capital, sometimes assisted by English residents in certain cities. Rugby was introduced to Perpignan, for example, by a pupil at the Lycée Michelet in Paris, on his return to the Collège de Perpignan in 1888.[2] Similarly the first game to be held in Lézignan was played in 1893 by students returning from their studies in Toulouse.[3] Carcassonne's first club was founded in 1899 by the sons of well-off families who had also learned the game while at the *lycée* in Toulouse. The high subscription fee ensured that the club's members came from similar backgrounds to its founders and kept the riff-raff at bay.[4] Paris's rugby supremacy began to be challenged. Until the appearance of the Bordeaux club, Stade Bordelais, in the 1899 final, the French championship had been dominated by Parisian teams. But from then on Bordeaux appeared in every championship final up to 1911 except one. Clubs from Toulouse and Lyon and even from the smaller cities of Perpignan, Bayonne and Tarbes were also finalists in the period leading up to the First World War, illustrating the application and ability which players in the south-west had quickly developed. As rugby spread geographically, so its players gradually began to represent a wider spectrum. Partly as a result of the creation of clubs at the workplace, rugby was able to cross the social divide. Throughout France, but particularly in the south, the game began to attract players - and, just as significantly, spectators - from all walks of life.

By the time war broke out in 1914, rugby's growing popularity was already showing signs of the troubles which would afflict the game in later years. Paul Voivenel, a doctor and official who, like other notables of the French Rugby Union, also wrote regularly on the sport, described with easily detectable irony the worrying situation in the south: "The crowds took to the game with exaggerated passion. Already the big clubs were arguing over players. As if by chance famous players became owners of cafés in towns bitten by the rugby bug ... As if by chance Englishmen settled in provincial towns and trained teams in which they were the best players."[5]

Instances of violence both on and off the pitch were being recorded. "Troublesome incidents" were reported, for example, at the match between Racing Club Narbonne and the Association Sportive of Carcassonne in 1912.[6] Referees were becoming the focus of crowd hostility. A warning to match officials was typically sounded by a Toulouse journalist writing in *Rugby*: "If you referee a match at Carcassonne and the home team gets beaten, it will be you who first feels the weight of that defeat."[7]

In the period immediately following the First World War rugby reached a peak of popular appeal in France. Indeed it was partly because of the war, when the call to arms brought about exchanges between soldiers that would not be possible in civilian life, that the game took hold to such an extent. Although the sport failed to sustain its early growth in certain areas such as the north, the rate at which it was taken up in other regions, particularly the south-west, was rapid. The total of 241 clubs in existence throughout France in 1919 leapt to a peak of 881 just four seasons later.[8] No longer a game played by a privileged minority in the larger cities, rugby was now also established in much smaller communities and had become accessible to all.

Rugby was not the only form of sporting activity which experienced a boom in public interest at this time. Athletics, cycling and soccer, which also originally came under the umbrella of the same governing body, the Union des Sociétés Françaises des Sports Athlétiques, all showed an upsurge in club membership. Much of this interest was to do with the increased amount of free time that the working man had at his disposal, following the reduction in the length of the working day. There was also a growing public awareness of the benefits of physical exercise, a notion which was still relatively new to the majority of the population. The media too had a part to play. Radio commentaries of international matches and finals were a regular occurrence from the mid-20s, while newspapers gave increased space to sport, leading eventually to the appearance of numerous specialist sports publications, from dailies to monthlies.

Geographically, the major expansion occurred within the triangle formed by Bordeaux, Bayonne and Perpignan, with the result that the south-west eventually came to be identified as rugby's stronghold. According to figures published for the season 1921-22 half of the clubs in France were located within this region.[9] Various reasons have been put forward for the game's success in this corner of France: the English presence in such places as Bordeaux and Pau, for example.[10] The popularity in the Bordeaux area of a sport resembling touch rugby, known as *barette*, may have led to the early assimilation of the English game. Political and religious connections have even been suggested: some have detected a preference for rugby in predominantly republican areas, whereas strongly catholic and royalist regions appeared to favour soccer.[11] The origins of the enthusiasm for rugby in certain parts of France are complex, but among them must surely be - though this is not exclusive to these regions - the correspondence between the tough, physical character of work in these areas and the nature of the game itself.

Such a phenomenal increase in the sport in so short a period brought problems. The growth in the number of active participants was accompanied by a similar explosion in terms of spectators. If the working man now had more time to play sport, he also had the leisure to watch matches and the means to do so. The money which spectators handed over at the turnstile every Sunday allowed club officials to have the funds at their disposal to create winning teams. Players could be paid bonuses as a greater incentive to victory and new players could be bought to strengthen the team. In short rugby was becoming professionalised.

But sport must also be organised and administered at a level beyond the purely local. The rugby section of the old USFSA had broken away to create the Fédération Française de Rugby, established in 1920 to cater for its specific needs. Though a specific governing body was clearly desirable and necessary, its officials soon found difficulties - at an ideological level, apart from anything else - in keeping pace with grass-roots developments. One of the new organisation's responsibilities was to administer the championship in which, at the first stage, clubs would compete against one another on a regional basis in order then to qualify for the second phase, which was organised on a national level. This quite logical format gave rise to immense difficulties of regulation. The phenomenon of modern sport, as it had developed in the late nineteenth and early twentieth centuries, had resulted in games becoming clearly codified, with precise rules and adjudication. But the spirit of those older, much more chaotic games played between neighbouring communities had not been lost either. If anything the partisanship was enhanced by the mushrooming of clubs which became the sudden focus of their community's pride and identity.

Crowd figures for the championship final reveal the escalating interest which the competition aroused. Spectators at the early finals were numbered usually in their hundreds, but the 1903 final, played at Bordeaux, and that of 1905, held at Toulouse, drew crowds of 5,000 and 6,000 respectively. By 1909 the final was being watched by a crowd of 15,000 - a figure which remained more or less constant until the outbreak of war. By the time the championship resumed in 1920, crowds had risen again to an average of 20,000.

The replayed championship final of 1925, contested by Carcassonne and Perpignan, who had fought out a scoreless draw a week earlier, also showed how emotions stirred by rugby could run out of control. No doubt the very confined spaces of the Narbonne stadium had something to do with it. The ground was so packed that large numbers of spectators stood close up to the touchlines while others were perched on the roof of the main stand. The hot weather, in contrast to the torrential downpour of the previous week, also brought the enthusiasms of the 20,000 crowd to the surface. It soon became clear that the fans' incitement of their teams and the players' response to such polarity of emotions threatened to reduce the game to an unregulated battle between two communities. After only a quarter of an hour's play fighting broke out between spectators on the touchline, the first of several disturbances. A brilliant 70-metre try scored by the Perpignan centre Roger Ramis just before half-time would determine the outcome of the game, but not before brawling between players had ensured that this final would be remembered for the wrong reasons. Such was the atmosphere that the referee, exasperated by the interruptions in play, took the unusual step of making an announcement through the public address system that he would abandon the match if the crowd persisted in inciting the players. All of this caused the FFR president, Octave Léry, to reflect: "Is there any other spectacle which is able to stir the crowd to such an extent and provoke such outbursts of enthusiasm and passion? I do not believe there is."[12] The correspondent of the *Miroir des Sports* put it more strongly. "Played like this," he wrote, "rugby is more akin to the ancient games of the Roman circuses."

The intense local rivalry bred by rugby's championship led to practices which the sport's governing body was unable to effectively control. Ambitious club officials, responding to the demands of the public and armed with the money paid by partisan crowds, set about strengthening their teams as well as trying to make sure that they looked after the interests of their own players. The amateur ethos, one of the pillars of the rugby establishment both in France and Britain, became severely compromised, not to say ignored. Players switched from one club to another, attracted by offers from chairmen who could afford to pay good money. Meanwhile the Federation, despite promising measures to control the movement of players, looked in danger of losing its grip on the game.

The most spectacular example of this migration occurred in 1926, when almost half of the US Perpignan team and their coach, Gilbert Brutus, decamped in order to improve the fortunes of the Quillan club, some 50 miles west of Perpignan in the neighbouring *département* of Aude. They were lured there by the generosity of the club's great patron and chairman, Jean Bourrel, owner of the hat-making factories which were based in the town and on which the local wealth was largely founded. This small town, surrounded on almost all sides by the thickly wooded foothills of the Pyrenees, put together such a convincing alloy of a rugby team that it appeared in consecutive championship finals between 1928 and 1930.

Quillan's record had been preceded by US Perpignan, who had achieved a similar feat between 1924 and 1926. A rift in the Perpignan club after their defeat in the 1926 final was exploited by Bourrel - a predecessor of the millionaire chairman now common in football and, increasingly, rugby league - who quickly signed up seven of their players. Quillan began a swift rise through the divisions, thanks to their imported players, though they also had the merit of playing in an attractive, attacking style which stood out at a time of generalised brutality and negative play.

Their greatest test came the following season when the *émigrés* returned to Perpignan to play a championship match in March 1927. In front of a fiercely one-sided crowd eager to see the home side punish the mercenary deserters, a violent match took place which more resembled a bullfight than a game of rugby. It resulted in the death, albeit accidental, of the Quillan hooker, Gaston Rivière, following the collapse of a scrum. Such turmoil was not unusual. Some six months later, a purely domestic fracas broke out when the two main rivals from the same city, US Perpignan and the Quins, met in a stormy game where no fewer than ten players were sent off.

Incidents such as these and the overall decline in standards moved the journalist and FFR official Dr Paul Voivenel to write an apocalyptic article headed *"Le Rugby de muerte"*.[13] The analogy with the *corrida* was well chosen. Voivenel, seeing greed, unscrupulousness and a win-at-all-costs attitude all around him, spoke of the serious, even criminal consequences of the path rugby had taken.

"Rugby has become a brutal game in which money has corrupted virtually everything," he wrote. Remarking how clubs came to find themselves with spiralling budgets, the writer looked back with affection to that early period when rugby was played purely for its own sake by players who were apparently bred to know how to behave themselves.

"Our old student game of rugby has become a sport which for many has become a business," he continued. "The rewards are seen in terms of money. Once, rugby fanatics, like the players, formed a certain aristocracy. Nowadays entire towns are whipped up into the frenzy of a mob and the importance of the result becomes wildly exaggerated ..."

Voivenel wrote of the consequences of what he called the *"crime sportif"*. Referees or visiting fans might be maimed as a result of violence at matches and a similar fate could befall players taken out by opponents bent on asserting their superiority by whatever means. His comments would prove prophetic, and for a second reason, too. For its present crimes, he predicted, rugby would "pay dearly, very dearly. Like at the bullfights."

At least one of the teams the writer must have had in mind contested the 1929 championship final. After losing the 1928 final to Pau by 6-4, Quillan won through to the final again the following year when they met Lézignan, their local rivals. Lézignan had narrowly won a stormy semi-final, beating Béziers 9-6 after extra time. It was yet another match marked by ill-temper and crowd scenes. Among the many instances of dirty play which were reported, including gouging, one foul by a Lézignan forward, unpunished by the referee, led to an all-in brawl, which in turn led to a pitch invasion by spectators. Play was held up for several minutes before continuing in the same brutal manner as before. "In the midst of a tumult impossible to describe," wrote one journalist, "the game resumed, violent, bitter, with no redeeming features."[14] A cartoon alongside the match report expressed even more vividly the aggressiveness shown by both players and public. The referee cowers in a corner of the dressing-room, the fist of an enraged fan comes through the wall, while a club official puts his head round the door to tell the referee, "We've only got a local bobby to help you get out of the ground. You'd be better off sending for a solicitor to make your will!"[15]

For the first time, then, two clubs from the same area - one of them, Quillan, situated 30 miles to the south of Carcassonne, the other 25 miles to the east - contested the championship final of France. The ultimate honour in French club rugby had never been contested by teams from towns so small - Quillan numbered around 2500 inhabitants, Lézignan 5000. Here was the proof of how the game of rugby had outstripped its exclusive origins, had been taken over by the working classes and had touched the remotest corners of the provinces.

The two teams however were quite different. The Union Sportive Quillanaise was a team of handsomely rewarded outsiders who played an open style of rugby. For FC Lézignan, by contrast, it was a matter of great pride that almost all their players were locally produced and, particularly in the forwards, who were their great strength, had all the toughness of people who spent their days working the local vineyards of the Corbières. Only their coach, the ex-international forward Jean Sébédio, who had previously built up a fearsome reputation at Carcassonne, was an outsider. A Basque, Sébédio had earned the nickname "Sultan" because of his service in the Syrian campaign and his authoritative manner. On his international debut in 1913 he had become the first working-class player to be selected in the France XV.[16]

A leading article in *La Dépêche* signalled the unprecedented nature of the finalists: "Old hands will compare this industrial village and the small town surrounded by vineyards with the great cities of the past which alone achieved the honour of the final. But there's nothing mysterious about the success of these small towns...

"Take a land where the people are exuberant in spirit and muscular in body ... pick twenty or so strong lads from an area limited by the local accent, build around them the enthusiasm of the local population, put a good coach in charge of them, look after the material needs of everyone, keep up their pride in their jersey and you'll have a XV of the highest rank..."[17]

The match turned out to have even more than the usual intensity of a local derby as the two teams fought - sometimes literally - for supremacy. Thanks to their forwards, Lézignan monopolised possession in the first half and scored an early try although their attacking play was generally poor. At 8-0 mid-way through the second half Lézignan looked to have the trophy within their grasp. Their coach Sébédio turned round to the Quillan officials in the stand and waved a handful of banknotes in front of them. "You see, I can pay players too if I want," he shouted.[18] His boast was premature. The speed and quality of the Quillan side saw them draw level with Lézignan before the centre Baillette scored a sensational long-distance try to give Quillan an 11-8 victory. Quillan's class and willingness to play a more expansive game had won the day, but far from improving rugby's reputation their triumph only added to the game's troubles as, at the end of the match, fighting broke out both on and off the pitch. "It is unfortunate that this final should have been played in such a violent and brutal manner," wrote Gaston Bénac in *L'Auto*. "Rugby in Languedoc is worthy of better than the bad-tempered play we have seen today."[19] The general condemnation was not mitigated by the fact that the winner had been the side more willing to play an open game. Quite the contrary. The victory of Quillan, a small-town side that had got to the top by more or less overt professionalism, had, in some eyes, merely devalued France's major competition.

Big-match incidents - and there were plenty of them - led experienced observers to talk of a crisis within rugby and to fear for the future of the sport. The credibility of the Fédération Française de Rugby, which appeared either incapable or unwilling to deal effectively with deteriorating standards of play, sportsmanship and public behaviour at its matches, was becoming more and more strained. To make matters worse, it found itself with a mutiny on its hands. Taking the initiative when the governing body seemed incapable, six of the top clubs, including US Perpignan, decided to organise their own breakaway competition in an attempt to promote higher standards.

It was one of a growing number of dilemmas which tested the Federation's authority. The sport was becoming a victim of its own popularity because it was inadequately controlled. As well as the shamateurism ("looking after the material needs of everyone", as the leader writer of *La Dépêche* had quite openly put it), the illegal approaches to players, the barely concealed inducements made to them and the almost unregulated transfers from one club to another, the standard of play had seriously declined. The win-at-all-costs attitude brought with it negative tactics and brutality. Foul play was rife. Fighting among both players and spectators was commonplace. Referees, subjected to verbal and sometimes physical abuse on all sides, were unable to impose authority. Even journalists did not escape the displeasure of a fiercely partisan public if their reports failed to match the views of their readers. The consequence of all this was that the game gradually began to decline in popularity, with the loss of some eighty clubs in the three years following the peak of 1923.

Then in May 1930 yet another incident took place which had serious repercussions for the Federation. In the championship semi-final between Pau and Agen, the Agen winger, the eighteen-year old schoolboy Michel Pradié, died as a result of a late tackle by his opposite number, the international Jean Taillantou. Although malicious intent was never satisfactorily established in the judicial enquiry which followed, Taillantou was fined and sentenced to a suspended three-month prison sentence. Nor did the Federation escape criticism. Rugby's governing body, as well as the Comité National des Sports which oversaw sport in France, were both held responsible for the events of that tragic day and made to give assurances regarding their future control of matches. But Pradié's death was not an isolated incident. Three other players had died on the rugby field during the previous autumn, causing questions to be asked in Parliament.

The truth was that the Federation was not equal to the task demanded of it. The occasional spectacular step, such as banning players or even whole clubs - both Lézignan and Quillan were excluded from the championship, but later re-admitted - revealed a desperate kind of authority which did not have a lasting effect.

Contemptuous of the falling standards of play and behaviour and dismayed at the attitude of the Federation, clubs began to take matters into their own hands. The six clubs who had earlier dissociated themselves from the parent body were soon to be joined by six others. These were the clubs with long traditions and numerous titles behind them who shunned the kind of barbarism which often resulted whenever they played against some of the smaller clubs. In the season 1930-31 the twelve clubs - Stade Français, Aviron Bayonnais, Stade Bordelais, Biarritz Olympique, AS Carcassonne, FC Grenoble, SUA Limoges, FC Lyon, Stade Nantais, Section Paloise (Pau), US Perpignan and Stade Toulousain, to be joined later by US Narbonnaise and Stadoceste Tarbais - formed their own association, known as the Union Française de Rugby Amateur. Their separation from the FFR became final in December 1930, when each club resigned its membership. They would not rejoin the main body until two seasons later.

Theirs was a revolt against the excesses bred by the championship, its professionalism and its brutality. By playing amongst themselves they would be able, they believed, to uphold certain standards and principles, including, as the title of their association suggested, that of amateurism. Matches played amongst the Twelve would be conducted in the proper spirit, with due regard to fair play and with an emphasis on open play. League positions would be determined by an accumulation of points scored rather than by points for winning. Despite the undisputed quality of their rugby, clubs such as Quillan - held up as an example of a side expensively assembled and almost as quickly dissolved once the money ran out - represented the antithesis of the Twelve's commandments. In fact one of the demands which UFRA had earlier made to the FFR was to put a check on clubs which were assembled for publicity purposes, or, in other words, heavily sponsored.

The FFR chairman, Octave Léry, in an attempt to forestall the breakaway movement, had floated the idea of abolishing the championship, since it appeared to be at the root of all French rugby's evils. Léry knew, however, that such a proposal would never gain the necessary support to be carried. He decided against standing for office again when his term ran out and was succeeded by Roger Dantou. The new chairman told delegates that the door would remain open for the return of the prodigals. "But we must dismiss from the outset," he added, "anything which is contrary to our dignity and to our sporting democracy, which is opposed to an oligarchy which would be disastrous for French rugby."[20] The interests of the majority would therefore not be sacrificed to the demands of the few. Fine words, but which expressed no desire to get to grips with the problem.

UFRA's new organisation proved however that it was no more immune to outside forces than the clubs which remained loyal to the Federation. The amateur principle, which UFRA had incorporated into its name, was much less evidently upheld than at first appeared. From the start the Twelve had demanded the scrapping of the recently-introduced system of freezing gate receipts and subsequent distribution of the revenue among all clubs. The system clearly benefited the smaller clubs at the expense of the big guns who pulled in the crowds. It very much appeared as if the Twelve's principles were not so noble after all. One of UFRA's prime movers, Perpignan's Marcel Laborde, even went so far as to declare that amateurism, the symbol of his organisation, was simply an illusion. "In order to keep our players amateur," he is said to have remarked, "we have to pay them twice as much."

The Federation was then hit by another shock wave, this time from across the Channel. The British Unions had been dissatisfied for some time about the way the game of rugby was being played in France - which it seemed to regard as a kind of colonial outpost - and decided to step in. The accusing finger was pointed at France for two reasons: money and violence. The British had reached the same conclusion as the UFRAclubs in identifying the underlying cause as the championship, which had brought about, they believed, an unhealthy appetite for winning, which in turn had led to the various excesses for which the French had acquired such a bad reputation. Apart from the breaching of amateurism, other practices which the British considered underhand because they were a purely French invention were the substitution of injured players and - an unofficial forerunner of the sin-bin - sendings-off which were only temporary.

It was no surprise that the British and UFRA wagged their fingers in harmony at the FFR. After all much of the dirt had been dished by the Twelve. UFRA, whose clubs were full of reforming zeal, had written to the

RFU denouncing the professionalism, brutality, poaching of players and other illegalities fostered by the championship. The British took note.[21] As far as international competition was concerned, the Home Unions no doubt also asked themselves whether France was worth having as a member of the Five Nations - and particularly so since the UFRA clubs had withdrawn their players from international selection. In the 48 matches played following the First World War, the French had won just eleven and drawn two and generally finished bottom of the table. Not only was France the weakest of the five countries, but their conduct at international level had also been causing concern for some time.

As early as 1913 the British - more precisely the Scots - had felt it necessary to take their French counterparts to task over their behaviour. The match between France and Scotland, played at the Parc des Princes on January 1st, 1913, had drawn a record 25,000 crowd expecting to see the home side repeat their famous victory over the Scots of two years earlier. It was not for the quality of the play that the game, won 25-3 by Scotland, would go down in the annals, but for the incident known as "*l'affaire* Baxter", after the English referee who controlled the fixture. Baxter's fastidious handling of the match and supercilious manner had enraged the spectators, who booed their response every time he whistled the numerous French infringements. At the end of the match thousands of spectators ran on to the pitch, a number of them setting upon Baxter, who had to be protected by the combined efforts of players and mounted police. Scottish players were struck by stones.[22]

An unruly demonstration followed, with spectators making their way through Paris to end up besieging the offices of the newspaper *L'Auto* in protest. The Scottish Rugby Union naturally took a very dim view of all this. The Union's honorary secretary, W A Smith, wrote in strong terms to his opposite number and fellow-Scot, Cyril Rutherford, who acted as the FFR's international secretary. As a preamble to the main thrust of the argument, Smith compared the attitudes of French spectators and players with their Scottish counterparts. "Here [in Scotland] the game has never forgotten its traditions," he wrote, "and our spectators have had the advantage of growing up with it. [In France] on the other hand, the game can only be played in front of spectators who do not realise what rugby football means when it is played in a spirit which is appropriate to its traditions."[23] But that was not to excuse the French. As a result of the "reprehensible" behaviour of the spectators and the unsatisfactory stewarding arrangements, the Scottish Rugby Union took the decision to cancel fixtures with the French, having nothing more to do with them until 1918, when the end of the war managed to bring about a greater sense of fraternity.

International relations remained fragile, however. The match between France and Wales in April 1930, played in chaotic conditions before a 50,000-strong Parisian crowd, the biggest ever for a rugby match in France, left a particularly bad odour. A victory for the French in their final match of the international season would have seen them win the Five Nations tournament for the first time. Never had there been such public interest, with tickets changing hands on the black market for several times the face value. Fans without tickets broke down barriers to get in and Colombes was packed to the rafters well before kick-off time. But France's hopes dived as Wales took control with an 11-0 lead. After Bioussa had earlier crossed but failed to ground the ball properly, France had a chance to hit back when Gérald went over following a Galia break. The referee, to the crowd's despair and disgust, brought play back for a forward pass. The French spectators, outraged after seeing Wales score from what appeared to them to be a similar infringement, soon made their feelings known to the English referee, who, in the eyes of the French, could not possibly be neutral, being British like the Welsh. The game had been full of instances of dirty play and brawling, with players on both sides requiring attention for cuts, among them the Welsh hooker, who had nine stitches inserted after receiving a kick in the face. The match had once again shown the unacceptable face of rugby.

With considerable understatement, the Welsh president in his post-match speech declared that this violent match had done nothing to foster good relations between the two countries. The press also condemned the brutality of this game, referred to in a leading article in *Le Temps* as *"la guerre sportive"*. A particularly damning commentary came from the Press Association's correspondent, who wrote: "The Frenchmen were broken on the wheel of their own highly-strung temperament. It would certainly have been a paradox if France had won today's match, for their Rugby was only a travesty of the game as Englishmen understand it ... The match served to emphasise France's failure to grasp the finer points of the Rugby game."[24] For the correspondent of *The Times,* this was nothing new. "An attractive game at Colombes is a very rare spectacle," he wrote. "Frenchmen who are keen supporters of the Rugby game ... are showing some alarm lest the international matches played here should be allowed to degenerate to the level of their own regional championships, in which some of them see the true cause of the decline."[25]

The British Unions were now rapidly losing patience with the troublesome French, to whom they had twice previously expressed their disappointment at the way rugby was being played and run in France. The France-Wales match could easily have proved to be the final straw although the official breaking-point came very soon after the relatively incident-free return match at Swansea the following season. It was not for dirty play that the French were now being upbraided, but for their poor performance in losing 35-3. With UFRA players unavailable for selection, the national side had become significantly weakened and the Federation was heavily criticised in the press the next day for its failure to bring about a settlement.

A prescient comment was made in *Le Matin*: "It is absolutely necessary that the French Rugby split be mended and that unity should prevail if we are to be spared such humiliations as that which occurred at Swansea... It is possible that the International Rugby Federation will refuse to accept France as a member of the international championship."[26]

On the same day, March 2nd 1931, the British Unions, who had indeed taken a close interest in the conflict between the FFR and UFRA, made public the decision which they had reached a fortnight earlier. They wrote to their French counterparts, informing them that there would be no matches played either at club or international level between British and French teams from the end of the season. An official statement by the Rugby Football Union, issued on behalf of the joint committee of the English, Scottish, Irish and Welsh unions, read: "After examination of documentary evidence furnished by the French Federation and the dissentient clubs, we are compelled to state that, owing to the unsatisfactory condition of the game of Rugby Football as managed and played in France, neither our Union nor the clubs or Unions under its jurisdiction will be able to fulfil fixtures with France or French clubs at home or away after the end of the season unless and until we are satisfied that the control and conduct of the game has been placed on a satisfactory basis in all essentials."

In *The Times* the next day Cyril Rutherford, the Scot who acted as honorary international secretary of the French Federation, was reported as saying that the ban had been brought about mainly by the split between the Federation and UFRA. The Federation had regarded the twelve clubs as "the worst offenders in the matter of professionalism. When the Federation had instituted a system of pooling gate receipts these important clubs had broken away under the guise of wishing to reform the game." Rutherford thought that the championship, in British eyes the root cause of the misdemeanours, would have to go, and be replaced by "a series of local competitions run on the lines of the London Hospitals Cup." His recommendation, ironic in retrospect, was that "[the French] must get away from championship methods and follow British ideas."

Chapter Three
THE PLAYMAKERS

The combination of the British Unions' sanctions and the apparently inconsequential decision to disband the Quillan team was to have huge consequences for French rugby. After the defeat by Agen in the 1930 championship final Quillan's chairman, Jean Bourrel, began to scale down his expensively assembled team, claiming that it was costing him too much. Since in professional sport the demand for top players never ceases - and French rugby was professional in all but name - there was no lack of interest in a number of Quillan players who figured among the best in France.

Quillan's international second row or back row forward, Jean Galia, consequently found the path to his door busy with rival club representatives making offers. But it was Galia's fellow-Catalan, Ernest Camo, who was to play a decisive role in both their future careers. Camo had been contacted by a former colleague at US Perpignan, the prop forward Camille Montade, who had been playing for the past two seasons at Villeneuve-sur-Lot, a town situated mid-way between Toulouse and Bordeaux. Montade's call had led to talks between Galia, Camo and a Villeneuve director over dinner at the Casino at Canet-Plage, near Perpignan, before a persuasive welcome from the chairman on their visit to the club itself. Galia, a businessman as well as a rugby player, quickly sized up the potential of Villeneuve's offer. The club's standards were rising, even if they fell short of what he was used to and those of other clubs anxious to recruit him. But Galia had been involved in the rise of Quillan from a club of little significance to national champions. It crossed his mind that, with the right approach, the same thing could be done at Villeneuve, where there was already the basis of a good side. That had obviously occurred to the Villeneuve directors too.

Villeneuve had had a successful season in 1929-30, in which they had drawn their match against Quillan. But Galia's apparent decision to join them, announced in the last days of August 1930, was a sensation that appeared to fulfil the ambitions of the Villeneuve committee and their supporters. The international forward had also promised to bring with him a Catalan three-quarter whose name was being kept a close secret.

But while Villeneuve thought they had their man, Galia was keeping his options open. In the first week of September he was reported as saying that he had not yet made the final decision. According to newspaper reports, he had told an official of one of his former clubs, the Toulouse-based TOEC, that if he could find an outlet for the family wholesale fruit and vegetable business in either Toulouse or Paris he would not hesitate to move there because those were the two cities which attracted him most.[1] Villeneuve was beginning to look like Plan B. Among the many rumours which began to circulate during the month of September 1930 was one which claimed that Galia, who had given up his amateur heavyweight boxing title to concentrate on rugby with Quillan, was about to enter the ring again and might even turn pro.[2]

Camo, who was to put together a book of reminiscences about his playing days with Galia, records that "serious offers" were made to the two players by other clubs.[3] But in the end they made a combined decision to join the Club Athlétique Villeneuvois, despite, he adds obliquely, last-minute attempts to persuade them against it.

The pair lost no time in setting up a business in their new surroundings. Soon after arriving in Villeneuve Galia and Camo took over the lease of a shop at number 34, rue de Paris, trading in sports goods and hats, which was both a sign of the times and a remarkable coincidence, given that their previous club chairman owned one of the biggest hat-making businesses in France. A further coincidence was that their former team-mate and fellow-Catalan, the international centre Marcel Baillette, had also left Quillan to set up shop at Toulon. Galia, however, was not destined to spend his days serving behind a counter. Nor did Camo, despite the fact that he had been a baker. They took someone on to look after the shop for them, and the business was soon thriving.[4]

The commercial venture was simplicity itself compared with the main reason they had come to Villeneuve. Transfers between clubs were regulated by the FFR, which also granted players licences to play. In order to prevent open recruitment by one club from another, top-level players wanting a move between first-grade clubs had, in theory, to sit out a two-year qualification period. What actually took place could be quite different. In just one of scores of examples, *Midi-Olympique* reported, alongside an article which recorded the signing of Galia and Camo for Villeneuve, an alleged inducement for another, unnamed player to switch clubs. The newspaper had no doubt been tipped off by a Toulouse bank employee as the player in question cashed a cheque for 10,000 francs drawn against the account of a big industrial concern in the Lyon-Saint-Etienne area, which was "assisting" the player with travelling and relocation expenses. "A perfectly normal transaction," commented *Midi-Olympique* ironically. "Who could take exception to that? Not even Monsieur Dantou [president of the FFR], who looks on paternally as the mass exodus of unemployed southern players continues towards those blessed lands where banknotes are distributed with such magnanimity."[5] It added a warning, however, that the British Rugby Union (some six months before they decided to ostracise the money-grubbing French) took a different view of matters and was beginning to be increasingly concerned at the number of transfers which were dealt with like those of "English professionals" - in other words, rugby league players.

As Villeneuve became anxious to know whether they had, after all, got their man in Galia, the FFR reconvened its players' registration commission and pledged to rid the sport of the touting and recruiting which had become such common practice. It would throw out, it declared, any requests for transfer which were in the least bit suspicious. Among the first victims of the purge, it was feared, would be Galia and his colleague Camo. As the inquiry dragged on, Galia threatened to look to one of the "Twelve" clubs if the FFR did not give him permission to play for Villeneuve. He did in fact sound out Stade Toulousain, though his application was rejected by UFRA, which did not want to set the precedent of acting as a haven for banned players. Meanwhile his new club declared that they would apply for permission to join the new organisation if Galia's registration was not sanctioned.

Galia was finally granted his licence to play for Villeneuve in the first week of January 1931, after sitting out the first three months of the season. He lost no time in making an impact, along with his partner Camo, who was called up to make his international debut as a back-rower in the 3-0 win against Ireland in the same month. In the following match against Scotland at Murrayfield, the Villeneuve club was represented by three players - Camo, Galia, who was now back to full fitness, and, making his international debut, the remarkable 18-year old scrum-half, Max Rousié.

In spite of its international representatives, the Villeneuve side did not achieve immediate good results. Camo recalled the difficulty which Galia, who had begun to impose his authority, had had in getting some of the local players, who resented the new arrivals, to train as seriously as he wanted. "In their eyes we were outsiders," Camo recalled, "two trouble-makers who had only come to Villeneuve out of self-interest."[6] But among the Villeneuve public, Galia in particular had made an enormous impression. This smallish town which had had relatively little to cheer about suddenly found in its midst France's top international forward who happened to be a boxing champ as well. With Camo and the local prodigy Rousié also figuring in the international line-up, Villeneuve had never had so much greatness thrust upon it.

Villeneuve-sur-Lot, with a population of some 25,000 inhabitants, owes its existence to the English occupying army of the thirteenth century who laid the foundations of this fortified town on the banks of the river Lot. In the 1930s Villeneuve was very much the hub of the agricultural industry in the region, its processing factories dealing with the locally-produced fruit and vegetables. And like Quillan before it, Villeneuve had sporting ambitions beyond its size. The arrival of Jean Galia was destined to alter the scale of things even further. As one account later put it, Villeneuve would become rugby's Sarajevo, a reference to an event which triggered the First World War.[7]

With France being banned from major international competition, however, Galia began to lose interest in playing for his country, which was limited to little more than the annual match against Germany, a third-rate rugby-playing nation. Instead he devoted himself to his business affairs - not only the sports shop, but also a cinema in Villeneuve in which he had become a partner and then another in Toulouse. Business matters were a valid reason, but Galia's refusal of international selection did not go down well with the authorities.

As Camo pointed out, Galia had no time for mediocrity. He would not be satisfied if the Villeneuve side achieved nothing greater than the regional championship. With the nucleus of their three international players, CA Villeneuvois had reached the quarter-finals of the national championship in 1931-32, but Galia knew that the addition of a top-class back would make all the difference. Such a player had already come on to the scene. François Noguères, a full-back or centre with US Perpignan, had guested with Villeneuve while stationed at the barracks at Agen, some 20 miles to the south. If it is surprising that Noguères should end up doing his military service so far away from his home town it is even more unusual that the Agen club, winners of the championship final against Quillan in 1930, did not manage to persuade him to play for them rather than Villeneuve.

But in the 20-year old Noguères Villeneuve saw an important acquisition and they were anxious to retain his services on his demobilisation in October 1932 though Perpignan were equally keen to have him back. Galia and Montade made contact with him again, paying him a visit in his home town of Le Boulou, where he worked in the local cork-making industry. Sometime afterwards Noguères received the telegram which has since passed into legend and which apparently read: "Travelling expenses reimbursed". It was signed "Jean". Those few innocuous words would affect French rugby profoundly.

The explanation for that brief telegram is not so simple and differing versions of the story have been put forward. Noël Altèze, the historian of rugby in Perpignan, has given perhaps the most plausible and reliable variation.[8] "I never saw the telegram and I doubt whether, apart from Moïse Baills[9] and Marcel Laborde, anyone else in Perpignan had sight of it. Certain people thought that it was a post office employee who intercepted the telegram. But that story must be false. In my opinion, on receiving the telegram, François Noguères, who, like all the players at USP, idolised Marcel Laborde, wanted to seek his advice. So he handed over the telegram to Moïse Baills, the club secretary and an employee at Perpignan station, who passed it on to Marcel Laborde. That is what I have always heard said by those involved with the club. I suppose that Marcel Laborde, who didn't want to lose a player as talented as Noguères, alerted the FFR, which at the time was emerging from the split with UFRA." Laborde, with the previous loss of players to Quillan still vivid in his memory and using whatever means he could to prevent the further drain of players away from his Perpignan club, would have presented the telegram to the FFR as evidence of the veiled professionalism which the governing body was being urged to eliminate from the game.

An additional twist to the story alleges that Noguères received a money order to the value of 5000 francs, but, not wanting to incriminate himself, sent it to the Federation, who passed it on to Villeneuve, who sent it back to the Federation, after which it seems to have disappeared. Augustin Saltraille told Altèze that he remembered that the sum of 6000 francs received by Noguères was immediately sent by the player to the Federation.[10]

The FFR, interpreting the "travelling expenses" as a euphemism, seized the opportunity to show that it was putting its house in order. Brought up short by the British, the governing body needed to give evidence of action if it was to be re-admitted to the top level of international competition. It was announced on November 16th 1932 that Galia would be expelled and that Noguères and the Villeneuve directors would be suspended. The club would not be allowed to play any more official matches until the end of the season. But the Federation officials could never have envisaged the consequences of their decision, which began with an indignant Galia completely refuting the charges laid against him.

François Noguères, however, did not deny that there had been some exchange of correspondence. "A telegram was intercepted by the US Perpignan officials, who didn't want me to leave the club," he stated. "On the station platform, the club secretary, Maurice Vails [sic], shouted to me, 'Don't go or you'll be disqualified.' So I turned back, unpacked my cases and rejoined USP - though not for long, because the storm reached the FFR and I was quickly suspended."[11]

Whatever the exact details of the matter - and they now seem lost for ever with their actors - the essence of the affair is clearly that there was rivalry between people of the same background but of different loyalties. Was Galia framed? He never accepted guilt, and it seems unlikely that he would have committed such an indiscretion.

"Jean always denied having sent the telegram," his widow said. "What the Rugby Federation could never stomach was to be told publicly that rugby was not an amateur sport, that everyone knew it and turned a blind eye to it and that it would be fairer and more moral to admit the facts, both for players and officials. He was never forgiven for that but he didn't care."[12]

His supporters in Villeneuve thought he had been set up, regarding it as beyond belief that Galia could be so imprudent. Two of those in close contact with him at the time, however, Noguères himself and Camo, who might have been expected to jump to the defence of their team-mate, are at best equivocal. Camo, avoiding controversy as usual in his record of the period, gave the rather opaque verdict: "Perhaps Villeneuve were a little careless."[13]

It may be that Galia, in his own mind at least, simply denied having done anything wrong, which is a different matter. In any event he was certainly unhappy about being the victim of a new and unconvincing puritanism on the part of the Federation. And with some justification. Marcel Laborde, the probable instigator of the FFR's action, pointed out: "If Noguères had sold his 'services' to Villeneuve instead of returning to his job and family, nothing would have been said. Dantou [the FFR president] would have covered the matter up as he has done with so many other cases and Noguères would have become an international. It remains to be seen whether, after acting like this, the Federation will resume relations with the English and regain its prestige."[14]

As Laborde pointed out, examples such as this were legion. The Federation official Dr Voivenel wrote of one case which had happened even before the First World War where a certain winger from Toulouse was prevented from joining a Catalan club by his own father, who sent the compromising papers to FFR officials.[15] Galia himself had signed for Quillan for a reported sum of 80,000 francs six years before the present charges were laid against him. Who had bothered to point the finger then? But that was before France was shunned by the British, before Galia had declined international selection and before the FFR had been forced to try to regain some credibility. What was now certain was that Galia would be looking for an opportunity to retaliate.

The Rugby Football League had been considering for some time the possibility of introducing their game into France and had set up a working party in April 1933 to look at the viability of the project. Six months later, on October 3rd 1933, a five-man delegation arrived in Paris to make specific arrangements. Their plans coincided with the arrival of the Australian touring team, whose co-manager, Harry Sunderland, a journalist with a reputation for a pioneering spirit, joined the Paris delegation.

A predecessor had taken a similar initiative twelve years earlier. SG Ball, manager of the 1921 Australian tourists, had also made the trip to Paris in order to try to open up France to rugby league, while the chairman of the Northern Union, as it then was, Willie Fillan of Huddersfield, attempted to make arrangements for an exhibition match to be staged there at the Stade

Pershing. But the chairman had had to deal with "a communication of an adverse nature subsequently received",[16] namely the French Rugby Union Federation's declared intention to boycott the stadium if rugby league should be played there. Negotiations dragged on until well after the Australians had returned home, with an England-Wales match being considered as late as March 1922.[17] It was even decided, naively, to consult the secretary of the FFR, Cyril Rutherford, but predictably the enquiry came to nothing.

A decade earlier, another ultimately fruitless suggestion that France might be ready for the thirteen-a-side game was received by the Northern Union. The possibility of staging an exhibition match there was put forward by a Mr Bureau, who had contacted the English headquarters of the game, writing that the French rugby clubs apparently allowed payment for broken time and that in his opinion "their sympathies are more towards the system of the Northern Union than that of the Rugby Union, though little is actually known of the Northern Union in France."[18]

When Harry Sunderland finally saw developments taking shape in the autumn of 1933, he began to see the realisation of a long-held ambition. Two and a half years earlier he had tried to persuade the Rugby Football League to appoint him as a prototype development officer with special responsibility for introducing the game to London and France - an enormous task, even for someone of his enthusiasm and ebullience. Eventually in May 1931 the Council cabled their unanimous verdict to him: "Regret that in our opinion your ideas of Rugby League expansion in areas concerned do not warrant outlay of type indicated by you in your letter of March 31 at present time."[19]

At around that same period, the secession of the UFRA clubs from the French Federation had led to speculation that rugby league was about to be promoted in France. The Rugby Football League's principled stance was given by its secretary, John Wilson, who stated: "The Rugby League does not take the view that malcontents in the Rugby Union anywhere should be welcomed merely for the sake of it. If at any time we find that there is a real desire on the part of a body of French rugby clubs to embrace the Rugby League rules we should be bound to consider the proposal, but the first step would have to be made by the French themselves."

The attitude expressed by Wilson, characterised by the gentlemanly values of an already bygone era, contrasted tellingly with the new-world dynamism of the man who would assist the push across the Channel. Harry Sunderland was not to be put off easily and kept up the pressure by, among other things, a circular letter to the press, in which his sense of frustration is all too apparent.

"I know that some of you people feel that you should not do any propaganda in France," he wrote, "but I would like to point out that there would never have been any rugby league in Australia if somebody had not broken away.

"It is all right for you people to take up the attitude that it would be 'infra dig' for you to move in France. But that policy will never make our code advance.

"I am sure that the present opportunity is one which should be grasped," he continued, going on to advise against conciliation with the French Rugby Union who had stood in the way of the previous attempt to introduce rugby league to France. "I would risk what would be said by those people who have never done anything for our game and never will, and who oppose us at every turn, even to the extent of arranging a boycott on the ground in Paris in 1921-22."

Events in France since the 1931 international ban by the British Rugby Unions had opened up new possibilities, which were mooted in the French press. On March 22nd 1933, chairman Walter Popplewell travelled to London to meet two journalists, André Fournier and Robert Perrier, to discuss the idea of promoting rugby league in France. Perrier, of the daily sports newspaper, *L'Auto*, found that rugby league's poor reputation in France was quite unfounded and was simply the result of accepting the opinion "with which we have been inculcated by the austere governors of the Rugby Union." What Perrier saw instead, after travelling north, was "a federation that is strong, prosperous and perfectly organised to control both professional and amateur rugby." When the two Frenchmen broached the possibility of establishing rugby league in their country, the League's representatives reiterated their stance that it would not be sporting to take advantage of the Rugby Union's difficulties. If the French Federation wished to make a proposal, then they would be willing to enter into association, though already the talk was moving on hypothetically to the possibility of sending an English team to play an exhibition match against France.

The following month the sub-committee was set up. Now there was much more commitment to the idea. "Ordinarily I am a cautious man," said Wilson. "I want to see the plan clearly before I make a move. In this matter of extending the rugby league game to France, however, I believe that the time is opportune for us to make a move forward."

Alongside Sunderland and Wilson in the working party were three men who were, or would become, chairmen of the RFL - Joe Lewthwaite of Hunslet, Bramley's Walter Popplewell and Wilfred Gabbatt of Barrow. They found, though, that the French Federation would not entertain any idea of collaboration with the Rugby League, and was concentrating its efforts instead on convincing the British Rugby Unions of its good faith in an attempt to restore international relations. Perrier wrote of the dictatorial attitude of the Rugby Union, and concluded that logically French rugby union and British rugby league should share the same platform since they were seeking the same ends. It was not through Perrier, however, but through other connections that the Rugby League began to explore the

French option. Not even rugby provided the common ground, but cycling, at which John Wilson had represented his country at the 1912 Olympic Games in Stockholm. By that means he had come to know Victor Breyer, an official of the International Cycling Federation and managing editor of the Paris-based *Echo des Sports,* a newspaper at whose offices the delegation now arrived to discuss future plans.

According to the journalist Gaston Bénac, Wilson and Breyer had met the previous year in Paris, when they had attended the world championship boxing match which ended in victory for France's Marcel Thil.[20] Spending the evening in the company of several Parisian journalists, Wilson is said to have put forward the idea of introducing rugby league to France and gained Breyer's immediate interest. The circulation war between sports newspapers was intense and editors and proprietors were always keen to make new connections, particularly since some of them also had interests in the management of sports stadiums.

A year on, Breyer agreed, as the man with the local knowledge, to look into the arrangements for staging an exhibition match in Paris. The Stade Buffalo, with which Breyer was connected, was not, however, to be used. The French Rugby Union, some of whose clubs also played matches there, made threats which resulted, paradoxically, in the booking of the municipally-owned Stade Pershing - the same stadium which the union men had also threatened to boycott twelve years earlier. This time Breyer simply put down the deposit and Sunderland and Wilson occupied themselves with organising the event.

The RFL representatives made a good combination, Sunderland with his drive and evident enthusiasm complementing Wilson's administrative ability and attention to detail. By the end of October it had been agreed that the match would involve an England XIII playing against the Australians, who by that stage would be nearing the end of their tour, which began at the end of August.

The preparations were gathering momentum, with a friend and colleague of Breyer's, Charles Bernat, being appointed to promote the event. Five weeks beforehand, Sunderland and Wilson made the journey to Paris again to host a press luncheon, which they afterwards considered very successful.

It was Breyer also who put the RFLofficials in touch with Maurice Blein, a 28-year-old journalist at a publication called *Sporting,* whose offices were situated in the appropriately-named rue Notre Dame des Victoires. They asked him his views on introducing rugby league to France.

"I told them it had to be skilful and attractive to play and watch," Blein recalled, "otherwise they wouldn't be able to persuade players to want to play it." And, Blein went on to point out, French players had also been earning more money as amateurs than they would probably ever have earned as professionals.

The Rugby League officials then asked Blein who, among the French rugby players of the day, would be most capable of leading a rugby league team on tour to England. "Without the slightest hesitation I gave them the name of Jean Galia," he said.[21]

Whether Blein's answer proved conclusive is open to doubt. The Rugby League delegates would certainly have wanted to hear more than one view. It was reported that two other international players had been considered: Eugène Ribère, captain of the championship-winning Quillan side and France; and another former captain of the French international side, the winger Adolphe Jauréguy, of the Stade Français club, who was one of the French rugby establishment's most respected figures and a very unlikely convert to rugby league.[22]

John Wilson dutifully recorded the progress made on the arrangements for the match, scheduled for December 31st. "We had a long talk with M. Blein, a young and enterprising Parisian pressman who speaks English perfectly," he noted. "At night, dinner and conference in M. Breyer's flat (Breyer, Bernat, Sunderland and Secretary), where all match arrangements were discussed and decided upon. Admissions 5, 10, 15 and 20 francs. To spend £100-£130 on advertising.

"The general opinion in Paris amongst pressmen is that there will be a large gate, many declaring that the Stade will not be big enough to hold the crowd."[23]

The plans had been carefully laid but no-one had taken account of the weather. The year 1933 went out in a blizzard. The ground at Stade Pershing was frozen and snow was in the air, but the match had to go ahead. In spite of the weather, around 10,000 people, paying a total of around £650, had made the effort to get to this stadium on the outskirts of Paris and were eager to see for themselves this new form of rugby from across the Channel, about which they had heard so much.

It was the Australians who adapted best to the difficult conditions, despite the fact that nine of the side had played against Wales the day before. The Kangaroos gave a commanding display to thrill the crowd, who applauded and cheered every move. The centre Dave Brown led the onslaught with 30 points from four tries and nine goals, while the Aussie forwards were also very impressive, scoring eight tries between them through their short inter-passing and alert backing-up. The final score of 63-13 - consolation for the Australians' defeats in all three Tests in England - suggests an exhibition match rather than a full-blooded international. But though England's contribution was well below standard, the match created a great impression on all those who saw it.

The Warrington secretary, Bob Anderton, who acted as one of the touch judges, was one of those to report the match a huge success - a "miracle" in fact - considering the weather and difficulty of access to the stadium.

Anderton was particularly impressed with the enthusiasm of the spectators, saying he had rarely seen anything like it at home and adding: "We stayed behind to see the France v Germany rugby union match on the Monday and although France won there was nothing like the enthusiasm shown at our match, when the spectators ran on to the field, carried off Brown and mobbed the players. The police had great difficulty holding them back."[24]

The match was big news and was commented on in all the French newspapers and by all the usual observers. The president of the International Rugby Federation reacted sniffily, considering 13-a-side rugby less of a mental than a physical game. "It is less diversified and owing to the lack of combination it is quickly exhausted as a spectacle capable of arousing emotion," he concluded.[25] Few others expressed such reservations. Loud in his praise like many others, the former rugby union international Marcel de Laborderie (not to be confused with the Perpignan official, Marcel Laborde) welcomed the initiative. "We went to the match with an open mind," he wrote, "and we got our money's worth. This 13-a-side game is splendid rugby. When you go to see an exhibition of this style, in which one brilliant attack follows another, you have the essence of rugby - the handling game. There is no doubt that these two teams showed us what rugby can really be."[26]

The former chairman of the FFR, Octave Léry, called it a "very spectacular sport". One of the directors of the Agen rugby union club, the great rival of Villeneuve, found the match "infinitely more pleasing than rugby union games".[27]

In Victor Breyer's newspaper, *L'Echo des Sports*, Louis Delblat, whose background was in soccer but who would play a significant role in setting up rugby league in France, remarked: "For me it was the revelation of a new game, which is not the rugby we know ..." But Delblat added a cautionary comment which ought not to have gone unheeded: "This new game needs a new name so that there is no confusion in people's minds. I hope this wish will be considered by those who are trying to launch the game in France and who will succeed because truly they are offering something which is here to stay."[28]

The provincial press was equally enthusiastic. "What a fine exhibition was provided yesterday by the Australians," ran the report in the Perpignan newspaper, *L'Indépendant*. "The ball flew from one pair of hands to another and there was always a player available to take the play forward from any position. All the players are fantastically skilful."[29]

Even more significant was the reaction of another interested observer. As a forward himself, Jean Galia was astounded by the fitness, mobility and intelligent passing of the Australian pack. For one not easily impressed or lavish with his praise, his comments revealed his enthusiasm for the new game. "It was a game of great beauty, marvellously played, making for a splendid spectacle," he told reporters. "It was magnificent," he told his friend Camo. "The handling was masterly, the attacking play was astounding - that's what rugby league is about."[30] And at the post-match dinner at the Restaurant Marguery, Galia made public his determination to raise the first French rugby league team, which would tour England three months later. Already banned from playing by the FFR, Galia resigned as a member the following day.

As *The Times* reported on the third of January: "The immediate success in French sporting circles of Sunday's rugby league match between England and Australia .... has been the deciding factor in the decision to introduce the game to France. Mr John Wilson and M Jean Galia today signed an agreement under which M Galia will form and captain a French team which will play four matches in England during March..."

Wilson's informal meetings with numerous top rugby players and officials over that weekend had convinced him that rugby league would soon be taken up in France. He was left in no doubt about their indignation at the international ban imposed by the British rugby union authorities. He again insisted, though, that the overtures to the introduction of rugby league into France had come from the French themselves. "Galia has had the idea of forming a rugby league team in his mind for some time," he told one reporter. "He is brimful of enthusiasm and thinks our game is eminently suited to the French style of play."[31]

Succesful though it had been, the Paris exhibition match was simply a starting-point. The formation of the team was now the priority but it presented problems of its own. Though many in France had seen rugby league as the way ahead, most regarded the venture as a high-risk project. *L'Auto* was sceptical about the new game's chances of success, putting forward the practical difficulties of training a team, once assembled, in such a short space of time and predicting that it would be heavily defeated, which would consequently reduce public interest.

But Galia set to work. Most of the next two months were spent driving backwards and forwards across France from his Villeneuve base in an attempt to convince other players to join him in the venture. Camo wrote how Galia would often arrive back at his flat above the shop as dawn approached, having driven through the night after some meeting with a prospective team-mate.

It seems strange that Camo himself did not join him. "I would have liked to go with him and I'm sure that would have given him great pleasure," he wrote, "but he knew that it wasn't yet possible and that I had to keep to my commitments towards the Villeneuve club which had not yet crossed the Rubicon."[32]

Nor had the rising young star of Villeneuve, the prodigiously talented Max Rousié, yet signed up. "Max came many times to see me to talk about it," said

Camo. "I tried to reason with him, although I wanted to go as much as he did."

In fact, no Villeneuve player was to join the pioneering group, despite the fact that directors of the club had been banned by the FFR. Was it because they, the players, feared the same fate? Representatives from the great rugby stronghold of Perpignan were also conspicuously absent. Galia spent a couple of days there and left accompanied by Maurice ("Tom") Porra, the only local player he had managed to recruit, though even he had been playing in Lyon.[33] Others on his wanted list, such as Noguères, Bardes and Serre, had remained loyal to their club. The chairman of USA Perpignan, as the club was now known since its merger with the Quins, told *L'Auto* that Noguères, who was still suspended from playing, had been offered 15,000 francs and a share of the profits to join Galia but had fallen in with USAP's ultimatum to stay with the club. "Galia wants to exact revenge on the Federation," said Monsieur Bazia, before launching a sideswipe at *L'Auto*'s drive against shamateurism in rugby: "Your campaign is misplaced. It's ridiculous to incriminate young men like ours who all work in Perpignan or the surrounding area. We never give them money. Of course we give them lunch or a drink or dinner, but that's all."[34]

Breyer and Bernat had now become anxious about Galia's venture. They wrote to the RFL to express their concern, pointing out that Galia seemed to be having some difficulty in fixing up his team. One of the problems seemed to be that many of those Galia was sounding out were, just as Maurice Blein had indicated, already earning more as amateurs than they were being offered to become professional rugby league players.

Neither Breyer nor Bernat had been able to get in touch with Galia and thought that someone should be sent to France to look into the situation. John Wilson duly travelled to Villeneuve to receive a progress report, as well as finding time to try on a beret at the premises of Messrs Galia and Camo. He also met two local figures who would play an important role in the formation of a rugby league club in France: Georges Bordeneuve, the mayor of Villeneuve-sur-Lot, formerly chairman of the CA Villeneuvois, and another former club director, Dr Léon Vinson, with whom Wilson was based during his stay. Both of the Villeneuve directors had been convinced for some time that rugby league was the way ahead for their club. Vinson went further, expressing the view that the best way to fight against shamateurism and violence in French rugby was to support the expansion of professional rugby league.

The mild-mannered Wilson made clear to Galia his concern about the difficulties the Frenchman was experiencing in convincing players to join him. Wilson, for one, must occasionally have doubted the wisdom of the enterprise. It was clear that, despite the enthusiasm shown for the exhibition match, it was quite a different matter to ask players to jeopardize a more certain future in rugby union. And for one man to recruit a squad capable of competing against English teams was no easy task either, particularly since time was short. But Galia, with his strong sense of conviction and persuasive powers, finally came up with the men he needed.

One of them was Antonin Barbazanges, a colleague of Galia's in the Quillan team which lost the 1930 final and an international stand-off, although he played more usually in the threequarter line. Barbazanges was probably one of the first to know of Galia's plans, claiming that Galia had asked him to go to the England-Australia match. Galia had shown him a letter of invitation from John Wilson, and, some time later, a second letter of inviting him to take a French rugby league team to England.

Like a number of other players, Barbazanges had been refused permission to play by the French Rugby Union Federation. After the Quillan team began to split up, he joined Roanne, but then fell foul of a rule which prevented him moving on to another club.

"At that time there was the two-year rule, which meant that you had to sit out two years before you could move between the top clubs, though if you had played with a big club you could join a minor club. I had left Roanne and had come to Beaune, in the Côte d'Or. I wanted to play for Dijon but I couldn't get permission. I got in touch with the secretary of the Federation. 'If it was up to me, I would give you permission,' he told me. 'But you'll create a precedent, particularly with a name like yours, which is bound to be noticed. Not only that, but you're an international player and if you are allowed to play, everybody else is going to be clamouring for permission too.'

"Because I wasn't able to play I agreed to meet Galia. He arranged to meet me at Chalon-sur-Saône, and we spent the evening discussing what would happen. He offered me the chance to join him and I said yes. I just wanted to play, that's all."[35]

Galia recruited other international players such as Robert Samatan, a winger with Villeneuve's rivals, Agen, who had also played against Galia's Quillan in the 1930 final. In the forwards were the international front-rowers, Jean Duhau of Bordeaux, Tom Porra, who had lined up for Lézignan in the 1929 final before moving to FC Lyon and then had come under suspicion following a proposed move to Agen. Alongside Porra in the 1929 Lézignan team was a third front-row recruit, Lolo Fabre. Lézignan's players, including another member of Galia's team, the threequarter Gaston Amila, had been banned by the Federation after a particularly brutal match against Montferrand. The forward strength of Galia's squad was increased by the recruitment of international second-rower Charles Petit of the SU Lorrain club and back-rower François Récaborde from Pau who had also faced Quillan in a championship final, with the Section Paloise in 1928, and who had been banned for life in 1930 for abusing the referee in that fateful championship semi-final against Agen. Récaborde confirmed to a local Pau newspaper that each player had been guaranteed 10,000 francs each plus a share of the profits.[36]

They were joined by Georges Blanc (Saint-Jean-de-Luz), Joseph Carrère (Narbonne), Jean Cassagneau (Quillan), Henri Dechavanne (Roanne), Laurent Lambert (Avignon), Charles Mathon (Oyonnax), François Nouel (Aviron Bayonnais) and Jean-Marie Vignal (Toulouse). Of the party of seventeen ("I know those 17 names by heart" said Barbazanges), eleven had been suspended or disqualified by the French Federation.

One of Galia's longest journeys took him from the south-west across France to the town of Oyonnax in the Jura mountains, where he stayed for three days with Charles Mathon, stand-off and captain of the Club Sportif Oyonnax and an international trialist. Mathon was not one of those who had fallen foul of the FFR's sanctions and it took some time for him to agree to enlist with Galia. Money was one of the subjects discussed but it was not the financial reward which decided him. He was concerned only to further his playing career.[37]

Nor was Laurent Lambert one of those who had been banned. He was simply full of enthusiasm to play a different kind of rugby. "I met Jean Galia on the platform of Avignon station," he recalled. "I would have accepted whatever he offered and when he started talking about going to England, for me it was like another world. Particularly when he gave me five one-thousand franc notes!

"But it was the sense of adventure that gripped me more. I had been playing on the wing at Avignon and I knew that I would never make progress because I hardly ever got the ball. But at the same time you had to be confident of your own ability to be part of a group like that because they were all top players."[38]

Not the least of Galia's concerns would be to get a return on the advances paid out to the players he had recruited. Lambert's 5,000 francs were probably an advance on the flat-rate payment of 10,000 francs per player, plus a share of any tour profits. Galia appears to have put the money up himself, a view confirmed by journalist Gaston Bénac ("...it was he who financed the tour," Bénac wrote, albeit ten years after the event).[39] However, there were assumptions made in the press that the English had funded it.[40] A document in the RFL archives confirms that the Rugby Football League underwrote the tour. Written by the secretary, John Wilson, on the notepaper of the Hotel Bedford in Paris, where the English officials were staying for the exhibition match at Stade Pershing, and dated January 2nd 1934, the document states:

"It is hereby agreed between M Galia and the Rugby Football League that M Galia brings a team of French Rugby Football players of first class calibre to England led by himself to play at least 4 matches as under.

"The party to arrive in Leeds on Monday or Tuesday March 5 or 6 and play:

March 10 v Club
March 14 v Club
March 17 v Representative team
March 21 v London Highfield
"These dates to be subject to mutual revision if found necessary.

"It is agreed between M Galia and the Rugby League that the French team take 60% of the nett gates with a guarantee that their share will not be less than Francs 60,000 (sixty thousand francs).

"It is further agreed that an England team visit Paris and play a France v England International match there against a team selected by M Galia, the gate receipts in this match to be either as above (60%-40%)or equally divided 50%-50%.

"The whole of this agreement is subject to confirmation by the Council of the Rugby Football League at their meeting in Leeds on Jan 11 1934.

Signed J Galia
For the Rugby Football League
Signed Walter Popplewell
John Wilson, Secretary."

The band of adventurers finally came together at the buffet of the Gare d'Orsay in Paris on Friday, March 2nd. Journalists were there, anxious to identify the recruits to the group and to ask questions. The international forward Jean Duhau was present, despite the efforts of his union colleagues to dissuade him. So was another international, Charles Petit, whose appearance came as a great surprise to the press, who plied him with questions. As the party left for their base, the Hotel Bohy-Lafayette, Galia had not yet arrived. A phone call came through to Charles Bernat to say that he would not be able to reach Paris until the next morning. He had been held up trying to persuade Charles Mathon to join him.

The next day there was a training session at the Stade Buffalo and the day after that a friendly match against a Paris side which laid claim to being the first to play rugby league in France. The pioneers spent the rest of the weekend nervously but optimistically anticipating their tour of England. Some of them had never been outside France before and, apart from their training sessions, none of them had ever played rugby league.

Chapter Four
GALIA'S BOYS

It was much more than a tour that had been organised for Galia and his team. The first steps his players would make in that opening match at Wigan, played only days after their arrival, would signal the crossover into a new sport, the foundation of a new association, the acceptance of a new sporting philosophy and culture and a contribution which would enrich the existing game. The French Rugby Union Federation, acting under the searchlight directed at it by the British Unions, had unwittingly created conditions for the new game to take root in and Jean Galia would prove less than compliant towards its attempt to prove its scrupulousness. Revenge was a natural consequence of the Catalan's wounded pride.

Outside the group of people directly involved, Galia's plan of introducing rugby league to France was considered to have little chance of success. As a direct challenge to the French Rugby Union, established in the previous century and whose clubs were widespread throughout France, it appeared a puny threat. Not only the French Federation, but the strength and formidable power of the British unions seemed altogether too heavy an opponent, even for such a determined champion as Galia.

With no infrastructure to rely on apart from the limited assistance of Breyer and Bernat and the circumscribed support of the RFL, Galia had to draw on his own individual commitment even to see the first stage of the project through. The lack of all the personnel that would today be considered essential made the task so much harder. Refusals and possible threats would have deterred others and, as an intelligent man, Galia must have known doubts but his single-minded determination to seize the opportunity rose above other considerations. In Galia, the already well-developed will to win became allied to a determination to restore his self-esteem.

As each player was successively recruited, the growing sense of strength in building the team seemed to confirm that the enterprise was justified. But the possibility of failure and the accumulated setbacks simply increased the responsibility which was ultimately Galia's. It was he with whom the venture was most obviously identified. The scale of the undertaking was remarkable for any individual but especially for a 28-year old player who would not only captain the team but have to assemble it himself.

All who knew Galia attest to the strength of his character, which was evident not only in the way he played rugby, but also in his business life and in his other sport of boxing. Unlike a number of his colleagues, for him sport was not a means of social elevation or even a necessary way of earning a living. He came from a family with extensive interests in the fruit and vegetable trade in the town of Ille-sur-Têt, some twenty miles to the west of Perpignan, whose 5,000 inhabitants were mainly employed in agriculture.

The contrast between the sun-bleached south-west of France and blackened Leeds was unmistakable. Though not in human terms, for there was an enthusiastic crowd, estimated at several hundred, waiting at the city station to greet them on that Monday evening, the fifth of March. An informal civic reception hosted by the Lord Mayor was put on and many indefatigable young boys begged autographs.

The journey by train from Paris and the stormy ferry crossing had left the players tired and, conscious that they would soon need all the energy they could muster, they went to bed as soon as the reception was over. A training session had been planned for ten o'clock next morning, but, to give the tourists time to adjust, it was put back until the afternoon. Despite the high spirits and the enthusiasm for the adventure, the arrival in England, which for some of the squad was at first a bewildering experience, created a sense of nervousness and made the players fully realise the importance of the enterprise. Galia expressed it like a professional. "We are apprehensive about our first experiences in rugby league," he told reporters through an interpreter, "but by the time we leave England we hope to show that we have a liking for the game and an ability to play it."[1]

Galia and his men - eleven exiles and five adventurers, as Gaston Amila described the band - were at last launched on their voyage of initiation. The relatively carefree attitude, the willingness to seize the challenge come what may were now tempered by the realities of the month they had ahead of them in England. The necessarily rapid adaptation to a new game and a colder, damper climate, life in a city centre, the difference in food, not to mention the lack of wine and, for some, a feeling of disorientation that bordered on homesickness - all these factors had to be faced, even before the matches were played. This was life as a professional rugby league player, in which the performance is all, but where so much can conspire to affect that performance. "I must admit," said Gaston Amila, "that at first everything was very difficult."[2]

After the squad had undergone the first training sessions at the Stade Buffalo in Paris, the former rugby union international, Marcel de Laborderie, was quoted as saying that he was particularly impressed with the backs and thought they would quickly adapt. *The Yorkshire Post*'s Paris correspondent added: "I do not hesitate to say that this team is at any rate the equal of the French rugby union side, if not better." But what do they know of rugby who only rugby union know?

Well-intentioned as they were, the Paris training sessions could not prepare the newcomers for the rigours of English rugby league. Jonty Parkin simply called his new charges "a likely-looking lot" and looked forward to making them into a real rugby league team.[3] The former Great Britain and Wakefield Trinity captain, together with the Welsh forward Joe Thompson, a three-times tourist to Australia who took over as Leeds coach mid-way through the French visit, would have their first opportunity of sizing up the Frenchmen on the Tuesday afternoon between 2.30 and 4 p.m. The two coaches, assisted by Leeds trainer Bright Heyhurst, had a good deal to do in a short time. Their main priorities were to instruct the newcomers in the specific aspects of rugby league, such as the play-the-ball, the scrum - two areas which would concern them for some time - and the many rule differences between the two codes of rugby. They would also have to ensure that the players curbed their impulse to kick the ball, and particularly directly into touch. Handicapped by a lack of French, Parkin and Thompson had to demonstrate by example.

After the individual instruction, the players went into a practice game, joined by their mentors. For the first time, the three or four hundred spectators began to find an answer to their curiosity about whether these Frenchmen could ever make a success of this game. They loudly applauded the speed and handling of the backs and of many of the forwards. The coaches were impressed too, although both were concerned about the lack of time available, especially to drill some defensive pattern into the Frenchmen.

The observing *Yorkshire Post* reporter was keen to emphasise the influence of Galia, describing him as "a positive glutton for the hardest of work" and "a complete footballer" who was full of "remarkable enthusiasm". He went on: "Galia dominated everything, not so much because he was in charge and would have his men work on the lines he set down, but because he was here, there and everywhere in the play. And, best of all, his great keenness fired the men who have followed him in this admittedly bold venture."

That evening, in his room at the Griffin Hotel, just across the road from the railway station where they had arrived the day before, Charles Mathon wrote home to his wife Marcelle: "It is six o'clock and we have just returned from a training session with an English coach, which we shall be doing every day. I've never seen anything like the reception we were given here. Everyone is very kind and helpful." As Mathon suggested, the players had been set much more at ease since their arrival by the friendliness and co-operation of their hosts. But there were many questions still to be answered.

Would the crash course in rugby league that the English coaches were putting them through be enough to enable them at least not to become a laughing-stock in the difficult matches ahead? Some of the players who had been banned hadn't even played rugby union for some time - would their fitness hold up? And how would such a small squad cope if there were injuries?

With only seventeen players, who were due to play four matches on tour, Galia's men would only just make up sufficient numbers for a modern-day squad. Those pioneers have become recognised as the apostles of rugby league in France, but only two weeks before departure two other players were announced as members of the party. For some reason Gérald - the pseudonym of a young Toulouse player whose parents refused to let him go to England; not to be confused with the international centre of the same name - and Lémond (Chalon-sur-Saône) missed the trip and future fame.[4] The international forward Bioussa was another who had been pencilled in on Galia's list but had had second thoughts.

Nowadays a touring team is accompanied by its coterie of managers, medics, baggage men and other assistants, whose job it is to smooth the players' passage so that they have only to concern themselves with the playing of the game. Galia's men, or Galia's Boys, as they became known, were joined by just two other members of the party. Maurice Blein, the journalist who was the same age as Galia, interpreted for the Frenchmen, and Charles Bernat, Victor Breyer's colleague who had long been associated with soccer in Paris both as a player and administrator, acted as manager. Even though Blein and Bernat looked after the group, it is quite clear that in any important matters, such as finance, it was Galia who was very much in control.

It is difficult to believe, in the present era, that the majority of Galia's squad had never even seen rugby league played. They fell in with him after being convinced by his description of the England-Australia exhibition match and the opportunities which the "neo-rugby" offered. The first match they saw with their own eyes took place on the afternoon of Wednesday, 7th March at a leaden Crown Flatt, where Dewsbury were easily beaten by Salford, winners by 35-5.

The next day began on a more sombre and reflective note as the party paid their respects to the war dead by marching the short distance from their hotel to the War Memorial, where Galia laid a wreath. But later the Frenchmen were able to put into practice something of what they had learned from the previous day's match. A more authentic training session was organised for them, involving members of the Leeds squad. With the exception of Vignal, who watched the first part of the game from the bench, and Amila, Petit and Fabre, who lined up in opposition, the French team took on a Leeds side which also included, apart from the two coaches, Brough,

Harris, Davies, Parker, Busch, Jubb, Green and Jones. Around 3,000 keenly interested spectators turned up to watch and see how the first non-English-speaking rugby league players would fare. Once again, the Frenchmen surprised the crowd by their handling skill, which was commented on not only by the Leeds players but also by none other than all-time great Harold Wagstaff, who was there to see for himself what to make of these Frenchmen. He was reported to have been much impressed by their ability to handle the ball quickly and also by their support play.[5]

The French themselves, however, were under no illusions about how much they still had to learn and they in turn were astonished at the high standards which seemed to be taken for granted among the Leeds players. Maurice Blein later spoke about how his side had been taken aback by the speed of the game, compared to what they had been used to in rugby union. They were also impressed by the Englishmen's range of attacking skills, with their dummies, swerves, sidesteps and change of pace, but most of all the Frenchmen feared the English defensive capabilities. A rigorous attitude to tackling was something which the visitors would soon have to learn to adopt themselves.

The Rugby Football League could hardly have prepared a tougher initiation into the game than the fixture arranged for Galia and his team against the strength of Wigan - who were to end the season as championship winners - just four days after their arrival in England. Although played on the same weekend as the third round Challenge Cup-ties - Wigan had been knocked out in the previous round - the match would guarantee maximum publicity and ensure a healthy attendance to offset some of the costs of the tour. But it was hardly an even contest to pitch some of English rugby league's best professionals against a side which was completely new to the game, had never played together before and had not even played much rugby union recently.

No wonder the French were nervous in their Central Park dressing-room on that Saturday, 10th March, wondering what exactly was being prepared for them. Wigan captain Jim Sullivan came in five minutes before kick-off to wish them good luck. It's unlikely that the sight of the Wigan star, despite his kind words, would have increased their confidence. Blein later admitted he had never suffered as much as before that match. The RFL secretary, John Wilson, watching from the stand, confessed he felt shivers running down his spine as he tried not to envisage the whole enterprise falling apart at the first stage.

The opening stanza of the match did nothing to assuage those fears. In poor weather and with no sense of the collective positioning which only match practice can bring, the Frenchmen spent the opening quarter of the game chasing cherry-and-white shadows, buying dummies wholesale, tackling thin air and making the serious mistake of kicking directly to full-back Sullivan. Within six minutes of kick-off, Wigan were eight points up and another Sullivan goal put them 10-0 ahead after a quarter of an hour. A total collapse looked imminent as the Frenchmen appeared to be well out of their depth. The wisdom of playing this match looked in grave doubt.

Nervously at first the Frenchmen began to show something of their more enterprising play, putting some good handling moves together. Their quick backs started to make breaks. Confidence soon increased when prop-forward Georges Blanc crossed the Wigan line to post France's first-ever try in rugby league.

Galia, playing in the second row, lost no time in making his presence felt, setting a captain's example with his defence and intelligent passing. More than that, he encouraged his players to make up by sheer effort and determination what they lacked in familiarity with the game. As Wigan, though playing for the usual terms, began to take unaccustomed liberties, the French moved into their stride, motivated by Galia's alternate pleadings, threats and cajoling. Each time his side stood behind the goal-line after a Wigan try, Galia would walk among his men, reminding them of the seriousness of their purpose, making it clear there would be no contracts when they got home if they didn't improve.

It had an effect. Trailing by only 18-14 at the interval, the French levelled the scores on the hour. With Galia, who had not played any sort of rugby match for over a year, scoring two tries himself, they took the lead three minutes from full time and were heading for an extraordinary victory. But a face-saving try by winger Jack Morley, converted by Sullivan to take his tally to six, restored Wigan's pride at 30-27. Nevertheless France had scored seven tries to six and created a very favourable impression among the 8,000 crowd, most of whom had come as sceptics but had gone away persuaded of the possibilities which the Frenchmen had suddenly opened up for their game.

One match report concluded: "The Frenchmen's style is admirably suited in that it is based mainly on attack, though for defensive purposes they have a lot to learn, especially in positional play. They handled splendidly, rarely wasted a ball, passed to each other with marked intelligence and finished strongly."

Galia's men had achieved more than they could have hoped for in that opening match. Their performance had given all those involved in the undertaking an increased sense of purpose and perhaps even destiny.

Although the two codes of rugby were in some ways closer then than now - which allowed for the Frenchmen's relatively quick transition - the differences which the French noted could just as well apply today. "At rugby union you could find touch and have a rest," said Barbazanges, "because that would stop the play. At rugby league that wasn't possible. Suppose there's a play-the-ball, you have to get into position; suppose you run 40 metres, there's another play-the-ball and you have to get into position again. Or you get hit and it might be hard to recover immediately. You certainly have to be in top condition to play this game."[6]

Fate, or rather the organisers of the tourists' intinerary, decreed that the French should sample another aspect of English culture by spending the night at Blackpool rather than returning to Leeds. It wasn't the only reason why the lengthening of the tour was already being discussed. Galia's party wanted to learn as much as they could while in England and so two more matches were added to the agenda - against Salford, whom they had watched beating Dewsbury, and Hull.

Firm plans were already being drawn up for the first rugby league match to be played in France involving French players. Victor Breyer wrote to the RFL agreeing to a France-England match at the Buffalo Velodrome on April 15th, but he pointed out that a break with the French Rugby Union was a consequence of it. He therefore asked the Rugby League to discuss an agreement with the stadium manager, Louis Delblat, not only about the use of the ground but also about the whole future of rugby league in France. When Delblat arrived in England a contract was duly signed which guaranteed that all representative matches played in Paris would be staged at the Buffalo Stadium, whose management now became closely linked with the fledgling rugby league movement and who would take ten per cent of receipts from matches held there.

Breyer's letter was discussed at a meeting of the Rugby League Council which was combined with an official reception for the French tourists at the Griffin Hotel. There were speeches and presentations, and comparisons were made between the French initiative and the Northern breakaway of 1895, which, for some of those in attendance, was still relatively fresh in the memory. The vice-chairman, Joe Lewthwaite, officially welcoming the Frenchmen into the rugby league fold, recalled the motives of the decisive move 39 years earlier, drawing a parallel with the present situation in France. The Northern clubs, he insisted, had wanted everything to be clean and above board, being determined that honesty should prevail. As a result of their resolve, they now had a great game which they could be proud of and had no reason to regret their decision.

Responding to the welcome they had been given, Jean Galia, through Maurice Blein, who interpreted for him, outlined the size of the venture. "When I undertook the task of assembling a team, there were those who said it could not be done," he said. "Well, as you now see, it has been done and we now look forward to establishing the game in France with an organised championship and perhaps also a cup competition. We know that the task ahead is still a great one and that there is much hard work ahead but I believe it can be done."

The confident tone was relayed by Charles Bernat, who spoke of the imminent formation of a French Rugby League Council and outlined his own commitment to the game. As a former player and official of a top club, he had been involved with football for some forty years but now had thrown in his lot with rugby league, so convinced was he of its future success.

A further analogy with 1895 was made by Maurice Blein, who stated that broken-time payments to players would be welcomed in France in place of the "shamateurism" which was widespread. It was an apposite comment at a time when the French sports daily, *L'Auto*, among others, had been devoting large amounts of space to allegations of professionalism and corruption within the FFR, which naturally denied the accusations. Encouragingly for the proper development of rugby league, Blein also promised that the amateur area of the game would be given as much attention as the so-called professional side.[7]

For the second match of their tour, the Frenchmen returned to what was almost like home ground. But even though they had become familiar with the Leeds team in practice sessions, Galia's team would find them tough opposition in a full-blown match. Once again bad weather affected both the size of the crowd - eventually given as 7,000 - as well as the playing conditions, so that the Headingley turf soon turned to mud, and the leather ball became difficult to use. Amazingly in view of the conditions it was the Frenchmen's handling skills which drew praise from observers. "I was immensely impressed by the way they can gather the ball from the ground without breaking their run," was one appreciative comment. "They handled with a skill and sureness that has not been equalled at Headingley all season," said another. It was clear that Galia had taken the Australian forward play, with their close support work which he had witnessed at Stade Pershing, as a model for his own pack. But it was their lack of defence which again was the Frenchmen's downfall, with Leeds winger Stan Smith racing in for four tries as his side rattled up 25 points with little opposition. French naivety allowed breaks down the blind side and the second row gave no crossfield cover, but Galia again rallied his men effectively, making a try for Barbazanges, scoring another himself and generally motivating his players so well that they came back to score three tries in the last quarter of the match to give respectability to a final score of 25-17. The Leeds players insisted that they had never been able to take their opposition lightly and were in awe of the ease with which the Frenchmen handled the ball, despite the raw conditions. The watching Rugby League officials were even more convinced that French crowds would be impressed enough by this style of rugby to make the venture ultimately successful.

The unrelenting rain which followed the tourists to their next match at Warrington against a Rugby League XIII did not deter over 11,000 fans from turning up to see the Frenchmen's attacking skills pitted against the know-how of some of the League's top players. Once more the visitors' inexperience in defence led to their third defeat, this time by 32-16, with St

Helens winger Alf Ellaby repeating Stan Smith's feat of scoring four tries. Not to be outdone, his French counterpart, Laurent Lambert, added two more to his own tally, but it was the try he made for Charles Mathon which had the crowd cheering longest. Sprinting down the touchline from near half-way he kicked ahead past Sullivan, regathered and, as the cover defence approached, he lobbed a perfect pass inside at the last second for Mathon to cross for the try of the match.

Galia's team had the advantage of watching their next opponents the day before they were due to play against them. In now-familar conditions of wind and rain, this time at Mount Pleasant, they watched the mid-table side London Highfield beat Batley 7-5 before Wednesday's floodlit match at the White City Stadium.

Either the English weather or English food, or a combination of both, began to have a deleterious effect on the Frenchmen. Gaston Amila admitted that what they missed most, surprise of surprises, was French cooking and, for him at least, a bottle or two of his native Corbières wine. "Galia told us some barrels which he had ordered would be arriving shortly," Amila recalled, "but of course they never did. He was just having us on."[8] Then, soon after the party arrived in London, François Nouel was taken to hospital suffering from stomach pains, thought to be the onset of appendicitis, and at least four other players required medical attention, although all except Nouel were declared fit to play against Highfield.

Nouel's temporary discomfort did not affect his impression of what he had experienced in England. He wrote to his friends at the Aviron Bayonnais rugby union club describing rugby league in highly complimentary terms. It was no coincidence that two of his former team-mates, Ainciart and Celhay, gave notice of their intention to leave the club, presumably to follow in Nouel's footsteps, which caused a local sensation. They later retracted their resignation but the Bayonne club did not appreciate what the two players unconvincingly claimed had only been an April fool joke.

Despite their unfamiliarity with playing under floodlights and with a white ball, the French came close to achieving their first victory. Amila came into the side for his first match in place of Nouel and played in his customary beret but the outstanding player on the French side was the big front-rower Charles Petit who cut an even more imposing figure. Galia once again led the way, scoring a fine try. With considerable improvement in defence, the touring side was leading 17-14 with two minutes remaining. From a penalty close to the French line, however, the London side scrambled a try to draw level and a fine conversion from wide out gave them victory.

Though two matches were added to the tour, Galia's men were already beginning to think of the return home and the task which lay ahead. Once the party had regained its Leeds base, Galia, together with Bernat and Blein, met RFL officials for further discussions. A written undertaking to assist the development of the game in France was requested of the Rugby League, so that prospective interested parties would have a clear indication of future planning. In addition to the France-England match to be played in Paris, other arrangements for tours were discussed and agreed on in principle, as was the official setting-up of the French Rugby League.

The RFL also gave their commitment to underwriting the present tour expenses, so that if the receipts from matches were to prove insufficent, the Council would compensate Galia and his players. Lewthwaite and Wilson attempted to ascertain from Galia what financial agreement he had made with his team so that a satisfactory agreement could be settled on. Galia was having none of it. The Council minutes record for the 26th of March, the day before departure: "As it had been impossible so far to get from Jean Galia the details of the contract he had with his players, the Committee deputed the Vice-Chairman and the Secretary to effect a settlement before the departure of the party." It is not recorded what agreement was made, only that Jonty Parkin, Joe Thompson and Bright Heyhurst were each granted £5 for their services to the tourists.

On March 21st, while the tourists were in London, Galia drew up a written contract which was intended to bind the pioneers to his team and the future French Rugby League for the next two seasons. Various stipulations were made, including fines for indiscipline, as well as a financial agreement. In the series of exhibition matches to be played in France, which Galia already had in mind, the sixteen pioneers would share equally 70 per cent of half of the gate receipts, once expenses had been deducted. Galia himself was authorised to take from ten to thirty per cent of the sum "as recompense for the great effort which he alone has made."

With just the two additional matches left to play, Galia had called on all his squad members except one, who was not to play at all on the tour. The ex-rugby union international hooker, Lolo Fabre, never quite earned the right to call himself a pioneer. Galia had been angry with Fabre from the moment they assembled in Paris because the Lézignan hooker, despite his promises to train intensively, had shown up looking grossly overweight and out of condition. He might have been left behind if it had not been for his assurances that he would train hard in England, and the fact that seventeen men would be better than sixteen. Once the squad began their training sessions, it was obvious that Fabre would be of little use, as he barely managed to complete a warm-up lap of the Headingley pitch - to the amusement of his team-mates and the annoyance of the captain. In one respect only did he manage to earn the respect of his colleagues - for the amount of food he managed to tuck away at each meal.

Yet by the time they played the fifth match - against Hull on Saturday, 24th March - seventeen players had been used. With injuries having taken their toll, the Frenchmen were short of players. Thanks to Walter Popplewell, the Bramley chairman, they were able to call on a Bramley A-team player who did more than make up the numbers. Playing under a pseudonym - variously reported as Eugene Vignials (a variation on the name of an actual member of the party, Jean-Marie Vignal) and Virginals, which looks like a transmission error - the half-back scored a try and kicked four goals to help the French to their first-ever victory. Showing increased fitness, they finished strongly, scoring ten decisive points in the last ten minutes, with a brilliant solo effort by Amila from his own quarter to seal the famous win by 26-23.

The final match, played on Monday, 26th March against the league leaders and previous season's champions, Salford, was a different proposition. Once again the injury-hit Frenchmen had to borrow a player, the Cumberland loose-forward Dalton, who played in the centre under his own name, but when they lost Porra early in the second half with a collar-bone injury, Galia's twelve men could not cope with the pace and variety of the Salford attack. Despite their captain's customary coaxing and his own exemplary efforts, the Frenchmen lost by 35-13 before a crowd of 7,000.

The six-match tour had resulted in one win and five defeats, with 116 points scored and 164 against. Half-a-dozen players, including Galia himself, had played in all the matches. The tour receipts had now risen to £2000, of which the French share would be just less than half. It is recorded that each French player received £35. The financial success of the tour was, though necessary, of secondary importance to the growing belief that France now represented a viable area for the expansion of the game. Thoughts moved quickly ahead to the forthcoming France-England match in Paris on April 15th and a short tour by a Yorkshire select team.

Although the pioneering players themselves had entered into the venture without really being aware of what it would entail, either in the short term or in the long term, they were now certain that their future lay in rugby league. "There was an exceptionally high morale among us," said Amila, "because we knew and could foresee that something unique, a phenomenon, was about to happen. This noble, manly, uncompromising game was made for us and the French temperament. We were absolutely convinced that it would take off and that the new game would soon capture the imagination of our fellow-countrymen."[9]

Galia's men left Leeds at 8 a.m. on Tuesday, 27th March - accompanied by RFL officials as far as Victoria - three weeks and one day after their arrival. They had clearly left an impression on English rugby league for it was not long before secretary John Wilson was having to give assurances that English clubs would not be allowed to poach French players.

The English tour marked a watershed in the sporting lives of Galia's players. It would also mark a turning point both in the history of international rugby league and the nature of rugby in France. "We have no doubts," said Galia, looking ahead to the impending exhibition matches back home, "about the interest that will be roused by the visit of this side to the south of France, the home of French rugby. As the interest created by the international match will be carried on by the Leeds tour, the way will be steadily prepared for the effort that will be made in the summer to begin a French Rugby League championship."[10]

Chapter Five
FIRST STEPS

Though the tourists' initiation into rugby league had been hard enough, the difficulty now lay in transferring what had been learned into the players' home environment. Galia, who alone among the pioneers had an overview of the enterprise, understood better than any the immediate need to build on what the English tour had taught them. The first steps towards mastering the new sport had begun, but only sixteen Frenchmen had ever played it and so far there were no clubs in France where they could play the game again or where they could introduce others to it. Most significant, rugby league had yet to find a public, without which professional sport cannot exist.

An important advance was made when the sport's governing body, to be known as the Ligue Française de Rugby à Treize, was formed and the process of legal recognition began when Charles Bernat lodged its articles of association at the Préfecture de Police in Paris on April 6th 1934. The first chairman of the new body was François Cadoret, the mayor and parliamentary deputy of Riec-sur-Bélon in Britanny, who was widely known in sporting circles. The Ligue's committee consisted of three representatives from Villeneuve, Georges Bordeneuve, the mayor, and Dr Léon Vinson, who were both nominated as vice-chairmen, as well as Jean Galia himself; and from Paris Messrs Bernat (secretary), Delblat (treasurer), Blein, Durand, Gondelier, Launier, Machavoine and Meunier, although the last-named was not mentioned in the report in *L'Auto* of the first official meeting which took place on April 16th. Most of the members were connected either with the press or with the Buffalo Stadium. All were friends or colleagues of Victor Breyer, who chose not to join them in a formal role, preferring to work independently in the background.

The Ligue's honorary president was Jean Payra[1], parliamentary deputy of the Pyrénées Orientales and a well-known figure in rugby in his native Perpignan, where he had been both captain and president of the ASP rugby union club. It had been widely announced that Jean Bourrel, the influential former patron of the Quillan rugby union club for which Galia had played, would also join the committee, but his name was not among those announced at that first constitutional meeting. Whatever involvement either Bourrel or Payra had was peripheral and short-lived. Other officials would also be replaced as the game became established and the impetus shifted away from the capital to the south.

As word spread about the English exploits of Galia's pioneers and as people began to look forward to watching France play against England, others began to convert to the new sport or at least try their hand at it. Two Parisian amateur clubs were quickly formed and were engaged to play a curtain-raiser before the France-England match: they were Sport Olympique de Paris, coached by François Nouel, and the student side, Quartier Etudiants Club. Outside the capital, and even before the international match had been played, the early signs were that more than a dozen teams would form a professional rugby league competition.

By one o'clock on the afternoon of Sunday, April 15th, a large crowd, which would swell to capacity, filled the Buffalo Stadium for the curtain-raiser to the first international rugby league match to be played between France and England. Sport Olympique de Paris, which had its origins in a bar in the rue de la Roquette, was a scratch side which Galia used as opposition for his representative teams whenever they were in Paris. They would meet the Quartier Etudiants Club again in the final of the first Paris amateur rugby league championship. The student side was a colourful outfit and included three players who would go on to find fame as a government minister, a composer and a singer. According to the account given by journalist Henri Garcia, the QEC winger, Loys van Lee, was the first Frenchman to score a try in a rugby league match in France - and in circumstances which were literally hair-raising. Playing under a pseudonym and wearing a disguise consisting of a wig and beard, the speedy winger was racing down the touchline towards the tryline when an Olympique player made a last-ditch attempt to prevent him scoring. Stretching out a hand to collar him, the would-be tackler caught van Lee's wig and as the winger dived over the line, the horrified defender, thinking he had scalped his opposite number, fainted with fright.[2]

As the time for the main event came closer, the excitement - not just at the match about to start but for French rugby league generally - was heightened when the presence of the young rugby union star, Max Rousié, was spotted among the spectators. Then, in contrast with the England-Australia match almost four months before, the teams emerged into warm sunshine and ideal conditions for a demonstration of fast, open football.

Though it was a surprise that Galia had not recruited the new players that he had promised, the thirteen pioneers on duty put up a strong fight against their formidable opponents. France scored first through Lambert but trailed

15-3 at half-time. After the interval they put pressure on England, twice coming within two points of the English lead as Duhau scored two tries, both converted by the prop-forward himself. Galia received a hero's welcome and massive applause when he scored his try, as the contest and the atmosphere grew in intensity. But the spectators appreciated also the fine skills shown by England and in particular applauded a virtuoso try-scoring effort by stand-off Emlyn Jenkins, which, converted by Jim Sullivan, was probably the decisive score in England's 32-21 victory. To their credit France had scored five tries to England's six, though Sullivan's seven goals extended the winning margin.

The 20,000 spectators paid gate receipts of 160,000 francs, or just over £2,000, which cheered the officials of both countries. There were handshakes and back-slapping all round as the final whistle blew on a match which had been a clear success. Victor Breyer commented: "We knew how much depended on this game. We had to satisfy a critical crowd whose idea of rugby league is built on what they saw in the England-Australia game. I think the players of both sides satisfied everyone today and I am certain there is a very bright future for the game in our country. The people will want the game after what they have seen today."[3]

That the French public was far more concerned with what happened on the pitch than off was made clear by the guest speaker, representing the Ministry of Sport, at the celebration dinner which followed the match. Open professionalism, he maintained, was the surest means to do away with shamateurism. Followers of sport in France, he assured his audience, were unconcerned by whether players were paid or not, so long as they played.

The next day the first meeting of the committee of the newly-formed Ligue Française de Rugby à XIII was held at the Restaurant Prunier. It was an appropriate place, for the fruit of the *prunier* (plum-tree) contributes greatly to the wealth of Villeneuve-sur-Lot, whose mayor, Georges Bordeneuve, now joined the committee as a vice-president. His first duty was to announce that the Villeneuve club, of which he was chairman and Jean Galia the major influence, had converted to rugby league and that he had bought the local stadium to ensure the game could be played there.

Galia, a co-opted member of the committee, promised that many more clubs would follow, after all the interest created by the France-England game, and brandished a bundle of letters from both clubs and individual players asking about joining the new movement. Encouraging as all this was, the committee, chaired by François Cadoret, decided it must first deal with more prosaic work involving the recruiting and training of referees, the translation into French of the rules, and public relations.

John Wilson, who attended the meeting, was much impressed with the thoroughness of the new administration and the enthusiasm it brought to the work in hand. "When we came to France for the match at the Buffalo

Stadium," he said, "we hoped that the weekend would prove historic. There seems to be no doubt about it now." He was also pleased to be able to report back to the Council that the RFL's share of the receipts from the international match had already covered their costs towards launching the French initiative as well as the extra payments made to Galia's players during their tour of England the previous month.[4]

The French public, brought up on the international rugby union matches which had not now been played for the past three years, responded with the same enthusiasm which Galia himself had exhibited at that first match between England and the Australians. Some did not. Certain rugby union officials who had been in attendance had attempted to rubbish the game, but provoked an opposite effect from nearby spectators who threatened them with misfortune. There were other, more official attempts to stifle the infant sport and to punish those who had assisted its birth. Players who had not already been banned by the French Rugby Union before they went off to England now received official notice of their ostracism. Potentially much more harmful were the attempts to prevent the game being played, even on the municipally-owned grounds which made up the majority of venues in France.

And who would have resorted to this kind of subterfuge? Members of the general public who simply preferred their rugby to be played with line-outs, rucks, mauls and fifteen men? Spectators who rose in indignation against open and honest professionalism? No, the public had plenty to gain and nothing to lose, whereas those who held positions of power and status within the existing rugby union framework had every reason to see their status threatened. They refused to modify their position and took appropriate - that is, self-interested - action. Rugby union, which by mismanagement had degenerated both on the field and off, was intent on bringing rugby league down as well.

It should all have been a matter of personal choice, as a columnist in *L'Auto* neatly suggested.

"Do you like rugby league better than rugby union?" he asked.

"Do you prefer Normandy sole to lobster *à l'américaine*?

"Are the mountains more beautiful than the sea?

"Personally I enjoyed the game that 26 young men played on Sunday at the Buffalo Stadium.

"It was lively, keenly contested, full of incident, athletic without being brutal ...

"But that doesn't stop me from liking the round ball game, from appreciating a good basketball match or being interested in a game of hockey.

"And that wouldn't stop me either from enthusing about a robust forward game peppered with attacking three-quarter play, according to the rules of fair play - if I was offered it. But where are the snows of yesteryear?

Where is your rugby, Dantou?" he enquired of the FFR president.[5]

Perhaps Galia had anticipated a little local difficulty when he wired to the RFL the arrangements for the forthcoming tour of France by the Yorkshire select side. "I confirm that the Yorkshire Selection touring team's games will be played before friendly crowds," his telegram informed Rugby League officials, most probably referring to the unruly reputation which rugby union crowds had earned for themselves over the years. Galia clearly was anxious to assure the RFL that similar behaviour would not be tolerated at rugby league matches.

Provisional arrangements for the tour had been drawn up while Galia was still in England. Naturally, the main concern was to take matches to as wide an area as possible within the short time available, to identify those cities where there was an established following for rugby and at which rugby league clubs might eventually be located. The original schedule had Paris, Vichy or Dijon, Agen and Pau as venues. The final arrangements took matches to Lyon, Paris, Villeneuve, Bordeaux and Pau. Perpignan, that hotbed which was Galia's native territory, was left out of the itinerary, although he claimed that the greatest difficulty lay in deciding which places to leave out, so huge was the demand to host the matches. A request had even been received from Italy, where a consortium wanted to discuss putting on a match in Rome between the touring side and a combined French and Italian team, although the interest expressed never quite took shape.

The Yorkshire Selection was put together as such at the request of the French, who were concerned that the public should see it as having representative status. In effect it consisted of those Leeds players whom Galia's men by now knew so well, plus two players loaned by York. By the end of the tour the two teams would be on intimate terms after having played against each other a further five times in two weeks. The eighteen Yorkshiremen, accompanied by Joe Thompson as team manager, two directors, and referee Harding of Manchester, travelled via Paris to Lyon, playing their first match at a stadium at Villeurbanne on Tuesday, the first of May.

This opening match fell foul of poor weather conditions which reduced the crowd to around 6,000 spectators, who nevertheless responded keenly to the game, won by the Yorkshire team by 35-22. The match was remarkable also for the rugby league debut of the phenomenon that was Max Rousié, who lost no time at all in settling to the new code and scored a hat-trick of tries. On the return to Paris for Saturday's match at the Stade Buffalo, similar weather and a similar-sized crowd greeted the tourists. In a match kicked off by the world middleweight boxing champion, Marcel Thil, the Frenchmen again went down, this time by 27-19, but, as at Lyon, Rousié gave some indication of what a force he would become in his new sport, scoring a try within five minutes of the start.

The Yorkshiremen travelled south for the second half of the tour, playing the following day in beautiful weather at Galia's home ground. On this fine Sunday, the sixth of May, sports fans from as far afield as Bordeaux made their way to Villeneuve's Pont de Marot stadium, some of them by rail, at the special half-price fares for the occasion. The gates were opened at one o'clock, three hours before the main match, and people brought chairs, stools and ladders, either to sit or stand on, as the stadium did not have terracing. The crowd, estimated at over 10,000, including numerous guests of honour, was the biggest Villeneuve had ever seen for a sporting event, with gate receipts twice as great as the previous best.

Following a curtain-raiser played by two teams of *minimes* (under-fourteens), who had been coached by Galia himself, the main event kicked off at 4.15, after the formal presentation of teams to the visiting government dignitaries and others. The big crowd soon warmed to the virtuoso display of rugby skills paraded before them.

"The Englishmen," wrote Henri Hoursiangou, sports editor of the Bordeaux paper *La Petite Gironde*, "played with assurance, coolness and remarkable speed to score tries which hitherto we have not had the pleasure of admiring in any other international side. They played like magicians." The spectators were soon craning their necks to follow every dashing move, enthusiastically applauding the free-flowing exhibition. They were ecstatic about the high-scoring game in which the play moved from end to end and side to side, and in which Galia, the local hero, now a figure of national importance, and his men played their own prominent role. Though the final score of 51-38 suggests a rather carefree attitude to defence, the crowd was left in no doubt about the spectacular nature of the new sport. "Do you want to know what the public's impression was of this match?" asked Hoursiangou. "It's not difficult to judge. They left the stadium enchanted. This match will long be remembered by all who saw it."[6]

An even bigger crowd of 13,000 spectators turned up for the game at Bordeaux on the Thursday and were thrilled as the Frenchmen almost reversed a half-time deficit of 21-2 before losing by 34-28. And if they finally ran out of steam in the last match at Pau, going down by 65-29, another capacity crowd was delighted by the fast, open play in heatwave conditions. The Leeds players, less used to this kind of weather, almost played themselves to a standstill. No player on the field was applauded more than Stan Smith, who enraptured the fans as he flew down the wing.

The tour had brought in the crowds and had more than covered costs, although it was reported that the Leeds directors, with typical Headingley largesse, "were not at all concerned about the financial side".[7] Simply they were pleased to have played a significant part in strengthening the position of rugby league in France and bringing the game to a wider audience, with gratifying results. But the financial viability of rugby league was a vital aspect of its establishment: this tour had earned almost 300,000 francs, with a net profit of almost 70,000 francs.

"The progress is greater than anything we had hoped for," announced John Wilson, who had joined the party after the Challenge Cup final. "Everywhere we went there were shoals of applications for admission to the League - from clubs as well as players. The French Rugby League's difficulty is to decide what to do with all the applications."[8]

At the same time as the Yorkshire side and Galia's men were winning over the fans in Pau, a meeting of the French Rugby Union took place at Toulouse. Remarkably, they had been studying a proposal to set up a 13-a-side league. The first move had apparently come from the newly-formed Ligue Française who might have been looking for a reconciliation. Odd as it may sound, in view of the handling of Galia and other disqualified players and directors by the FFR, a member of the Ligue, Delblat, with one eye on his business as manager of the Stade Buffalo, had originally tried to pre-empt possible conflict between the two bodies. Shortly after the Ligue had been formed he took care to explain that the name (League, not Federation) was chosen so as to show that the new association had not been set up in opposition to the existing FFR. Newspaper reports suggest that the hostility emanated from one side only. The Rugby Football League's attitude towards expansion in France, despite Harry Sunderland's urgings, had been cautious and strictly non-confrontational. In March 1934, as Galia was arriving in England with the pioneering tourists, the RFL had contacted the FFR to suggest collaboration in introducing rugby league into France.

"The Rugby League," wrote secretary Wilson to the Federation chairman, "would much prefer to avoid creating a dissident movement or appearing to be in revolt against the authority which your Federation represents as the governing body of rugby football in France. To this effect my Committee is not only willing but is keen to establish relations with yours with a view to finding the means of coming to an agreement. They are now ready to make all possible concessions in order to avoid a clash of interests which they consider can only end badly. I should be very much obliged if you would let me know your views on this matter."[9]

The suggestion was quickly thrown out. Without batting its one eyelid, the committee declared: "The Federation has decided to ignore professional rugby, considering it incompatible with the traditions of amateurism of the French Rugby Federation."[10] A choice remark.

The FFR's treasurer, Monsieur Rolland, later paid tribute to the virtuoso displays of rugby league he had seen for himself in England, but appeared more than willing to believe certain assumptions. "Rugby league, being palpably faster than rugby union, demands athletes who undergo strict training several times a week, which is incompatible with the daily demands placed on a young man to provide a living for himself and his family... In order to play the game well players must have no other preoccupation, in other words they must be professionals. Let me also counter the objection that there are amateurs in the Rugby League. Alas there are not, since these ruggers [sic] receive broken-time payments."[11]

The French Rugby Union not only did not want anything to do with rugby league, it would also make sure it stood in the way of anyone who did. The union authorities would "disqualify" any ground on which "professional rugby" (rugby league) was played. They showed they could move quickly when they needed to. After action by the FFR against the Stade Pershing and the Stade Buffalo in Paris, the directors of the SABordeaux club who had taken part in organising, a couple of days before, the match between Yorkshire and France - only the sixth rugby league match to be staged in France - were banned. The FFR also invited clubs to provide them with the names of all those players or officials who had been involved in negotiations with the Ligue. The French Rugby Union, in particularly vindictive mood, promised that if clubs provided this information only those people named would be struck off. If a club did not comply and its players were later found to be guilty of involvement with the *treizistes* the whole club would be suspended.[12]

Their actions were taken against a backdrop of allegations which had been made principally by *L'Auto* - the journalist Robert Perrier had played a leading investigative role - at the time Galia was recruiting players for his pioneering tour of England. "Should one be an accomplice to dishonesty in sport by hiding the truth?" asked a leading article which served to introduce a page full of attacks, launched by Galia's renegades, Samatan, Porra, Carrère and Fabre, on the Federation's attitude to shamateurism. The attitude of leading clubs towards paying players was called into question by these allegations, one of which, made by Samatan, insisted that the FFR itself had paid a bonus of 1000 francs per player after an international match against England. Samatan went on give details of approaches made to him by such clubs as Stade Toulousain, Carcassonne, Quillan and Agen, even producing a letter from the Agen chairman bidding for his signature against two other clubs. There were steaming denials, of course, though Monsieur de Luze, former chairman of UFRA, chairman of Stade Bordelais and member of the Federation's disciplinary committee, found "nothing unusual" in the revelations, pointing to his own reports of the previous year which made a similar point but which the FFR had refused even to discuss.[13]

As *L'Auto* knew perfectly well, it was all bad timing for the French authorities, whose officials would shortly be travelling to London to try to convince the British that France was now clean enough to be allowed to compete again at international level. But the British rugby union authorities decided to maintain their ban on international fixtures with France, still insisting that not enough had been done to purge the game of its French ills. The French, despite their posturing which simply looked like a calculation designed to catch the approval of their British counterparts, were not true enough amateurs. The Parisian newspaper *France-Soir* called the decision a "slap in the face".[14] The French Federation went on the defensive, claiming, through its president, that it would continue to do without the British, who were essentially only interested in themselves. With the possibility of rugby league, though still undeveloped, creating a new dimension in team sport in France, the conflict between the British and French Rugby Unions looked increasingly like a lumbering battle of dinosaurs.

The British Unions, however, were not all of a piece. Some irritation with the British stance was shown later by the Welsh, who, because their rugby is not the preserve of one comfortably-off social class, have traditionally found it easier to accommodate the notion of paying players, even if they have had qualms about owning up to it. Only half-heartedly sharing the other Unions' stand against the unruly French, the Welsh committee made it clear they thought that the British Rugby Unions' attitude was playing right into the hands of rugby league.

Chapter Six
THE VILLENEUVE INITIATIVE

The strength of character shown by Jean Galia and the respect in which his players held him were two of the qualities which proved that the RFL and Breyer and his associates were fully justified in choosing him to lead rugby league on to the playing fields of France.

Galia celebrated his 29th birthday during the pioneering tour of England, having been born on March 20th, 1905 at 86 avenue Pasteur, Ille-sur-Têt. His father, also named Jean, owned large areas of agricultural land, but Jean Galia *fils* was never really interested in the family business and much preferred sport - not only rugby, but also boxing, rowing and motor racing. As the son of a family which had acquired wealth, he was able to indulge his fondness for sports cars and Bugattis in particular. But his mother, Anna, who died before Jean reached twenty, disapproved of his sporting activities. She particularly hated rugby, which she regarded as too violent a sport. She disapproved of his interest in cars too and would lie down in front of Jean's Bugatti to prevent him from going out. Her protests seem to have had little effect.

The characteristic with which Catalans are perhaps above all associated is one which first springs to mind in those who knew Galia. He was, it's said, a proud man. On the rugby field his self-esteem was the motivation behind his single-minded determination to be the best.

Many Catalan players have learned their rugby on home territory before moving away to play for other clubs, but Galia, one of the finest, never played for a local club. Although he no doubt picked up something of the game in his native Ille-sur-Têt and played a couple of games with the neighbouring village team of Millas, his career as a senior player began during military service with the 2e Aérostiers in Toulouse, where he played for TOEC (Toulouse Olympique Employé Club).

As a young man of around twenty years of age, Galia, who had not been playing rugby seriously at the time, became interested in joining the

Perpignan club, USP, and started training with them. He was watched by an ex-international back-row player who had been captain of USP's 1921 championship-winning side, Fernand Vaquer. Known as "the Field-Marshal", which reflected his military background as well as his authoritarian manner, Vaquer expressed the view that Galia would never make the grade because, as he said in Catalan, *"Es pas camat"* - his legs were not strong enough. Galia later found out what had been said about him and went away feeling both hurt and resentful. He never returned to the club. Instead he set about proving himself elsewhere. That became his spur, so that by the age of 22 he was a member of France's international side and soon earned himself a reputation as the best forward in Europe in a side which in 1930 for the first time beat two of the Home Unions in consecutive matches.

The same smouldering resentment at his ban by the French Rugby Union later led to Galia's equally determined efforts in setting up rugby league. When the opportunity was offered he seized it because he recognised the potential of the sport and because he liked what he saw, but also because he was driven by a need to restore his pride at the same time as exacting revenge on those who had punished him. By such forces, typical of certain Latin temperaments, was Galia's inner strength sustained.

"He was," his widow said, "a very proud and distant man - in other words, a Catalan. But he was very generous and gave readily of himself. He had a very high ideal of what one owed to others."[1]

Galia had a highly-developed sense of self but also showed loyalty to true friends as well as inspiring others by his personality. Only those close to him would use the familiar *tu* when speaking to him. Others called him Monsieur Jean, including, apparently, some of the directors of the club. Those who knew him believed that one of the reasons the telegram to Noguères was a set-up was that Galia would never sign himself as simply "Jean".

In personal matters he was fastidious. He was always fashionably and immaculately dressed, changing his clothes two or three times a day, and never had a hair out of place. He preferred to dress in the casual English style and owned numerous cars which at various times included an Alfa Romeo and a Nash apart from the Bugatti. He moved easily in high social circles. Galia was as successful in business - of his own making, not the family's - as in sport. He eventually created a chain of cinemas in the south-west and had interests in a theatre, a music hall and cinematic production and distribution. He also owned property in Toulouse and in the Roussillon region.

Galia was no stranger to hard work, but the summer months of 1934, customarily the close season, proved a hectic period for him and the organisers of the new Ligue Française de Rugby à Treize. Not that there was any shortage of manpower. Those who had seen the demonstration games in April and May had been enthralled and word quickly spread. Players in their hundreds wanted to join up with rugby league, not just because, at the top level, payments were to be made openly rather than secretly, but because they liked the open, fast and spectacular nature of this game which put a high value on handling and running. The prospect of international competition with Britain and, in the future, with Australia and New Zealand, also gave a dimension which was closed off in rugby union. And it was not only at professional level that rugby league would make an impact. Although twelve professional clubs were expected to start the season, eighty amateur sides had given notice of their intention to play at a secondary level.

A meeting of the Ligue Française de Rugby à XIII was held in Paris on July 24th, at which the decision was taken to base the first-ever championship on soccer's pattern - which was logical since football was the closest example of an openly professional team sport. But one regulation which was endorsed was unique to rugby league. It concerned the qualification of players, who could be brought into a side as late as the day before a match - a ruling which was designed to accommodate the almost daily defection of players from rugby union.

With so many matters of importance to be decided in a very short period, meetings were a regular occurence during that summer. A general assembly of the Ligue Française was held on August 21st at the Hotel Régina in Toulouse, to which the clubs were able to send representatives so that final details for the inaugural season could be settled. With Georges Bordeneuve presiding and Joe Lewthwaite and John Wilson - who continued to be astounded by the success of the venture - in attendance to give advice on the many questions which arose, the meeting lasted over nine hours. It was eventually announced that the championship, to begin in October, would be contested by twelve clubs - Villeneuve, Albi, Bordeaux, Lyon, Perpignan, Pau, Paris Celtic, Sport Olympique de Paris, Roanne, Grenoble, Côte Basque and Béziers. The delegates were particularly happy to welcome the Perpignan club, to be known as the XIII Catalan, which had recently been formed and which represented an important piece in the jigsaw which was being put together. The obvious omission was Toulouse itself, where no suitable ground could be found for a club to be based. Fixtures for the season were arranged, a cup competition agreed on and a schedule of representative matches between Britain and France was drawn up. Plans were also put in place for an early-season tour by the English champions Salford as well as Hunslet. The French had expressed their wish that as many of their clubs as possible should host a match against a visiting English team. For those who regarded rugby league, despite all the evidence to the contrary, as merely a professionalised version of rugby union, the governing body's concern about the creation of the many more amateur clubs shows their commitment to establishing the new sport at all levels.

As might be expected with Jean Galia at its head, the Villeneuve-sur-Lot club was already setting the example for the rest to follow. Galia and the members of the club committee had already made a remarkable riposte to their ban by the French Rugby Union only a season ago. With chairman Bordeneuve rallying the members, the club quickly established itself as the front-runner both in its administration and its recruitment of players to the new cause. For this primary role Villeneuve earned the right to become known as the cradle of French rugby league.

Some of the former rugby union players of CA Villeneuvois, such as Camo, Barrès and Jean Rabot - not to mention Rousié, who had already joined up with Galia - were signed up to the new club whose official name was now Sport Athlétique Villeneuvois XIII. Other players were brought in from farther afield, as Galia, with his wide network of contacts and eye for talent, began to assemble a formidable team. As he had done before his pioneer tour Galia looked to his home territory for new players, this time with more success. Joining Villeneuve from Perpignan came Jean Daffis, Aimé Bardes, Martin Serre and, for his second spell - but this time in totally different circumstances - François Noguères. The SAV XIII clearly looked to have great potential.

This team would have another advantage over its rivals once the season got under way. Galia, believing that the most effective way for the newcomers to learn the game of rugby league would be to experience it at its source, set out for the second time in six months for the north of England.

After 26 hours' non-stop travel from Villeneuve, the squad of players, accompanied by Dr Léon Vinson and Charles Bernat, arrived at Leeds City station at around 8 p.m. on Friday, 7th September and set up their headquarters at the now-familiar Griffin Hotel. Their tour would take in six matches, beginning the day after arrival at Warrington. During the following ten days matches were scheduled to be played against Broughton Rangers in Manchester, Hull, a Yorkshire team at Keighley, then Oldham and Leeds. There was another major difference from the first tour in March. This time the wine arrived - which made the Frenchmen feel more at home - though only half-way through their stay.

In the first match at Warrington, Rousié, leading the side in the absence of the injured Galia, lost no time in stamping his authority on the game. Playing scrum-half he was at the centre of almost every French attacking move as well as showing a sound defence. Still with only half-a-dozen rugby league matches behind him, he proved irrepressible. Against Broughton Rangers he helped himself to four tries, as the Manchester side's defence found it impossible to contain him. Following up this performance with fourteen points against Hull, in a match in which he was unfortunate to be on the losing side, Rousié went on to score two tries and four goals against Yorkshire. From as early as the third minute the half-back entranced the Keighley crowd when instead of place-kicking a penalty goal he scored with a drop-kick from almost half-way. Once more the hero at Oldham, with two tries and five goals, Rousié was again outstanding in the final match at Leeds, where one particular try left the defence flat-footed and the crowd in no doubt that here was a player of the highest quality. From a scrum on the Leeds '25', Rousié passed to stand-off Cougnenc, ran around him to take the return pass and accelerated unstoppably towards the line. Such quickness of thought and action, combined with his excellent pass, strong kicking game and superb defence, led many to regard the Villeneuve scrum-half as already the complete footballer. Playing in all six matches, Rousié accounted for 76 of the 117 points scored by his team - and this in spite of the fact that he never once finished on the winning side.

At least two of those matches - against Oldham by a single point and against Hull in the last minute - were only narrowly lost. It was after the Hull game that Joe Thompson, who had continued to advise the Frenchmen, felt obliged to express a complaint on their behalf. Thompson had been approached by Galia and Rousié who both felt that in the Broughton Rangers and Hull matches intimidatory methods had been used against them. "They quite understand," said Thompson, "that rugby league is a strenuous game, entailing inevitable bumps. What they can't understand is why such tactics should be used against them when they have come here to learn."[2] This first sign of discord between British and French over standards of play was not entirely surprising. Most of the French players had played rugby union at some time or other in an atmosphere of far greater brutality. By contrast, the pioneers' tour and the matches played by the Yorkshire Selection in France had been characterised by the openness of the play as well as its fairness. It was almost inevitable, though, that some player somewhere should take it into his head to show the newcomers something of the darker side of this collision sport. John Wilson, however, while promising to investigate the matter and bring it before Council if need be, admitted he had seen only one incident in the Broughton match and nothing in the Hull game. The Hull chairman denied any such allegation and demanded a retraction.

It was also unfortunate for the Frenchmen that Galia, troubled by an ankle injury, was only able to lead from the front in two matches, where his inspirational and intelligent play made a good deal of difference in the forwards. Serre, the centre, suffered similar misfortune against Broughton Rangers and was unable to take any further part in their tour.

But, despite his side's record, Galia announced at the end that he was pleased with the progress that had been made. Winning matches had not been their major concern. The main objective had been to learn more about the game. One example of the Frenchmen's keenness to make the most of their stay was revealed when, immediately after the Warrington match, the five players who had not taken part came out on to the field to practise.

Many of the squad showed distinct promise at their new code of rugby. The centres, Noguères and Etienne Cougnenc, though very different in style, both looked capable of breaking down defences with their combination of subtlety, speed and strength. Among the forwards, Rabot, Camo, Daffis and Rousse were outstanding. But like their pioneering predecessors the Frenchmen had still to develop positional sense in defence, and often failed to appreciate the importance of possession. On several occasions an automatic impulse to kick, natural to players brought up on rugby union, simply gave the ball away.

It was Charles Bernat who expressed the hope, as the party left for home, that English player-coaches would go to France to teach the converts more about the game. Although financially as well as educationally profitable, the expedition had yielded a profit below that of the pioneering tour. Apart from the first match at Warrington, where there had been 10,000 spectators, the remaining fixtures attracted more modest crowds of around 5,000. Consequently the Frenchmen arrived home on September 22nd with just £15 bonus in their pockets, compared with the £35 received by their predecessors. It was a sign that the new game would not provide limitless opportunities to earn money and that players who decided to play it would have to have motives other than financial.

Chapter Seven
THE CATALAN CONNECTION

Though he had followed their fortunes for twenty-five years, the late journalist Guy Cassayet hesitated when it came to writing a special anniversary tribute to the Treize Catalan. Born further to the west of the Pyrenees in the Béarn, Cassayet, despite having shared a passion for rugby league for so long with the Catalans, had always regarded himself an outsider. He had never quite managed to come to terms with what he called "the sensitiveness and the occasionally superior attitude of the Catalan with his strong and often disconcerting reactions arising from normal, everyday talk about sport." Although his loyalty to his adopted environment eventually got the better of him so that he duly produced the article, Cassayet's concern was nevertheless a legitimate one.[1]

There is an analogy to be made between the Catalan character and the river which flows through Catalan territory, the Têt, which meanders peaceably through Galia's birthplace but, if the conditions are right, can rapidly be transformed into a raging torrent which needs to be taken very seriously. Never far below the relaxed exterior of those who live between the Têt and the sea there is a fervour which becomes abruptly apparent whenever certain subjects are broached. Rugby, because it calls into question personal and collective pride and honour, is one of them. For Catalans rugby represents the culture, almost as much as the language. It's played with an overwhelming sense of local identity, especially against outsiders.

Hanging in pride of place in Jacques Jorda's bar at Canet-Plage, the main coastal resort of Perpignan, there is a team photograph of the representative side, the Catalans de France, who beat the touring Australians by 20 points to five at Christmas, 1948. Although we were talking about a different period, Paul Déjean, captain of the Catalans that day, referred to it several times. It was a golden moment for himself, his team and his people - the finest showing of their rugby culture, a triumph of courage and subtlety over physical power.

The strength of Déjean's convictions tell you that he must have been a formidable opponent. As captain of France playing against the British Empire at Marseille in 1950, Déjean suffered broken ribs, a ruptured kidney and a cracked pelvis, but played on, even managing to kick a drop-goal. It was only when he collapsed in the shower after the match that the extent of his injuries became clear.

He talks about how you have to be fast to play this game. But physical qualities are only half of it. With clenched fist, Déjean thumps his chest. It takes heart, too.

He must have known Jacques Jorda for something like 25 years. A true Catalan, Jorda is a native of the ancient town of Elne where there was a twelfth century bishop of the same name, which was adopted from the River Jordan in the Holy Land by medieval crusaders. A stand-off with Saint-Estève and XIII Catalan, Jorda went on to coach both of those clubs, as well as Carcassonne and Pia, and had a relatively successful four years at the head of the national side. He comes over to join the conversation, which centres on the current standings at international level and the way the game is being played. "Defence is only the first requirement," Jorda insists, flicking my arm with the back of his hand to emphasise the point, before going on to make a stronger case for the finer attacking skills. Players must be able to express their abilities fully, he asserts. Attacking players of talent should be given free rein to put their abilities to work for the good of the team. Unpredictability is a virtue. Jorda recalls when France were unfortunate to lose 8-4 to Great Britain at Perpignan in 1990 before shocking the British with a 25-18 victory at Headingley. With satisfaction he quotes scrum-half Andy Gregory: "He said he didn't know what we were going to do next." Jorda takes Gregory's comment as praise, confirming his own belief in surprising the opposition by the unorthodox. He doesn't seem to recognise the ambiguity of the statement, which also implies a French failing. The English have always shaken their heads at what they perceive as French lack of planning, order and discipline.[2]

The need for self-expression, the quickness to respond, the seriousness of the endeavour, the loyalty to the chosen cause are all qualities which have been harnessed together to make Catalans into a fearsome team. Within their own territory, however, these same qualities have led to the establishment of factions, each convinced of the value of its own perception. It is an acceptable reason why Catalans have been inextricably involved with both the finest and the most ignominious moments in the history of rugby league in France.

There is hardly a town or village in Roussillon that has not produced at least one outstanding rugby player. Ille has Galia as its most famous son, Le Boulou produced Noguères, from Bages came Elie Brousse, from Collioure Jep Desclaux, Gaston Comes came from Millas, Eugène Ribère from Thuir - these are just a half a dozen names from the long list of international players of both codes. These stars from the constellation surrounding Perpignan would often be drawn towards the regional capital, which itself produced the likes of Déjean, Jo Maso and Roger Ramis. Perpignan has supported a multitude of rugby clubs for the best part of a century and that has bred intense local rivalry as well as resentment against clubs in other parts of the country, which tended to use the area as a recruiting-ground.

This was the scenario in which the quick-witted Marcel Laborde came to prominence as a rugby union official in the 1920s, before eventually acquiring a reputation as the grey eminence of French rugby league in the immediate pre-war era and beyond. Laborde, a lawyer by training and profession, left few indifferent to his bold yet subtle, persistent and eloquent championing of the cause.

But which cause? There have been many to point to the apparent inconsistencies in Laborde's allegiances and portray him as an opportunist who would have been at home in the corridors of power in medieval Florence. Many of his detractors came from outside Perpignan, the city where he assumed the post of secretary of the Chamber of Commerce after a period at the bar in Paris and as secretary of the *préfecture* of La Rochelle. He had his opponents on home ground too, in the city where the young Marcel had played the game as a boy and where everyone appeared to have an opinion on rugby.

Nicknamed *"Le Lapin"* (Rabbit), looking nothing like a rugby player with his slight build and Charlie Chaplin moustache, he had nevertheless been the tricky 16-year old scrum-half in the ASP team which had won the championship of Languedoc in 1905. But too frail in physique to play on into manhood, he had devoted his energies to the administration of the game instead, finding his true vocation by harrying his opponents and tenaciously and skilfully defending his own ground. He never married and never tired of telling his friends, "Rugby is my mistress."

A principle to which Laborde adhered with unfailing consistency was to protect Perpignan, and his own USP in particular, from poaching by other clubs who were only too willing to invest in Catalan talent. Those players who were nevertheless lured elsewhere generally went far afield. Very few joined up with the enemy on the doorstep. The great exception was Quillan, the champion team from the adjacent *département* of Aude.

The defeat of US Perpignan in the 1926 championship final by Stade Toulousain brought the divisions in the club to crisis point, with Laborde and the referee and international selector Gilbert Brutus on opposite sides. Brutus had played as a centre with USP and went on to coach the team to their 1925 championship victory. But just over a year later the coach decamped, together with several members of the USP side, to Quillan, where he joined up with that other Catalan with a point to prove, Jean Galia. Laborde's frustration was considerable as he saw the renegades become finalists themselves within two seasons, playing in a style which gave full rein to the stars' talents. Laborde's opposition to the poaching of players and the other illegal practices which were becoming increasingly prevalent in French rugby in the '20s and '30s led to his involvement in the creation of the Union Française du Rugby Amateur, the select group of clubs which set out to uphold stricter principles both on and off the field. It also provided him with a platform from which to denounce contemporary sporting evils. It was Laborde who took up the case against Galia, implicating him the Noguères affair which led eventually to Galia's expulsion by the FFR.[3]

Defeated in the 1926 final, Laborde's club had further cause for regret the following year. USP's derby match with Perpignan's other major club, the Quins, was played in an atmosphere of spite and brutality and achieved particular notoriety as a result of the sending-off of ten players. Laborde's memory of it was still vivid when, some six years later, a merger between the two clubs was proposed. Quite apart from their history of rivalry, there were perceived differences between the two: in general terms the USP were the "bowler hat" club, drawing members mainly from the Perpignan middle class, while the Quins, who inappropriately called themselves after the London club of the same name, were considered to be the working class "flat caps". The Quins had also maintained good relations with Quillan, the club to which so many USP players had defected.

The first game played in Perpignan between USP and Quillan since the departure of Brutus and his players was predictably ferocious but had unforeseen consequences. The death of Quillan's young hooker, Rivière, fatally injured in a scrum, gave rise to considerable ill-feeling among the French rugby public towards the Perpignan club. It was left largely to Laborde, as vice-chairman, to defend the club's difficult position, which he did with skill and vigour, replying eloquently to the attacks made on USP in the local and regional press.

Despite the rivalry and differences between Perpignan's two major clubs, the once unthinkable possibility of a merger began to gain support. There was evidently a good deal of potential in pooling the resources of two first division clubs within the same city. The idea of a merger was nothing new in Perpignan and Laborde had himself been instrumental in previous moves, when ASP (Association Sportive Perpignanaise) and SOP (Stade Olympien Perpignanais) had united to form the present USP.

When the first proposal of a USP-Quins deal was made there was hostility from both sides. A letter to the local press from the Quins committee, writing to protest about USP's decision to stage a match on the same day as theirs, showed the antipathy between the two just a fortnight after the merger was first suggested. Sneering at the turmoil within the club which had led to Laborde's resignation, the Quins officials wrote: "Their leaders may change, as resignation follows resignation, but the same fierce hatred, the same low jealousy, the same shabby behaviour is still in vogue at the heart of the so-called 'senior' club."

Nevertheless the merger between USP and the Quins went ahead on the fifth of May 1933 and a new club, known as USAP, was the outcome. The "Union" incorporated into the club's name, however, was not borne out by reality and Marcel Laborde was not to be part of it. Undercurrents of ill-feeling still washed around those figures associated with the two separate clubs of the past, and Laborde was the one who polarised members' emotions the most, to the extent that there were those former Quins officials who, recalling Laborde's tirades against them in defence of USP, wanted him to have nothing at all to do with the new club. Laborde had already resigned before the merger went through, sensing that he would find the new structure inimical to his beliefs. It is unlikely that the majority of officials of the new club would have wanted him on board. Whatever the reason, the result was that the one official of national stature was left out of the new organisation.

Laborde's administrative abilities would now be limited to his work as secretary of the Chamber of Commerce, where his competence was as highly regarded in the business community as it had formerly been in the sporting world. If Laborde did not immediately attempt to re-establish his authority in rugby, his overview of events was as penetrating as ever. The intellectual qualities which he had brought to bear, allied to years of experience in club administration, had given him an almost unrivalled position in pre-war French rugby. Even today there are few names from the intervening period who come to mind as being of similar stature.

Laborde claimed not to regret his absence from rugby. "I am an escapee from the prison that is sport today," he told *L'Auto*. "I know nothing, or rather I don't wish to know anything, about what is happening there. The lowering of moral standards in sport is only a reflection of the lowering of moral standards in society as a whole. We live in a country where dishonesty gives entitlement to public esteem."[4]

Commenting on accusations imputed to Jean Galia about shamateurism, Laborde went on: "Ask Monsieur Galia not what he and his friends received from Monsieur Bourrel, because there's nothing unusual about that. Instead, ask what all the recruiting agents, the intermediaries, the Federation's officials and the referees get..."

At the time this interview appeared, *L'Auto* was in the throes of the campaign against the veiled professionalism which abounded in French rugby and which had been brought into sharp focus by the openly professional rugby league team which Galia had raised.

"Personally I'm amazed at the surprise which your revelations have caused," commented Laborde. "In 1927 when I reported, with evidence to hand, the complicity of the Federation and the dealings of the Quillan club, the game's administrators closed their eyes and put their hands over their ears. It's just the same now ... They go after the small fry and ignore the big fish."

Laborde correctly set out the contemporary dilemma confronting modern sport in general and rugby in particular - one which rugby union was still struggling to come to terms with more than sixty years later. The principal actors in the drama which had been unfolding in French rugby since the twenties were the players and the club officials, while the spectators paid their money and, as spectators do, looked on.

"Rugby is either recreation or entertainment," he declared. "If it is entertainment it has to have impresarios and performers, who have to be paid. The public wants entertainment, there's no denying it. That is why professional rugby must have its place and that is why we should put an end, if possible - although I believe that it is not possible - to this widespread hypocrisy...

"They say that by abolishing the championship they will eliminate corruption. They will abolish the cause to eliminate the effect, that is undeniable, but they will also eliminate the interest it creates."

Laborde's long experience as a club administrator had provided him with all the proof anyone needed of the underhand practices which were common throughout rugby. The lot of a club director, he claimed, was like forced labour, with the poor official having to bow to the accepted practice of paying to support his club, in effect paying to ensure that his club might win. During his time he claimed to have seen all human baseness and all its ugliness. As for his own involvement, he had helped the social advancement of his players, had even recommended the ones who wanted to move on and whom he could not hope to retain. The Federation knew all of this because he had told them and had provided proof of various transactions, but they took no notice. "It is not the players who are at fault," he concluded. "It is the Federation which is corrupt."

The Federation, of course, lost no time in offering its "absolute and categorical denial of all allegations".[5]

The chance for Laborde to re-emerge as a figure of importance in French sport came a little more than one year after his dissociation from it. It coincided with the very point at which his former adversary, Jean Galia, was setting about re-asserting his own identity, to the chagrin of those who had attempted to negate it.

Certain other USP officials had felt badly let down by the decision to exclude Laborde from the new, merged club. Eventually they came together and made the decision to form yet another club which would be known by the revived name of Association Sportive Perpignanaise, the forerunner of USP and which had been national champions in 1914. It was constituted at the end of June, 1934, but, although it had officials in plenty, the new club had as yet to persuade players to join the venture. That was a second reason why Marcel Laborde came back into the picture. Laborde, more than any other club official, had a special relationship with the players, who revered him for his loyalty towards them. By instinct he was an amateur, preferring to help players advance their careers outside the game - which in his role as secretary to the Chamber of Commerce he was well able to do - rather than by means of the veiled professionalism that was all around him. But his honesty was also a quality which players respected him for and he in turn would later find no argument against the honest professionalism of rugby league. "He was an exceptional man, a great gentleman who was always very kind towards the players," said one such player, Paul Déjean. "You would kill for that fellow."

Laborde re-emerged into the spotlight to run the club along with other influential partners such as Dr Gaston Banet and the great international centre, now nearing the end of his career, Roger Ramis. But though constituted as a rugby union club, the new ASP would not play a single match.

At the same time Galia and the newly-formed Ligue Française de Rugby à XIII were heavily involved in organising the first French rugby league championship which would begin in the autumn. But although Galia had travelled far and wide across France, first when he was recruiting for his pioneering tour of England and second when organising venues for the Yorkshire tour, he had had little success in establishing rugby league in his home territory. And yet it was self-evident that the new competition would be the worse off for the absence of a Catalan team.

"Rugby league is a very attractive game," Galia had told the local newspaper, "because it is extremely fast. Two types of rugby player are particularly suited to it: the Catalans and the Basques. So I hope that rugby league will soon become established in Perpignan and that our compatriots will soon be able to appreciate it for themselves."[6] It was their approach to rugby union which led Galia to believe that players and clubs in those two regions would make a successful transition to rugby league. In Basque teams such as Aviron Bayonnais all the players, regardless of position, liked to attack like three-quarters. The Catalans, perhaps even more than the Basques, liked to improvise, particularly on the counter-attack and did not care for the technicalities of the forward-based game played by other clubs. The Basque region was now well on the way to forming its own club in Côte Basque XIII. But nothing had yet developed in or around Perpignan.

Galia first sounded out Dr Gaston Banet of the new ASP club. A further meeting was held between Galia, Banet and Marcel Laborde, who was no doubt invited as the most authoritative official of the breakaway club, though a possible association between Galia and Laborde looked, on the face of it, improbable. Galia: once rejected by Laborde's club, USP; star of the enemy team, Quillan; alleged poacher of the USP player, Noguères. Laborde:

defender of the Perpignan faith; stern critic of Galia's alleged involvement in the Noguères affair. Yet both quickly saw qualities in the other which they respected, qualities which would allow them both to advance. They left the meeting if not as friends at least as potential allies.

When questioned about his future association with professionals, Laborde, known to all as a defender of amateur principles, particularly since his involvement with UFRA, gave an explanation which he considered perfectly rational. He was, by his recent actions, simply encouraging and supporting his friends, he claimed.

"My preferences have always been for amateur rugby," he said, "but fully amateur. Unfortunately the times and people's attitudes wish it otherwise: I note that and lament it. But, things being as they are, professional rugby is the only means available of putting our young men to the test.

"Four years ago I said that we should make rugby professional for the professionals and leave amateur rugby to the others." Laborde's stand at that time against the corruption in rugby which led to the formation of UFRAhad now evolved into an apparently antithetical position. But he was, he maintained, at ease with his own conscience in wishing to see openness and honesty return to French rugby, an opportunity offered by rugby league.[7]

When Banet and Laborde reported back to the members of the ASP, approval was given to the plans discussed with Galia. Perpignan became the latest, powerful addition to the towns and cities which would support rugby league. Its importance was immediately evident and was recognised at the historic second general meeting of the Ligue Française du Rugby à XIII, held in Toulouse on August 21st.

"All the delegates were particularly pleased to applaud and welcome the Perpignan club, to be known as the Treize Catalan," reported the Toulouse newspaper, *La Dépêche*. "With the intelligent guidance and impetus of their chairman, Dr Banet, there is no doubt that the new game will develop and flourish in the Catalan region."

The presence of Marcel Laborde, the reluctant professional, was at least as significant in attracting players to the team. Very soon the new club had assembled a potentially formidable side, led by the former rugby union international Roger Ramis. After Galia had lured François Noguères and his two team-mates from his home village of Le Boulou, Martin Serre and Aimé Bardes, to join Villeneuve on their early-season English tour, an agreement was made so that the trio would return to give the XIII Catalan vital experience in the opening season which lay ahead.

It had not taken much effort to convince Serre and Bardes to convert to rugby league. Their treatment by the new, merged rugby union club, USAP, ensured it as much as anything. While Galia had been touring England with his pioneers in March, USAP suspended the two players. The club claimed that they had both demanded a large sum of money the day before they were due to play an important match against Narbonne. Two days later both players were banned for life by the FFR. The two players protested their innocence in a letter to the local paper.[8] The club president, Monsieur Bazia, who had recently told the press that his club never paid its players, came in for some stinging criticism from them. It was Bazia, they said, who had repeatedly offered money which they had never asked for. But since he never kept his promises they could not take him seriously. Their threat not to play against Narbonne was the result of their irritation concerning a backlog of travelling expenses amounting to 1,000 francs, which were long overdue and had been promised many times. Finally they accused him of trying to gain popularity by exploiting this incident for which he himself was responsible.

Against this kind of background Galia had recruited and would continue to sign up players, not just for his own club but for rugby league in general. He was happy to see Bardes, Serre and Noguères remain in Perpignan to help develop the game there. As a further gesture of goodwill, he spent a week in Perpignan leading the pre-season training sessions in the grounds of the Château de l'Esparrou at Canet, a property owned by a former chairman of USP and friend of Marcel Laborde. The Catalan connection was being used to positive effect. Catalans had already been the motivating force in the creation of the game in France. They would have an equally significant role to play in rugby league's future.

Chapter Eight
COUP D'ENVOI

By the time the first pass had been given in French rugby league's inaugural championship, a very significant number of players had embraced the new sport, not hesitating, to use a common phrase of the time, to cross the Rubicon. The FFR had told them - disingenuously, as it turned out - that there was no going back. But a number had already been suspended from playing rugby union and others, mindful of what rugby league had to offer, hardly considered it a risk, even if older heads could not foresee the new game's survival, let alone its success.

The players who took up the new rugby and were good enough welcomed the chance to be paid openly. Impressed by what they had seen or heard about, they felt they had little to lose. What was good for the likes of Max Rousié was good for them too.

Word got around quickly and it was positive. The two exhibition matches in Paris, followed by the Yorkshire tour which took rugby league into the heart of the country, had an immense effect. These matches proved that there was considerable public interest - and therefore financial support - for what many of those seeing the game for the first time took simply to be a faster and more open version of the game they already knew. If it was a well-established sport in England, as the refined skills of its exponents now demonstrated before French eyes, there was no reason why it could not become so in France. The contact with English teams, denied by the British Rugby Unions, not only gave the new sport of rugby league immediate credibility but also satisfied public demand for the international competition from which France had been more or less isolated. French eagerness to see their own favourites measure up to foreign stars is reflected in the enthusiastic previews which appeared in the French press.

Henri Hoursiangou, sports editor of *La Petite Gironde* but also former chairman of the steering committee from which the FFR was born, wrote with unexpected enthusiasm for a man with such previously strong links with the rugby establishment. Previewing the France-Yorkshire match at Villeneuve, he declared: "It is not presumptuous to predict that, as a sporting contest, the match at Villeneuve-sur-Lot will be a brilliant success." After detailing the quality of the players of both sides, spattering his prose with words like "sensational" and "absolutely remarkable", Hoursiangou went on to tell any readers who had not yet had the chance to see a rugby league match that it would be a revelation. He promised attacks and counter-attacks, uncompromising defence and a minimum of stoppages in a game of such clarity that even the uninitiated would be able to follow it with ease; a game of constantly increasing excitement which could not fail to win the spectators' approval.

International competition - which meant in effect matches between France and Britain - was a cornerstone on which the French Rugby League was built, and by French request. It was a priority item on the agenda of the Toulouse meeting, at which representative matches as well as Franco-British club matches were scheduled even before those of the domestic championship.

A whole programme of international fixtures was drawn up, with matches against England and Wales, as well as games which pitted the English league champions and cup-winners against their French counterparts. In addition there were to be three short tours of France by English sides. Salford, the reigning champions when Galia's pioneers had toured England, kept to their arrangement to become the first club side to play in France; Hunslet, the 1934 Cup-winners, would follow them; and an English select team which was still to be decided on would tour in the New Year.

English assistance came in various other forms. Referees were sent over to officiate at tour matches and were also invited to control domestic finals, since local referees were not yet sufficiently experienced to deal with big matches. Coaches - and particularly player-coaches - also came to teach the new game, particularly at clubs without players who had first-hand experience of playing against English opposition. Among the first were the Welshman, Tom Parker, who arrived at Bayonne from Wigan and went on to coach Albi, and Salford's Eddie Matthews, who coached Bordeaux, where he was followed by the New Zealander Lou Brown. Another New Zealander, Albert Falwasser, also arrived at Bordeaux via Rochdale.

Although plans had been made for an inaugural championship of twelve teams, the competition which started in October 1934 was contested by ten clubs: Racing Club d'Albi, Sport Olympique de Béziers, Bordeaux XIII, XIII Catalan, Côte Basque XIII, Union Sportive Lyon-Villeurbanne, Paris Rugby XIII, Pau XIII, Racing Club de Roanne and Sport Athlétique Villeneuve. Of the original twelve, Grenoble dropped out and from the initial plan to have at least two Paris teams, only one emerged. The non-starters fell victim to the most significant problem faced by the new sport - lack of grounds. The

Grenoble club had recruited two of Galia's pioneers, Antonin Barbazanges and Bob Samatan, as its star players - they eventually teamed up with Charles Mathon at Lyon-Villeurbanne - but the difficulty of finding a stadium in which to play proved insuperable. It was a problem which beset many of the newly-formed clubs and even forced the Ligue into considering building portable stands which might be erected on suitable pieces of land and then dismantled after a match, to be moved on to the next. But the prohibitive cost soon led them to abandon the idea.

The race against time to set up the championship, to recruit players and referees and to install clubs at appropriate stadiums came close to being lost. At the scheduled start of the season, some teams still had no ground to play on. For clubs such as Paris, Béziers, XIII Catalan and Côte Basque the dilemma was particularly serious. Paris XIII was unable to play a home match until December 9th. The Côte Basque club, based in the Bayonne-Biarritz area, spent the first half of the season up to the New Year without a stadium of its own, and, unhappily for a new club in a new game trying to establish local support, shared grounds with Pau, 100 km to the east, and even with Bordeaux, almost 200 km to the north. In addition to the travel to "home" matches - and its attendant costs - the wide location of clubs in the new championship meant that, for example, Côte Basque, in order to play a pre-season friendly at Roanne, set off by coach at one on the Saturday afternoon and only arrived at their destination, after a 900-kilometre journey, at five o'clock on the Sunday morning.

Not that Roanne had found it easy to find a stadium to play in, either. Long negotiations were finally settled when the president of the Ligue, the parliamentary deputy François Cadoret, intervened to persuade the mayor to overrule objections from leading rugby union figures and allow the rugby league club to play at the council-owned Parc des Sports.

For XIII Catalan, finding a stadium in Perpignan caused many headaches for officials and players alike. There was the inevitable clash with the rugby union club, USAP, which successfully stood in the way of the new club's attempts to hire a stadium. The result was that, during the whole of the first month of the inaugural season, XIII Catalan had to play away from home, thus denying the Perpignan public the chance to see for themselves the new sport which had been introduced into their midst.

Just before the season was due to start, an anxious but determined XIII Catalan board of directors wrote to the local newspaper in the following terms: "A whole clan of people has vowed to see us perish. Everything possible has been done to stifle rugby league in our city. The plot has been hatched by USAP. But their efforts are to no avail because XIII Catalan now has a team and soon will have a ground."[1]

It wasn't quite so simple. Training sessions took place either on a piece of spare land or in the more agreeable grounds of Château Lesparrou at Canet-

Plage, but which was situated some thirty minutes' drive away. The imminent arrival of the English flag-bearers, Salford, gave the search for a ground even greater urgency. Eventually a site was found, but it was one which bore no resemblance to a stadium. Volunteers were enlisted to demolish the house which stood on the land, to level and mark the ground and builders and joiners were hired to construct the stadium. The land on which only recently fruit trees and vegetables had been growing was transformed, by almost continuous effort over a period of just a fortnight, into a rugby league ground - even if the pitch consisted simply of bare earth. It is said that as the crowd entered the new stadium for the match against Salford, they passed the builders on their way out.[2] It had been a close-run thing but the club's efforts were rewarded by the biggest attendance and highest takings - 27,000 francs - ever known at a sporting event in the city of Perpignan - and on a Friday at that. Despite an expected defeat by the English champions, by 41 points to 16, the XIII Catalan side gave their public their money's worth from the outset. François Noguères, the brilliant young full-back or centre whose suspension by the French Rugby Union had been the indirect cause of rugby league's birth in France, created the opening for winger Aimé Bardes to score the first try of the match. It was an eloquent and symbolic moment for the future of the sport in the city which was to become a bastion of rugby league.

For their part, Salford, dubbed *"les Diables Rouges"*, gave wholehearted commitment. Harry Sunderland, covering their tour as much as an enthusiast and innovator as a journalist, reported that Salford were "ideal propagandists" for the game in France. Immediately after the final of the Lancashire Cup, they travelled to France to play six matches in two weeks, suffering in the process a financial deficit estimated at £350.

"They have done a tremendous amount of good," Sunderland wrote in *The Sports Post*, "and that £350 will come rolling back into somebody's coffers in years to come. The Rugby League will some day reap a harvest out of international fixtures, and future clubs to tour France will benefit from the spadework that Salford have done, just as they will also benefit from what Hunslet have helped to do at Bordeaux and Pau, and what Leeds did last autumn."

The Red Devils, officially credited as the first English club to tour France (since Leeds had used two York players on their May tour and had been billed as a Yorkshire Selection), created huge interest in the six centres where they played during the latter part of October and the first week of November. The skills of players such as Gus Risman and the international half-back pairing of Jenkins and Watkins whetted the appetite of the local crowd for what rugby league had to offer. The crowd of around 5,000 for the opening game in Paris had been disappointing but understandable after rugby union influence had engineered a last-minute change of venue, which accounted for substantially reduced takings.

The other five matches, played at Lyon, Béziers, Albi, Perpignan and Villeneuve, all of which Salford won, made an immediate impression on a public which had been starved of international competition. After Hunslet had played Bordeaux on October 28th - a match which the home side, strengthened by Rousié from Villeneuve and Rousse of Pau, won 38-23 - and Pau on November 1st, eight of the ten French championship clubs had received an English team within the first month of the competition. Only Côte Basque, which in any case was forced to play fixtures at Bordeaux and Pau, and Roanne were unable to host matches against the English, although Roanne was to be the venue for a match against a Northern Rugby League XIII which would make a short tour of the south-east in January.

Whatever difficulties the ten professional clubs experienced in setting up a base, the question of player recruitment was not a problem. They were queueing up to play rugby league. Within two months of the start of the season, top-class rugby union players from clubs such as Agen, Lézignan, Bègles, Lourdes, Biarritz and Bayonne were signing professional forms. Rugby union referees also joined the march towards the new code.

Albi, the second French club to become registered on rugby league's roll of honour, alone found difficulties in enlisting players. The city's major rugby union club had gone to some length to protect its playing strength, losing only two players to the rugby league club. RC Albi XIII, under the leadership of one of Galia's pioneers, Jean-Marie Vignal[3], recruited players from nearby Toulouse, which, to Galia's concern, lacked a rugby league club.

After friendly matches had been played during the second half of September, the first-ever round of championship matches was played on Sunday, 7th October, 1934. Galia's own Villeneuve side, which included Porra from the original seventeen he had taken on tour to England, but which had been substantially strengthened by the arrival of Rousié and other top players like Brinsolles, Cougnenc and Guiral, was one of the favourites to take the inaugural title, especially after their instructive English tour. In a high-scoring match which was played at the Pont de Marot, Villeneuve, because there was still no ground available in Perpignan, Galia's team handed out a lesson to XIII Catalan, coasting home by 48 points to 25.

Five matches should have been played that weekend. In fact there were only two other results: Pau's 28-14 defeat of Côte Basque and a victory for Bordeaux, by 26 points to 6, over Albi. The Paris club, reorganised following the difficulties of finding a stadium, was still not up and running.

If it had been an achievement simply to launch a rugby league championship, the need to put on matches which were not only entertaining but also evenly-contested and meaningful was a further obstacle. On only the second weekend Roanne scored fifteen tries in their 59-9 hammering of Béziers. It prompted the sharp observation in one newspaper: "What is allowed of amateurs cannot be tolerated from professionals."[4]

It was not a typical comment. Following a match in mid-November in which Bordeaux narrowly beat Villeneuve by 28-25, Henri Hoursiangou wrote: "Suppose it were possible to ask each of the 6,000 spectators at this match, 'Hand on heart, what do you think of this match in particular and rugby league in general?' We bet ten to one that not a single spectator would reply anything other than: 'This match? Splendid! Rugby league? The finest of outdoor sports!'"[5]

After the return match the following month, won 13-6 by Villeneuve, the same writer reported: "I don't know what took place on the rugby union grounds this afternoon but I very much doubt whether it was as good and as clean as this rugby league match at the Parc de Suzon.

"Let me tell you that it rained incessantly, that part of the pitch was a proper quagmire, that the ball was enveloped in mud and that in spite of these unfavourable conditions four thousand spectators witnessed a very fine match with some splendid passages of play.

"We already knew that even in bad weather rugby league loses none of its attractions but it was good to have the confirmation of it today.

"One can say that these two teams produced the maximum of good play in the most hateful circumstances imaginable for rugby."[6]

As professionals, it was the players' duty to provide a game worthy of the public's money. But the word professional, heavy with all kinds of symbolic significance throughout the period leading up to the creation of the French Rugby League and beyond, belied the actual state of affairs as far as financial reward was concerned. First of all, the state of open professionalism, as the former XIII Catalan player and coach, Tintin Saltraille, remarked, was only a regularisation of what had gone on in rugby union. Match bonuses, called *primes*, had been paid during the twenties and thirties, the amount paid out depending on the importance of the match and the result. A fixed salary was a long way from becoming a reality for all the new, professional rugby league players, the majority of whom continued only to draw their *prime* after the match as they had done when there had been fifteen a side. A star performer like Max Rousié, who could be relied on to pull the crowds in, whatever the circumstances, was an exception in terms of earning power. One example was his appearance for both Bordeaux and Pau against Hunslet at a fee of 500 francs per match.

For most it was a different story. At Pau contracts had been agreed with the players at the beginning of the season, but as a result of the cost of rebuilding the main stand at its Bourbaki stadium, the club found itself in financial difficulties. Players' contracts were cancelled and match payments were instituted in their place.

At Lyon, Charles Mathon, following Galia's exhortation to try to set up teams in all the viable cities, was entrusted with the job of getting a rugby league side established. Mathon, the former stand-off and captain of Club Sportif Oyonnax, an international trialist and a forces international, was one of those who had taken the most persuading by Galia to join the venture. He had not been banned, nor, apparently, was it the money on offer which tempted him. In fact he repudiated the press allegations about his own involvement in the shamateurism which was rife in rugby union.

The day after arriving in Leeds with Galia's team Mathon had written to his wife: "I was really annoyed when I arrived in Paris to read the rubbish attributed to the CSO and I pointed out to Galia that at Oyonnax it had never been a question of money and during my career I had only ever had offers from LOU [Lyon Olympique Universitaire]. You can imagine how amazed I was, the day after leaving for England, to see quotations coming from me. I almost felt like not going, I thought it was so ridiculous. They're going to have a strange opinion of me in Lyon, and they're certainly not going to be pleased about it."[7]

There were many others who, like Mathon, would switch over to rugby league because they saw the potential in sporting terms rather than financial. Mathon had also persuaded four other pioneers, Laurent Lambert, Antonin Barbazanges, Gaston Amila and Bob Samatan to join him. None of these were local players: Lambert, who was originally from Avignon, was living at St-Rémy de Provence; Amila came from Lézignan and Barbazanges and Samatan were from Toulouse.

They were joined, among others, by René Barnoud, a future international winger from Grenoble, who, a lithographer by profession, had fallen victim to technological advances in the printing industry and was out of work. When Mathon's letter arrived at the end of July, inviting him to become a professional rugby league player in Lyon, Barnoud seized the chance. He soon settled into one of the recently-built high-rise flats in Villeurbanne, an area which adjoins Lyon but is distinct from it - almost as Salford is to Manchester. Villeurbanne was a boom area and it was there that the US Lyon-Villeurbanne rugby league club was to be based.

The Lyon-Villeurbanne team, like others throughout France, were aware of their responsibilities as professional rugby league players, both on and off the pitch. Both Barnoud and Barbazanges recalled their efforts to drum up publicity in the early days, when they would tour the area in cars, announcing the match with loud-hailers, and pinning posters and banners to every available space. Barnoud, with his experience in the printing trade, wrote, illustrated and produced a kind of match programme, selling copies at 75 centimes to introduce the public both to rugby league in general and Lyon-Villeurbanne XIII in particular.

"We were," said Barnoud, "the representatives of a game which was new to France and we had to make an impression because rugby union, as a result of the fact that there were no more international matches, was in ruins. It was our concern to safeguard - a big word, but that's how it was - to safeguard rugby because we were able to have English teams come and play against us, and that meant a lot. In rugby union there were only matches against Germany, Italy and Romania - which counted for nothing.

"Of course the minute I started to play rugby league, I was automatically disqualified by the Rugby Union Federation, which was not the same as Galia's disqualification, because at union I hadn't been paid money. Galia had. There were several other big-name players who had been earning money and were banned by the Federation because at the time English rugby union had a tight hold on the French Federation.

"So when we went out to play we knew we had to entertain people. And when the teams were well matched it was a real spectacle. That first season we had an exceptional team at Lyon-Villeurbanne, coached by Charles Mathon."[8]

Mathon was more than coach or captain. It was he who saw to the numerous practical problems which arose, not the least of which was money. The arrangement struck with the club chairman guaranteed the players an initial signing-on fee, plus a share of match takings.

"The percentage of gate receipts we received was really minimal," commented Barnoud, "so we made a bit of money on our travelling expenses. We travelled third-class but instead of leaving at mid-day to get the train to go and play at Bordeaux, for example, we would leave at ten in the evening to avoid having to pay for a night in a hotel. We would pack sandwiches so that we didn't have to eat in a restaurant. Then we would share out the expenses - travel, hotel and evening meal - to make a bit of money. That's what you do when you're unemployed.

"I sold my furniture to have some money to live on. With the 4,000 francs signing-on fee I got I bought some furniture, and then I had to sell it again. We were supposed to be professionals but we weren't. We couldn't live on what we earned from playing rugby."[9]

"The outrageousness of the term 'professionalism', for which some of us had been banned by the French Rugby Union, provoked feelings of almost homicidal rage when on our journeys we by chance came across the rugby union 'amateurs'," Barnoud went on to write in his autobiography. "Pampered by their directors, they relaxed in their first-class couchettes, gorged themselves in the dining-car and were accommodated in first-class hotels. The purest of the pure, they looked down on us with the same kind of condescension that a company chairman might reserve for the lift-boy."[10]

Even training sessions took place in difficult conditions. At first the Lyon-Villeurbanne team simply trained on a piece of spare land until the municipal authorities decided to lease the Georges Lyvet stadium to the rugby league team, which plays there to this day. Thanks largely to the players' own promotional efforts and the increasing success of the team, eventually crowds of seven or eight thousand spectators would turn up on a Sunday. That was some achievement, considering that the long-established Lyon Olympique rugby union club, who had been champions of France two years earlier, also played in the vicinity.

The New Year of 1935 brought a further test of the French Rugby League's strength. The first international match since the establishment of the championship was to be played on January 1st at Bordeaux. The opponents, Wales, would ensure a stern contest.

From the team beaten by England in France's first-ever international match played the previous April, only four players retained their places - Galia, Porra, Duhau and Samatan. Into the side had come great attacking players in the shape of Rousié and Noguères and formidable packmen such as Rousse and Claudel, two of four representatives from Paris XIII.

Sullivan, by now a familiar figure in matches against the French, led Wales from full-back. The Wigan captain gave a typically outstanding performance, kicking four goals and creating his side's only try. But even his efforts could not prevent France from registering their first international victory by 18 points to 11 before 13,282 spectators who were thrilled to see the exploits of Galia's men come to fruition. Though Wales had at one stage been reduced to ten men through injury, nothing could detract from the individual brilliance of Galia and Rousié, who between them worked a fine try which was the outstanding moment of the match.

That game was to act as an introduction to the first official international that France would contest - against England on March 28th. A lock-out crowd of 20,000 turned up at the Stade Buffalo in Paris to see a French side which showed four changes take on the English, who, though perhaps not at their strongest, counted such talented players as Brough, Ellaby, Brogden, McCue and Hodgson among their ranks.

Again Galia and Rousié, the latter having switched to centre, were the stars of the piece. Setting the tone of his side's performance as he had done so many times before, Galia scored the game's first try, supporting good work by Noguères, so that France led 10-2 at half-time, following a converted try by winger Samatan. England came back to take a second-half lead despite resilient French defence before Rousié again made his mark, scoring the best try of the match with a dazzling run from his own half.

His Villeneuve team-mate, Camo, wrote later, and only slightly more evocatively with the passage of time, "The Tricolours were being pushed up against their own line by the English attacks. From a five metre scrum, France got the ball. Rousié, playing in the centre, took the ball, dummied, sidestepped, then after an astounding change of direction put the ball down under the posts. The ovation he received was indescribable."[11]

A late English try squared the match at 15-all but in other respects it was a huge triumph for the French Rugby League so soon after its inception. For

Max Rousié it was further confirmation that this enormously gifted player already had all the rugby league skills at his disposal. His display did not go unnoticed in England, where an agent offerred 200,000 francs for his signature on an English contract - an enormous sum at the time.

It is worth comparing Rousié's first international rugby league appearance with his debut in France's national rugby union side. Of that occasion, when France played Scotland in January 1931, it was reported that "...long before the end the players seemed as bored as the spectators."[12]

France's performance demanded that rugby league be now considered as part of French sporting culture. The national side's display helped to encourage more players to take the game up, more spectators to watch it and the media to give the sport more attention. Other propaganda matches, involving either French championship teams or touring sides, added to the impact. Apart from in cities where teams were already settled, one-off matches took place across France, from Grenoble in the east to Nantes in the west, and even beyond French shores as one army regiment played another in Haiphong, Indochina (now Vietnam).

The amateur section had risen from a complement of around twenty clubs at the start of the season to a hundred by the close, although at this early stage competition between clubs was still uneven, resulting in many one-sided matches, and the flow of players towards the professional clubs had yet to develop. Nevertheless the first amateur international match was staged at the Stade Buffalo, Paris, where 4,000 spectators watched their compatriots put on a creditable show in a 23-9 defeat by England.

As a remarkable first season drew to a close, confounding the critics who had claimed it would not even start, it would have been surprising if there had not been casualties along the way. In the professional championship, only two clubs - for various reasons, chief among which was the unavailability of stadiums - managed to complete all their 18 scheduled fixtures. Of the remaining eight, Béziers failed to last the course, withdrawing from the competition just three matches from the end of the season. Although they had finished bottom of the league, there was no shame to be found in their results. They had established a good following but the limitations of their stadium were a hindrance to their ambitions, or at least to those of their chairman who had only the previous season led a second division football club.

Jean Galia was able to take great satisfaction from the achievements of the inaugural season. Not the least of his pleasure was to be derived from the success of his own club, Villeneuve, the first winners of the championship, decided for the only time on points. (In future seasons the top clubs would play off for the championship title.) Bordeaux ended the season in second place, two points ahead of Lyon-Villeurbanne and Roanne, both of whom had played two matches fewer.

In the Cup, for which the trophy was donated by Lord Derby and which would henceforth bear his name, Lyon-Villeurbanne staged a second-half come-back to beat Galia's men 14-13 at Bordeaux and reach the final, while in the other semi-final at Toulouse, XIII Catalan accounted for Paris XIII by 22-15. The finalists were therefore Lyon-Villeurbanne and XIII Catalan, who met at Toulouse. The first half ended with both sides even at 7-all but, as in the semi, Mathon's team put the pressure on after the interval. Lyon overran the Perpignan side, scoring a further fifteen points without reply, thanks to tries from Lambert, Mathon and Amila, with three goals from Barnoud. The goal-kicking winger was to attribute his team's success to their captain-coach, Charles Mathon, the first player to hold the Lord Derby Cup aloft, who had raised his side's fitness to a level above that of their opponents, as well as leading by his own example. "We owed it all to him," said Barnoud.[13]

As Cup-winners Lyon-Villeurbanne took on the RFL Challenge Cup winners, Castleford, who had won the trophy for the first time at the expense of Huddersfield at Wembley. In front of 4,000 spectators at the Stade Buffalo in Paris, Lyon and Castleford appeared to be heading for a 21-all draw in a closely-fought, fast match. The French three-quarter line, outstanding with Barbazanges and Amila in the centre and Lambert and Barnoud on the wings, got the better of their English opponents, though the Castleford forwards had the edge over the French six. In the last minute, the Castleford centre and captain, Arthur Atkinson, a clear man of the match, went over for the try which gave his side a 24-21 victory. In a similarly even match at Bordeaux a week later, Swinton, the English champions, defeated Villeneuve by 27 points to 25 in front of 15,000 spectators.

The fact that France's top two teams could virtually match their mentors after just one season's competition was a resounding triumph. French rugby league's lightning progress on the pitch and moves towards stability off the field were both a vindication of its leaders' faith and determination as well as a rebuttal of those who said it couldn't be done. But not everyone was convinced enough to join in. There were still many who, instead of praising the pioneers' progress, stared balefully from their corner.

The US Perpignan team of 1921, champions of France at the 15-a-side game. Several of those pictured here would play decisive roles in rugby league some thirteen years later: Marcel Laborde (extreme left, wearing hat) became the driving force behind XIII Catalan; Jean Payra (third from left) was credited as the Ligue's first honorary president; the centre Roger Ramis (second player from left) became XIII Catalan's first coach.

Jep Pascot (back row, fifth player from left, looking sideways), on the other hand, used his position at Vichy to bring rugby league to a halt in 1940. Fernand Vacher, the captain (front row, third from left), famously offered the view that Jean Galia would never make it as a player. (Coll. N Altèze)

The CA Villeneuve XV of 1932 which was soon to undergo a profound transformation. The young full-back or centre François Noguères (front row, middle, directly in front of the two directors) was at the centre of the scandal which led to the ban placed on the player who brought him to the club, Jean Galia (back row, fourth player from left).

The official in the middle on the left, Georges Bordeneuve, the club chairman and mayor of Villeneuve, backed Galia's move to introduce rugby league by buying the stadium for the new Villeneuve rugby league club. Jean Barrès (immediately to the right of the two officials) became the secretary of the French Rugby League many years later, while Max Rousié (front row, sixth player from right) would become one of the game's greatest ever stars. (Coll. R Verdier)

The first page of the letter of agreement between the RFL and Jean Galia, outlining arrangements for the pioneering tour of England in March 1934. It was written by RFL secretary John Wilson on the notepaper of the Hotel Bedford, Paris, two days after the England-Australia match at Stade Pershing. (RFL archives)

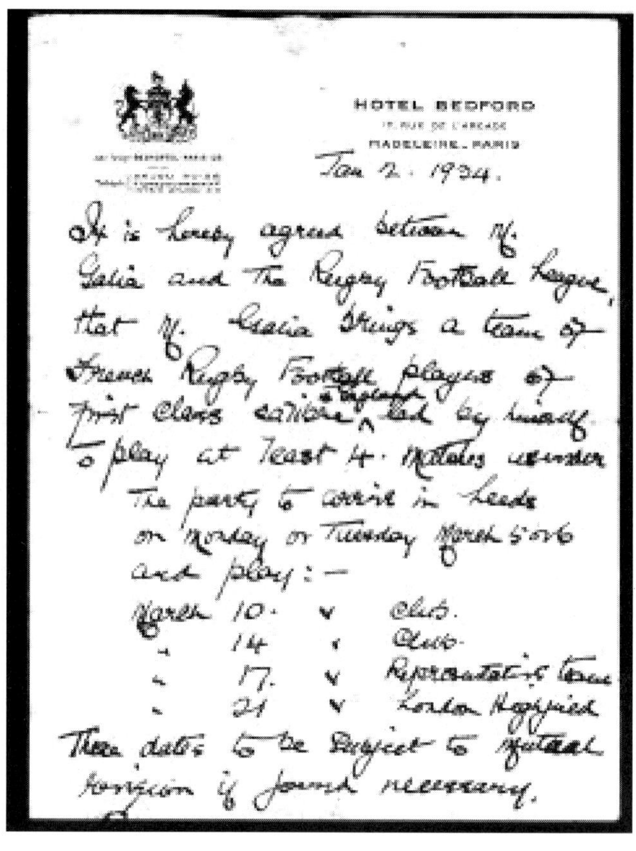

HOTEL BEDFORD
17, RUE DE L'ARCADE
MADELEINE – PARIS

Jan 2. 1934.

It is hereby agreed between M. Galia and The Rugby Football League, that M. Galia brings a team of French Rugby Football players of first class calibre to England led by himself to play at least 4 matches under

The party to arrive in Leeds on Monday or Tuesday March 5 or 6 and play:—

March 10. v Club.
" 14 v Club.
" 17. v Representative team
" 21 v London Highfield

These dates to be subject to mutual revision if found necessary.

The first Frenchmen ever to play rugby league: Jean Galia and his pioneers, March 1934. Back row (left to right): François Nouel, Léopold Fabre, Charles Mathon, Jean Duhau, Charles Petit, Henri Dechavanne, Maurice "Tom" Porra, Joseph Carrère, Georges Blanc. Front row (left to right): Jean Cassagneau, Laurent Lambert, Jean-Marie Vignal, Jean Galia, Gaston Amila, Antonin Barbazanges, Robert Samatan, François Récaborde.

Wigan captain Jim Sullivan is congratulated by Jean Galia at the end of the first-ever match played by a French rugby league team, 10th March 1934 at Central Park. Wigan won 30-27.

Galia's pioneers at a civic reception given by the mayor of Wigan on the morning of the match. Front row, from left to right: Henri Dechavanne, Jim Sullivan (Wigan capt.), Cllr James Horne, Jean Galia, Maurice "Tom" Porra. Second row: Gaston Amila, Laurent Lambert, James Walkden (chairman), Maurice Blein (interpreter), Jonty Parkin (coach). Third row: Lolo Fabre, Bright Heyhurst (masseur), Charles Bernat (manager), Antonin Barbazanges, Harry Sunderland.
Back row: Joseph Carrère, Georges Blanc, Charles Petit, Jean Cassagneau, Charles Mathon.

ABOVE: Jean Galia, pictured here at the wheel of his Bugatti, had a taste for fast cars. (Coll. M Galia Kaplan)

BELOW: Galia, a champion boxer as well as an international rugby player of both codes, seen here outside his family's fruit and vegetable business in his home town of Ille-sur-Têt. (Coll. M Galia Kaplan)

Galia, shown here on the river Lot, was a keen rower. (Coll. M Galia Kaplan)

The first French international team which played England at the Stade Buffalo, Paris, on April 15th 1934, losing 32-21. From left to right: Galia, Petit, Blanc, Duhau, Samatan, Nouel, Barbazanges, Porra, Récaborde, Mathon, Carrère, Cassagneau, Lambert.

An advertisement from Victor Breyer's Echo des Sports, announcing the first international between France and England, played at the Stade Buffalo, Paris. Two Parisian amateur clubs, Sport Olympique de Paris and Quartier Etudiants Club, played a curtain-raiser to the match.

The curtain-raiser to the first rugby league match played at Villeneuve, May 6th 1934. Two teams of under-14s took part, refereed by François Récaborde. Among the young players are the future journalist René Verdier and Jean Gironde, who was to be a star of the post-war Villeneuve side. Note the berets. (Coll. Mme Gironde)

The post-match dinner held at the Hôtel Gache, Villeneuve, on May 6th 1934 after the third game of the Yorkshire Selection team's tour. The Yorkshire players are seated on the left (inside row), the France team on the right (inside row). (Coll. R Verdier)

Captains Jean Galia and Jim Sullivan exchange pennants before the France-Wales match at Bordeaux on New Year's Day 1935. The French gained their first international victory, defeating Wales 18-11. (Coll. N Altèze)

The power of advertising: France's national squad endorses a make of hat, circa 1934. Almost a decade earlier Jean Bourrel's hat-manufacturing business had bankrolled the rugby union championship-winning Quillan club, of which Jean Galia was an important member.

The Lyon-Villeurbanne team on tour in England, September 1935. Five of Galia's pioneers figure in the side: Gaston Amila (back row, extreme left), Charles Petit (back row, third from left), Antonin Barbazanges (back row, third from right), Laurent Lambert (front, second from left), and Charles Mathon (front, middle).

The future internationals Joseph Griffard (back row, extreme right) and René Barnoud (front, third from left) also appear. The Lyon-Villeurbanne chairman, Joseph Pansera, who was murdered two years later, is seated next to Mathon with arms folded. (Coll. R Barnoud)

Charles Mathon, captain-coach of Lyon-Villeurbanne, clutching the Lord Derby Trophy awarded to the winners of the Coupe de France. Lyon-Villeurbanne became the inaugural holders of the trophy when they beat XIII Catalan 22-7 in the 1935 final. (Coll. Mme Mathon)

France v England at the Stade Buffalo, 16th February 1936. Galia (no. 11), with Barnoud (no. 5) outside him, moves in to tackle England stand-off Herbert. England won 25-7 in front of 21,300 spectators. (Miroir des Sports)

Two outstanding scrum-halves: Sylvain Bès (right) was signed by Jean Galia and became the linchpin of the Toulouse Olympique side, while Max Rousié, who also played stand-off, centre and full-back, was considered by many as the finest of all time.

On their 1938 tour of France the Australians suffered defeat at the Stade des Minimes, Toulouse at the hands of the Midi-Pyrénées representative side, losing 15-0. Here the Kangaroos manage to get the ball away despite the attentions of Sylvain Bès, the captain, while winger Etienne Cougnenc closes in.

Two up-and-coming Villeneuve players, Jep Lacoste and Jean Gironde, both protégés of Jean Galia, circa 1939. Note the French cockerel badge on the radiator grille of the car. (Coll. Mme Gironde)

Scenes from the 1937 Cup Final between Villeneuve and XIII Catalan at Bordeaux. Above: Maurice Bruneteaud, scorer of both Villeneuve tries, evades the XIII Catalan second-rower André Bruzy. Below: Villeneuve's Carbo and Brinsolles give chase. Villeneuve went on to win the Cup 12-6.

The most feared attacking duo in France: Roanne's Jean Dauger (left) and Max Rousié, who had been signed from Villeneuve. (Coll. R Verdier)

St Helens, 25th February 1939: in defeating England 12-9, the France XIII became the first French international rugby team of either code to win on English soil. (Back row, left to right), Marius Guiral, André Bruzy, Maurice Bruneteaud, Antoine Blain, Louis Brané, Henri Durand, Henri Gibert, Messrs Cadoret (president of the Ligue) and Pelot (treasurer); (front row, left to right) Etienne Cougnenc, François Noguères, Pierre Brinsolles, Jean Dauger, Max Rousié, Jep Desclaux, Raphaël Sarris. (Coll. L Bonnery)

The XIII Catalan side of 1937-38: (back row, left to right) Porra, Bruzy, Danoy, Forma, Gau, Bosc, Lloanci (official); (front, left to right) Ollet, Lavagne, Vaills, Noguères, Saltraille, Garcies, Quéroli.

A championship match between Toulouse Olympique and XIII Catalan, 1st February 1938. Martin Serre launches a Catalan attack as Toulouse scrum-half Sylvain Bès covers. Toulouse won 11-5.

The Albi team of 1937-38 which won the championship from seventh place. Back row (left to right): Rudin, Halard, Lataillade, Bousquet, Mounié, Sagné. Front (left to right): Lapeyre, Lopez, Desplats, Vignal, Castagnon, Combes, Jansous.

Marcel Laborde, the XIII Catalan official and the Ligue's executive chairman, who was summoned to Vichy in October 1940 by Jean Borotra to be told that rugby league was to be banned.

Colonel Joseph Pascot, a former rugby union international, Borotra's successor and an instigator of the ban on rugby league, at an official pre-match presentation during the Occupation. Here Pascot is introduced by Max Rousié to a team containing players who, like Rousié himself, had been compelled to convert from league to union.

Paul Barrière (left), recruited by Marcel Laborde to fight the treiziste cause in the immediate post-war period, pictured in the company of fellow-official Monsieur Quéheillard of Bordeaux and the former international forward Jean Duhau, coach of the national team.

After the Liberation, Carcassonne met Villeneuve in a charity match at the Parc des Princes, Paris. Here the Villeneuve winger Max Amblard makes a blindside break, supported by second-row Gaston Calixte (wearing scrum-cap) and loose-forward Maurice Bruneteaud. (Coll. Mme Gironde)

Chapter Nine
IRRECONCILABLE DIFFERENCES

The opening rugby league season of 1934-35 was more than two months away when the committee of Villeneuve's rugby union club, the Club Athlétique Villeneuvois, felt sufficiently threatened to want to make public the reason for their continued existence in the town.[1]

"The question is not whether Villeneuve will have a rugby league club or a rugby union club," the rugby union officials wrote in the local paper. "Put in such terms the problem is not clear. There is a risk - which may be the wish of some, although it is certainly not ours - of setting two organisations and groups of people against each other.

"To those who take pleasure in such shabby quarrels, we say quite clearly that, in pursuing their singular path, they do not serve sport.

"The CAV has a right to exist and, moreover, we have a duty not to let this organisation perish...

"The CAV will live on. Already the ill-intentioned, or, we prefer to think, ill-informed prophets of doom, have drafted out the funeral oration. Some, with a tone of ironic pity, others, with a hint of spite, have placed wreaths over the CAV declaring: the CAV cannot survive, it has no players, it has no ground; and giving, as their final argument, the great preoccupation of modern times, that it has no money...

"The CAV must live on; we will see to it. It is a club which has its own character and which is officially recognised... The CAV has a ground, it has matches to play, it has players, it has volunteers who take an interest in its welfare. It will strive to march on.

"We are jealous of no-one; we mean no harm to anyone; but for pity's sake let us now call a truce."

The rugby union club's plea revealed a remarkable situation in Villeneuve. Before the French Rugby League had even drawn up a fixture list, and after only one exhibition match had been played there, rugby union was fighting for survival. It depended for its future existence on those members of the club who had not thrown in their lot with Galia, Bordeneuve, Vinson and most of the rest.

The precocious dominance of rugby league in Villeneuve arose from the enthusiasm of the game's leading figures to strike out in a new direction after their rough treatment by rugby union's governing body. Bordeneuve in particular, as a civic leader, was keen to seize the opportunity to make his town and his club a model for the rest of rugby-conscious France. As for those who had preferred the security of the status quo they quickly found, as the letter showed, that their standing was very much reduced. "The *quinzistes* didn't count any longer," said René Verdier.[2] They would not be denied the right to continue, even if they were seen as sympathisers with a body which had dealt the town a severe blow. But their club would no longer be regarded with anything like the civic pride it had once enjoyed.

In a town of Villeneuve's modest size it was possible for a single sport to achieve the dominance which rugby league was about to enjoy. By contrast, another set of circumstances resulted in rugby league receiving a huge impetus in a city of greater strategic significance, Bordeaux.

When Bordeaux was lined up as a possible venue for one of the France-Yorkshire demonstration matches in May 1934, the FFR immediately took action to try to ensure that the city's most suitable stadium, the Parc des Sports de Suzon, should not be used as a rugby league venue. The stadium, which consisted of the usual rugby pitch and stands but also had facilities for tennis, basketball, swimming and pelota, was owned by shareholders, of whom some were also officials of the Sport Athlétique Bordelais rugby union club which had reached the championship semi-finals in 1927 and 1929. The club had requested a loan of 25,000 francs from the FFR to carry out refurbishment of the ground but had had no definite response. Once it was proposed to stage the rugby league match there, the stadium company leased the ground to the Ligue de Rugby à XIII and gave the rugby union club notice to quit. The FFR struck back by banning the ground for rugby union and suspending the committee of the SA Bordelais. The Federation's plan backfired. The France-Yorkshire match, played on May 10th, was a resounding success, with receipts of over 100,000 francs. Although the outcome of a general meeting of the SAB rugby union club, held three weeks later, was that the club should remain within the FFR rather than defect to the Ligue, many of those against the motion, including the leading administrators and players, decided to break away. The prime movers - the international forward Bonamy and the officials Darmaillac and Loze, the chairman - put forward a proposal which led to the creation of a rugby league club, to be known as Bordeaux XIII, and the demise of the rugby union club, which suddenly lost both its players and its ground. The Ligue was happy to step in where the FFR had dallied and agreed to advance the costs of ground renovation.[3]

As far as the development of rugby league was concerned, the Suzon stadium had a crucial role. It was reserved for the exclusive use of rugby league and was utilised to maximum effect. Not only were finals held there but clubs occasionally transferred their ordinary championship matches to Suzon, sure in the knowledge that the enthusiastic Bordeaux public would welcome their efforts and turn up in numbers to support them.

Mid-way through the first season, the Bordeaux secretary wrote to his counterpart at Albi and suggested that the fixture between the two clubs be played at Suzon, since Albi's ground happened to be unavailable that Sunday. He suggested that they would take at least 15,000 francs at the gate, whereas the best receipts at Albi had been just 5,500, and went on to quote some impressive figures for the opening part of the season. "We took 13,727 francs for the match against yourselves on October 7; 16,000 against Perpignan on October 21; against Villeneuve on November 18 we had receipts of 25,669 francs; against Côte Basque on November 25 we had 16,315. Even for a friendly match we exceed 12,000 francs, regardless of the opposition."

Bordeaux and Villeneuve became established in a very short period of time as rugby league strongholds. The fact that both clubs quickly found a permanent base was an important step towards achieving stability, since it facilitated the promotion of both the club and the game among the public.

Pau was another club which, by applying to the owners of a stadium used mainly for football, largely avoided confrontation with representatives of the rugby union club over where they would play. But that did not prevent the subject from becoming controversial in the columns of *L'Indépendant des Pyrénées*, which, like many local newspapers, picked up and reprinted the more spirited arguments from the specialist sporting press. Quoting from *France-Olympique*, one of numerous contemporary publications devoted exclusively to sport, the Pau newpaper published the following passage of startling naivety a month before rugby league's first season was due to start.

"Rugby league clubs, if they are powerful enough to buy up a stable of top players, should be rich enough to build new stadiums. It is too easy for them to come along and say to others: 'Get out of here. We want this place.'"

Although admitting that rugby league's rules made an interesting concept, the writer added his misgivings about the sport's implantation in France, criticising the methods by which it had come about.

"As they seem to want to make something new out of something old and with materials taken from their neighbour, we really don't see what there can be to make a fuss about...

"Rugby league, founded by malcontents, could only win malcontents to its cause. That is what has happened and continues to happen. There is nothing unusual in that. But one could never conceive that these malcontents, instead of simply playing this sport to which they attribute every virtue, should transform it into an instrument of war against existing rugby union organisations."

The writer, accusing rugby league of open warfare against rugby union, nevertheless admitted that it was wrong of the FFR to ban stadiums for use by rugby league clubs. "But," he continued, "the French Rugby League must not allow its new members, burning with a zeal which they could have put to better use in their old clubs, to harm rugby union clubs. In all of this, the rugby union clubs have sought to do no wrong in any way to those involved in rugby league and rugby league people should do the same and leave them in peace."[4]

It was a wild accusation, accurate only in its inference of ill feeling between the two codes. Since the first moment that thirteen players had lined up against thirteen others on a French field - even before then, in fact, if one takes into account attempts to stop the exhibition matches of 1921-22 and 1933 - the rugby union authorities had consistently acted with aggression.

The problems experienced at such places as Roanne or Perpignan, irksome as they had been, were comparatively minor, set against those encountered in Paris, where the FFR had its headquarters. Rugby union's governing body put pressure on its clubs to place whatever obstacles they could in rugby league's path. In addition it attempted to coerce other sporting bodies to ostracise and otherwise hinder the *treizistes*. Its machinations ran particularly deep in the capital, where the Stade Buffalo, "suspended" by the FFR immediately after the France-England match, became a minefield of hazards for Paris XIII.

The FFR had tried to spread its malign influence even beyond the bounds of rugby, instigating an agreement with other major sports federations to suspend those grounds which had been defiled by rugby league. Taking a lead from its Federation, the rugby section of the multi-sports club, the Stade Français, one of the oldest and most prestigious clubs in France and an original member of the breakaway UFRA organisation, influenced other sections of the club, notably football, to prevent the Stade Buffalo from staging rugby league matches.

By a contract with the Buffalo management, both the soccer and rugby union sections of the Stade Français had the right to play their matches at that stadium - a right which the union club duly asserted in order to prevent rugby league from being played there. The stadium manager, Louis Delblat, a founder member of the Ligue Française de Rugby à XIII, pointed out that the exclusivity applied only to the sports which the Stade Français practised and rugby league was not one of them. In any case, its rugby union team had only played one or two matches at Buffalo during the previous season, taking its big matches to other stadiums where it had no exclusive contract. Its football section, which played only as amateurs in the local Paris league, had little need of such a stadium. Delblat further pointed out that, if the rugby union section had given notice of its fixtures for the season, it could have had the first chance of booking the stadium for those dates. None had been forthcoming, yet it wanted to prevent rugby league from being played at all times.[5]

The conflict rumbled on through much of the curtailed existence of Paris XIII. One particularly unfortunate incident took place towards the beginning of the club's second season, in October 1935. Just before Paris XIII was due to play an important match against Galia's Villeneuve, the football section of the Stade Français claimed the right to play at the stadium that same day. Spectators who turned up at Buffalo to watch the rugby league match saw instead, fastened to the main gate, a hand-written notice which read: "The Paris v Villeneuve match will not take place at Buffalo and is cancelled."[6] Although the match was eventually re-scheduled for February, last-minute postponements did nothing to win the support of Parisians for rugby league.

The harrassing of rugby league by the FFR was consistent with rugby union's continued and unusually energetic efforts to deal with the effects of its own fundamental incompetence. That vigorous critic of the FFR, Marcel Laborde, believed corruption was so rife within that institution, the taint so deep that it was impossible to remove.

"Eight out of ten teams are - how shall I put it? - recompensed," he claimed. "Thirteen out of fifteen players owe their jobs and lifestyle to the game they play."[7]

Laborde admitted he was unable to understand the Federation's attitude towards what he called the birth of professional rugby. "They're trying to abort it instead of welcoming it. The League is the enemy and they're fighting it." With this stance, Laborde argued, the FFR was simply preparing the way for a resurgence of shamateurism within its own ranks. The Perpignan official criticised its committee for its shopkeeper's mentality, its preoccupation with petty rivalries, its concerns with money-making, with playing more and more matches, with numbers at the expense of quality.

This "war of players, war of grounds, war of influence" would, predicted Laborde, have a fatal outcome for the FFR and its standing in the sporting world. At least two paths could lead in this direction. The League could discredit the Rugby Union by going to the government minister responsible and denouncing union's financial practices as no different from rugby league's, except that they were done secretly. "This sporting fraud is simply financial fraud," claimed Laborde. Second, existing agreements between stadium management and the FFR could be replaced by similar agreements with the League, if that proved more profitable. By this means the FFR could be placed in a difficult and ultimately untenable position.

Admitting it was unlikely, Laborde's suggestion that both games should come under the same administration was a reiteration of what had earlier been suggested and turned down. But Laborde himself, unacquainted at that time with the game of rugby league, had been talking from a theoretical viewpoint which did not take into account the differences between the two sports.

He confessed: "For me it's not so much a matter of this rugby league, with which I am unfamiliar and which I wait to see for myself, as the establishment of a moral status for rugby."

Professional rugby, he proposed, should be incorporated as an extension of federal rugby, i.e. rugby union. If that did not happen, he suggested, both would collapse within two years at the most. "Unless," he added, "rugby league, supported by the English, wins the day."[8]

In the meantime the FFR continued to marshal its troops to fight Laborde's prediction, one of the rare examples of decisive action it proved capable of taking.

The Ligue Française de Rugby à XIII had made applications for official recognition by the Comité National des Sports, a semi-autonomous body made up of delegates from the existing sports federations. The purpose of the CNS was to act as an intermediary between the sporting organisations and the public authorities. Admission to this body would have put rugby league on a par with other sports played in France and given the game a much-enhanced status. Only one federation however was allowed to represent each sport. And rugby league had the greatest difficulty in making a claim for itself as a separate sport, rather than a variant of an existing one. Its applications to the CNS consequently remained without a definitive response. The FFR was still in a position to agree to take amateur rugby league under its wing even if it wanted nothing to do with the professional game. But if the FFR refused that responsibility, then the CNS would be automatically authorised to recognise rugby league as a separate organisation. "But what must not happen," wrote the journalist Marcel Oger, "is that the FFR be allowed to put off making a decision about its own position."[9]

The Federation had every interest in deferring a decision. A categorical refusal to accept rugby league into its own organisation would have given the new sport the independent and official status that would have made it an even more serious rival than it already was. Rugby league had to be kept out of the CNS at all costs. The FFR's pressure on other sports federations effectively established a cartel which would act not only to exclude rugby league from the CNS but to strangle the game's development. The alliance had consequences which would have appeared simply ridiculous if they had not also invaded individual freedoms.

To cite one example: in Nantes there were three rugby league clubs with around 150 strictly amateur players. A number of these players wanted to take part in the regional athletics championships. They found themselves barred from doing so because their clubs belonged to a federation - the

French Rugby League - which was not recognised by the CNS. When they then asked whether they could join athletics clubs in Nantes in order to compete they were told by the French Athletics Federation, which was bound by the CNS code, that they could not, because they belonged to an unofficial organisation. It didn't seem to occur to the established federations like Athletics that to turn potential participants away from their own sports was to contravene their own terms of reference.

The Athletics Federation had also banned the middle-distance runner, Jules Ladoumègue, for a minor breach of amateurism. World record-holder Ladoumègue however was invited to run, in July 1934, at a meeting in Albi organised by Maurice Metgé, the secretary of a sports club which embraced both athletics and rugby union. As a result, Metgé also was blacklisted by athletics' governing body and by extension all other federations. But Metgé's ban only increased his determination to launch the Albi rugby league club which was being planned at that time.

Marcel Oger continued to expose the absurdity of the official line. "Again we come up against the eternal problem," he wrote. "Rugby league is a sport which has a right to exist. The FFR will not recognise it. The FFR will not be responsible for administering it, not even for the strict amateurs. But at the same time the FFR claims that it governs and must govern all forms of rugby, which includes, of course, rugby league."[10]

By maintaining its obdurate attitude the CNS, Oger pointed out, was compromising its own credibility, while at the same time depriving young people of the right to take part even in officially recognised sports, as the would-be athletes of Nantes had discovered.

But the CNS remained steadfastly unimpressed by rugby league's request for official status, passing the buck yet again to the FFR, who, the Council reiterated, had sole authorisation for control of "rugby". The CNS chairman, Jules Rimet, president of the French Football Association, stated that he hoped that the FFR would make a decision. But the FFR would have no dealings with open professionalism. The attitude of both bodies was neatly summed up by *L'Auto*: "FFR XV: strategic inertia. CNS: inert strategy".[11]

The president of the FFR, Roger Dantou, inadvertently defeated his federation's own argument for wanting to control all forms of rugby played in France. He asked that his organisation be left in peace and not be expected to incorporate another rugby "which is completely different, in every respect, from orthodox rugby".[12] The CNS, however, maintained its original stance, refusing, in spite of the evidence, to see rugby league as an independent sport. That position stayed unchanged even after rugby league received government recognition in January 1938. Which is more than can be said of the FFR's perception of the game itself. "We will continue to claim that *Rugby à treize* is only a copy of real Rugby," commented Dantou, unhappy at the government's decision. At least his federation's opposition to this "copy" was entirely consistent. "If the Rugby Union in Britain would appreciate what we are doing against professional Rugby and resume relations with us it would be of the greatest help," he added.[13] Regardless of how popular the game became - in spite of such concerted attempts to shackle its steps - vested interests would ensure that, in the sporting community, rugby league players would remain pariahs.

Chapter Ten
BREAKTHROUGH

At the first annual congress of the Ligue Française de Rugby à XIII, held at Toulouse on July 27th and 28th, 1935, some impressive figures were announced. Those critics who branded rugby league as merely a professional form of the orthodox code would be made to reconsider as the congress chairman, Dr Vinson, announced more than a hundred amateur rugby league clubs in existence, plus another fifty student or schoolboy clubs. The figures showed the extent to which the game had already gripped the imagination of both the spectators who turned up to watch the ten professional clubs and of those who wanted to play the game themselves. Amateur clubs were springing up everywhere. There were now half-a-dozen in Paris, as many again in the Bordeaux area, while others from La Rochelle in the west to Lyon in the east were already in existence.

The professional league was expanded to fourteen clubs for the second season and was played in two pools of seven. To the nine survivors from the first season was added a second club in Paris, as Celtic de Paris finally got under way, to be joined by Dax, Agen, Périgueux (based in the home town of the FFR president, Roger Dantou) and Gallia de Toulouse (which had nothing to do with Jean Galia but took its name, as several other sports clubs did, from the Latin word for Gaul). The expansion proved too fast for some, however. Agen dropped out after three matches and the Toulouse club after just two, without a win between them.

This second season should have been one of consolidation, with the Ligue and its officials profiting from the initial wave of enthusiasm for rugby league and ensuring that the new sport began to establish a solid base. The development of the amateur game would be vital to the long-term survival of the sport. The integration of the professional clubs within their communities would be similarly imperative. But the collapse of the Agen and Toulouse clubs (both of which, however, would continue in the amateur divisions) showed that success would be far from automatic.

It was a time of conjecture, project-making, visions of the future, all of which were constrained by present problems. New clubs were envisaged at Marseille, Montpellier, Nantes, Limoges, Cognac and Biarritz among others. Largely owing to the difficulties of finding grounds to play at, only the Nantes club saw the light of day. In the existing professional ranks consideration was given to a merger between Pau and Côte Basque, the latter still without a home ground, although both clubs eventually continued their separate ways. There was also talk of the re-emergence of Béziers, but it did not materialise.

Contact with English sides remained very much part of the programme of development. Lyon-Villeurbanne, after three months' respite, undertook a Cup-winners' tour of England which began at St Helens, where the home team won an open, attractive game by 19 points to 10. Three days later the tourists played a return match against Castleford where they lost again, this time by 18-8, but created a very favourable impression on the 8,000 spectators. One match report, headed "How Rugby can be played" saw the game as "most entertaining and abounding in thrilling passing movements, the ball being taken from one end of the field to the other at amazing speeds."

Other spectacular displays of handling were seen at Craven Park, Barrow, where Mathon's team lost by a single point and at York, where a Rugby League XIII accounted for the touring side by 23-19. A reporter who covered the match referred in amazement to the Frenchmen's footwear. "It is a mystery how Amila shot two goals shod in a canvas sort of contraption resembling a running pump," he wrote, before making the following judgement on the French methods of play: "While I am envious of the French style - it is so entertaining, constructive and spectacular - I realise its frailty. Competitively, our dreadnought cup-tie methods would smash it to smithereens; but that does not prove it to be unworthy of modified adoption. A combination of the two would produce an ideal."

In the *Sports Echo*[1] one writer addressed an open letter to Charles Mathon, as the captain of the first authentic club side to tour England. It showed a fair understanding of the state of the game in France.

"When Galia turned his attention to the Rugby League code you quickly decided this was the game that fascinated you and although maintaining your reputation as a clever utility man, you have particularly impressed as a smart and thrustful outside half with a deceptive side-step....

"I know you are surely and firmly convinced that Rugby League is the favourite winter code of the future in your country. The return of your team to France coincides with the opening of the French season proper.

"There are 14 professional clubs, playing in two sections, and over 100 amateur clubs. This number would be even greater if more grounds were available.

"Many of them occupy municipally-owned enclosures and to use your own quotation: 'The Rugby Union people have ceased to trouble because they realise they cannot stop a rising tide.'"

During the close season, Lyon-Villeurbanne's forward strength, already considerable with the likes of Griffard, who had been singled out during the English tour as a fine, hard-working and constructive forward, was increased by the acquisition of another pioneer, Charles Petit, a Parisian by birth, a renowned former rugby union international and the captain-coach of Roanne in the first year of that club's existence. It was he who, according to Barbazanges, became a prototype of the development officer, teaching schoolchildren to play rugby league on their free afternoons.

The team certainly proved too strong for Bramley, who, with Leeds, were on tour in France in November. Lyon-Villeurbanne took the honours, winning 25-19 in a well-contested match (for which, incidentally, René Barnoud had produced the first issue of his *Treize* match programme). The game between Leeds and Bordeaux, played the same day, yielded gate receipts given as £1,000, while the match at Villeurbanne produced £666 - excellent figures, particularly for matches played on a Monday afternoon.

But this so-called professional sport did not provide a living for the vast majority of its players. At Villeurbanne the players' dissatisfaction with their terms turned to unrest as they failed to perceive a strict relationship between the size of the crowds and their own cut of the gate. The club chairman, Monsieur Pansera, in turn said that he was disillusioned with the attitude of the players. "They're wrong to want to kill the goose that lays the golden eggs," he declared, "particularly since they all have a paid job outside sport." Pansera announced that he had spent his own money keeping the club afloat and could not accept the players' increased demands. Eventually he decided he had had enough and sent his letter of resignation to the Ligue, saying he would demand transfer fees for the players and henceforth would spend his winters skiing.[2]

But Barnoud, who was unemployed, saw the matter in quite a different light and claimed that Pansera altered the gate receipts to suit his own purposes.

"We didn't take legal action against Pansera but agreed to support Mathon," Barnoud said. "He had written to each of us in order to form a kind of players' association which would defend our interests and demand a monthly salary, which would be the same for everyone, instead of a percentage of the receipts."[3]

The action was to rebound on the captain. An anonymous letter was sent to the Ligue giving details of the players' revolt. The remarkable result was that Charles Mathon, the founder, captain and coach of Lyon-Villeurbanne and a man described by Barnoud as "totally incapable of dishonesty" was banned from rugby league for life.

The problems associated with setting up rugby league in new areas were not confined to France. Similar events were unfolding in London, where the two clubs Acton & Willesden and Streatham & Mitcham were in deficit and were having to trim players' remuneration to prevent further losses. Perhaps the unfortunate Londoners were able to commiserate with their hosts, Lyon-Villeurbanne, whom they played in a combined London tour match in mid-April.

Two members of the London side, the New Zealanders George Nepia and Jack Cutbush, were also selected in the British Dominions (Other Nationalities) team which met France in Paris on April 26th. It was to be Galia's last match. A player whose personal pride would never allow him to slip below the standards he had set for himself, Galia told his Villeneuve club-mate, Jean Barrès, "I'm going to play one last big match then retire. I want to finish at the top."[4] And so he did, as France's best player in their 8-5 victory.

Earlier in the season the France team, following their victory over Wales at Bordeaux the previous January, travelled in optimistic mood for the return match at Llanelli, where a reported 30,000 crowd assembled from all over South Wales. The Welsh forwards, however, soon dominated their French counterparts to create the positions from which the likes of Gus Risman at centre would take full advantage. Handicapped by the absence of Galia in the forwards and despite the best efforts of Rousié, the Frenchmen revealed shortcomings in defence and experienced a crushing 41-7 defeat. Had Jim Sullivan been in goal-kicking form the defeat would have been even heavier, as the Welshmen ran in eleven tries.

France's international team fared slightly better against England. With a stronger set of forwards which included Galia, France was again defeated, by 25-7, but showed more determination in defence after opening the scoring with a Noguères try. Played before the Minister for the Navy, Monsieur Pietri, who would become an ally of rugby league, and 21,300 other spectators, the match gained further ground for the new game in the capital.

Even more significant was France's performance in the amateur international played at Halifax on Easter Monday. The inexperienced Frenchmen put up a stirring display against Englishmen from such strongholds of the amateur game as Kells, Oldham and St Helens before losing by 16-8. It was an indication of the all-important progress being made to establish rugby league outside the professional division in France.

One black cloud which troubled rugby league's previously clear skies appeared at Bordeaux during the course of a match against Côte Basque in March. The often violent and indisciplined play which had been associated with rugby union's championship had so far failed to infect rugby league, which, despite the relative hardness of the game, had kept a commendable record. As Tintin Saltraille put it, there was no deliberate brutality in rugby league. But a brawl between the Bordeaux and Basque players resulted in a touch judge being jostled and play being subject to long interruptions. At least the League's disciplinary committee acted decisively. The Côte Basque forward Bizauta was suspended for six months and fined 500 francs.

That sanction also put the Basque player out of his club's cup campaign, which culminated in the final at the Suzon stadium in Bordeaux, where Côte Basque met Galia's Villeneuve team, which included stars such as the full-back Guiral, loose-forward Bruneteaud, half-backs Cougnenc and Brinsolles, not to mention Max Rousié, playing in the centre. Villeneuve's half-time lead of 8-2, which included a Galia try, came under pressure in the second period. The Basques crossed the Villeneuve line three times in adding thirteen points to their total with none in reply to become winners of an exciting final, excellently refereed by Frank Peel of Bradford.

The Basques went on to give another good account of themselves against the English championship runners-up, Widnes, at Bayonne. Only a last-minute converted try allowed the Chemics to share the honours at 14-all.

The 1935-36 championship, unlike the previous year's, which had been decided on points, set the precedent for future years in being decided by play-offs. As in the Cup, the championship final was played at Bordeaux, despite the fact that the home club, narrow semi-final winners over Lyon-Villeurbanne, was involved. Their opponents were XIII Catalan, who quickly went about trying to make amends for their defeat in the Cup final the season before. The gates were shut an hour before kick-off and the anticipated close, thrilling match ensued, with the Catalans scoring five tries to four in a high-quality match which they won by 25-14.

But the pleasing standard of these matches could not disguise the fact that this second season had been far from easy, a point made realistically in the report given at the annual congress. The economic position of the professional clubs indicated that full-time professionalism among their players was a long way off. A resolution was passed to ensure that all players should have a job outside rugby league and that their remuneration should be regarded not as wages but as bonus payments. The reduction in the number of professional clubs from fourteen to ten also left its impression. In future only those clubs which could be shown to be based on a solid footing would be accepted into the top division.

Consequently the 1936-37 season would start in the same way as the inaugural season, with ten clubs. The only difference in the composition of the professional division from that first season was that Dax had taken the place of Béziers.

The early-season tour of England undertaken by Côte Basque characterised much of the method of French rugby league as it entered its third year of existence. The Basques' attacking style was regularly described as spectacular, with favourable comments being made about their speed and ball-handling, which was guaranteed to please the crowds. The Basques had some star performers in the skilful loose-forward Rousse and the small but tricky centre pair, Cussac and Sanz. But despite running Wigan close, thanks partly to the efforts of the ex-Wigan half-back Tom Parker who organised his Basque team-mates effectively, the Frenchmen fell some way short of winning their other matches against Bradford Northern, Hull KR and a Rugby League XIII. In that last match one particularly critical reporter described their defence as "glaringly inept" and lacking in teamwork.

"Every man tries his hardest," he continued, with faint praise. "After the manner of an enthusiastic schoolboy he wants to be where the ball is with the result that the position he should be in is unguarded; and an opponent intercepting a pass or snapping up the ball has merely to run strongly to be an almost certain scorer... The Frenchmen, too, 'buy the dummy' with ridiculous simplicity."

After a mere two years' experience, French players clearly still had a good deal to learn from their English mentors and just as much to unlearn from their union upbringing. They knew it and to that end the tours to and from England continued to multiply, while English referees now regularly officiated at top matches. Nevertheless at international level France emerged with credit in the encounter with Wales, losing 9-3 on a miserable December day at the Stade Buffalo in Paris, which now had an exclusive contract with the Ligue for international matches.

And where else but Paris would you find a rugby league team called Arts Décoratifs XIII? If the name suggests something more fanciful, whimsical or enigmatic than is usually associated with the thrusting realism of the Anglo-Saxon version of the thirteen-a-side game, it merely embraced that of a student club, who, as elsewhere in Paris, were keen to give rugby league a go, making their début in January 1937. What noble idealism is brought to mind by the name Treize Olympique Parisien, another torch-bearer for amateur rugby league in the capital, with an imposing registered address on the Place de la République! Or the more down-to-earth Treize Populaire Parisien, with its revolutionary echoes, though with a ground quite a long way removed from the Bastille.

Individual French players continued to make an impression both at home and in England. Without Galia, now retired, French teams might lack a collective direction at times in the face of their English opponents, as they did in the 1937 international at Halifax, which they lost 23-9. But there were some fearsome French forwards beginning to make their presence felt, including the likes of Porra, Galia's old sparring partner, Bruzy and Griffard, not to mention Rousse and Brané. The loose forward Maurice Bruneteaud had made the position his own with his excellent tackling and skilful handling. It was for the backs, though, that France was acquiring a reputation across the Channel. With fast, creative players like Noguères, Guiral, Samatan and Brinsolles, it was easy to see why. François Noguères became known throughout French rugby league by his nickname "Good", acquired when an English opponent had singled him out for praise, pointing to him, giving the thumbs-up and uttering his approval.

Above all it was the incomparable Rousié who unfailingly left his mark on any game he played in. In that 1937 international against England it was not for his creativity or strength in attack or for the solidity of his defence that he stood out, but for his kicking. This time it was the turn of the Halifax crowd to be amazed as the French captain, being awarded a penalty, prepared to take a drop-kick at goal from a position in the angle of half-way and the touchline. With his wide repertoire, Rousié had no difficulty in simply taking a few measured steps and sending the ball cleanly between the posts.

In the domestic championship, XIII Catalan proved what a force they had become, heading the league table comfortably, with Bordeaux in second place. For the second year in succession these two teams met in the championship final, which was again played at Bordeaux's home ground before a capacity crowd. But the similarities went no further, for the Perpignan team was convincingly beaten by 23-10. Nor did the Catalans fare much better in the final of the Cup, where they lost 12-6 to the previous season's runners-up, Villeneuve, for whom back-rower Bruneteaud scored the only two tries of the match.

A comparison between the championship finals in both rugby codes, played on the same day, is revealing. For the union match at Toulouse, 30,000 spectators paid a total of 280,000 francs in receipts. At Bordeaux just over 14,000 paying spectators accounted for receipts of 92,000 francs. Although for the second year running some 4,000 people were reported locked out of the rugby league final, there was still some ground to make up on the 15-a-side game, with its well-established traditions and access to superior facilities. Overall, however, rugby union was clearly less popular than it had been a decade earlier. In that time some three hundred clubs had folded,[5] some of them having transferred to rugby league, but most having withered away for lack of interest.

Rugby league, on the other hand, continued to progress. In the summer of 1937 the first-ever tour by the Australians was announced, creating a tremendous sense of anticipation. The tour would open up international competition even further to the French, who vividly remembered the compelling demonstration of rugby league which the Australians had given in that first-ever match in Paris on the last day of 1933.

At club level, Roanne, supported by its great patron, Claudius Devernois, was in the process of building a big-name team. A year earlier Villeneuve had caused a sensation by allowing Max Rousié to join Roanne for a reported transfer fee of 25,000 francs. Then, in August 1937, Devernois' club recruited two future stars, the Dauger brothers, from the Basque rugby union club, Aviron Bayonnais. The elder of the two, Robert, was already established as a stand-off, but it was the 17-year-old Jean of whom particularly great things were expected. He would not disappoint.

Even more significant was the fact that at last a viable professional club was in the process of being established in Toulouse, which Galia had first targeted in 1934. It was no surprise that Galia himself took on the responsibility of setting up this club, to be known as Toulouse Olympique. The Ligue gave formal recognition to the applications of both Toulouse and Nantes, which would swell the professional division to twelve clubs. And since gross income from gate receipts had doubled during the previous season, there was every reason for optimism.

But in the weeks preceding the opening of the 1937-38 season, Nantes gave up its aspirations to become a professional club. Once again, the problems associated with finding a suitable stadium proved insuperable. Nor was its squad considered strong enough to hold its own at professional level. In announcing this decision, the Ligue was, however, at pains to point out that it would continue to seek applications for professional clubs in the south-west.[6]

Encouraging news came in the form of the French Football Federation's decision to abandon the pact by which other sporting bodies, at the instigation of the FFR, had agreed to place a ban on any ground where rugby league had been played. Football clubs would now be free from this constraint and the French FA would be able to stage its big games in stadiums used by rugby league. One of the barriers placed in front of the new sport by the FFR was therefore diminished, as was one of the arguments which made the directors of municipal stadiums dither.[7] The position of the FFR itself of course was not altered by the footballers' move.

Meanwhile in the east the existence of the Lyon-Villeurbanne club was in jeopardy. The chairman, Joseph Pansera, had been murdered, gunned down outside his own house by a man who made off on a bicycle. In a case of almost farcical mistaken identity, René Barnoud was questioned as a suspect before eventually being released. Some time later it was discovered that Pansera, as a result of his involvement in arms-trafficking, had fallen foul of mobsters from Marseille. According to Barnoud, Pansera had used his position with the Lyon-Villeurbanne rugby league club as a cover of respectability for his shady dealings.

In spite of the upheaval, the Villeurbanne club managed to carry on with a new committee in place, installed after the Ligue had commissioned a report on the administration of the club. With Galia's initiative in Toulouse, the number of professional clubs now rose to eleven. For some time, Galia's business interests had centred on Toulouse, which clearly offered greater commercial opportunities than Villeneuve. His Toulouse side made its championship debut three weeks late, on October 24th, in a derby match against Albi.

"The appearance of Toulouse Olympique XIII has really caused a sensation," it was reported. "And all the more so since Jean Galia has put the team together with the greatest secrecy."[8] But it would take Galia's men some time to find their feet. They lost this first game by 44-14 and again two weeks later by a virtually identical score to Côte Basque.

The creation of a new rugby league club in Toulouse was not the only activity Galia was to become involved in. Even more ambitious than his cinema interests was a new sporting venture he decided to commit himself to. In 1938 Galia spent some two months in the United States and New York in particular. The purpose of the visit was to raise two American football teams to play a series of exhibition matches in France the following year. Not satisfied with having brought rugby league to France, Galia began trying to establish a second major team sport and set up matches in major French cities as a launching-pad for the introduction of gridiron. He had some initial success - Marseille was one city which hosted an American football game in December 1939, drawing 15,000 spectators.[9] But it was bad timing. The war prevented Galia from seeing the project through.

From the *treiziste* point of view Galia's attempts at setting up American football in France poses a problem - at least in retrospect, if not at the time. Jean Galia is one of rugby league's great heroes, acclaimed as the founder of the game in France, where he succeeded, despite considerable obstacles and while still a player himself, in providing rugby league with its only base on the continent of Europe. The fact that he was now making efforts, just four years later, to repeat the exercise in a different sport does not lessen his original achievement but may perhaps diminish the man in the eyes of some.

We prefer our sporting heroes not to be burdened with complexities: our admiration is then unfettered. Galia unfortunately was not a simple character. Forceful and very determined, he was necessarily involved with others of a similar disposition. Top players must have mental as well as physical strength, and Galia was in constant contact with them all. One such player was the hooker, Maurice "Tom" Porra, who, after the pioneers' tour of England, joined Galia at Villeneuve. Porra, a Catalan like Galia, had a reputation as an iron man and, like most hookers, had his own way of seeing things. During one training session in the course of the second season at Villeneuve, Galia, the captain-coach, called Porra to order. Porra took offence and stormed off into the dressing-room. Galia followed and asked for an explanation for Porra's outburst. What exactly happened next is unclear, but it appears that Galia, the former boxing champion, threw a punch which Porra dodged, was knocked off balance and hit his head on the corner of a bench. Others then burst in to stop the fight. Who threw the first punch depends on which account of the incident is given, but the outcome is the same. Porra was suspended for two months and Galia was not seen either at the club or in the town for some days afterwards - time enough, it is said, either for his wounded pride or his black eye to heal.

The incident became part of the folklore of the early years of rugby league in Villeneuve. The details of the story may vary, but its essence is not disputed. In fact other dressing-room disputes between Galia and his players have also been told.

"I never knew why," recalled the former Lyon-Villeurbanne player, René Barnoud, "but I myself saw Jean Galia and Charles Mathon having a big argument in the changing-room at a France versus the Rest match. Mathon was telling Galia he was dishonest and they came to blows.

"To achieve what he did, he had to have a strong character. And of course he couldn't expect everyone to approve of everything he did. There was a lot of jealousy. I was there when the fight took place between him and Mathon, who was quite the opposite of Galia, and there was certainly some trouble about money after the tour which he and the pioneers made to England."[10]

Galia's conviction about whatever he undertook was revealed in many ways. He liked to get his own way, even with those on his own side. Discussing a forthcoming local derby match with two of the Villeneuve committee, Galia expressed his fears about the damage a certain opposition centre might cause and proposed putting a hard-case second-rower opposite him to sort him out, but the club officials opposed the idea. When Sunday came, the second-rower started the game in the middle of the back line, as Galia had proposed, staying there just long enough to flatten the centre - of whom no more was seen - before moving back into the pack. Villeneuve duly won the match and when the two directors came to offer their congratulations, Galia replied that, in the heat of the action, he hadn't had time to notice the positional change which had taken place. "Still, the main thing is that we won," he concluded.

As a rugby union international, Galia had stood out, when forwards were not generally appreciated for their attacking ability, as a second row capable of making breaks and possessing the handling skills to create play for others. He lost no time in making the transition to a top rugby league back-row forward. He had to. At 29 there was no time to lose and he needed to pass on what he acquired to the many other players who were making the crossover. As the English tour had shown, he soon made an impression, leading by example both in defence, where he was ubiquitous, and attack, where his speed of thought and intelligence were key assets.

Galia proved to be an astute and inventive coach capable of bringing out the best in individuals. He was also ahead of his time in the development of young players. Largely due to his initial influence the Villeneuve club became known as the Academy, successfully producing players who swept all before them at junior level, many of them going on to form the backbone of the senior team. After rugby league had been in existence for just three years the Villeneuve area could boast a significant number of junior players who had never played any other kind of rugby.[11]

"Jean Galia and his fellow-players used to meet in the cafés around the Porte de Paris," recalled René Verdier, "where we, as schoolboys of about 13 or 14, used to play on a piece of spare land. We used to put our jerseys, which we had saved up to buy, over our school clothes and play there either before or after school. The right bank of the river Lot would play against the left bank. Galia had the idea of asking us to play the curtain-raiser before Villeneuve's first-ever rugby league match against the Yorkshire team in May, 1934, and he acted as our coach.

"But one day we were late for vespers at church, where I was a server. The canon noticed our football socks under our surplices and soon realised the reason for our lateness. 'You are not fit to take communion, you boys who play this game of savages,' he said. We were worried because we had to serve at mass the next morning but we also wanted to play rugby," said Verdier, recounting what was possibly the first sanction taken against rugby league players. "Fortunately a priest who was a friend of Monsieur de Perricot, one of the club directors, interceded on our behalf and so we were able both to serve at church and play.

"We all had a sleepless night before that match because we were so excited. But the fact that Galia asked us to play that curtain-raiser match - which at the time was most unusual for a junior team - shows that he was already interested in the future and the development of young players."[12]

Among those who played that day were a number who went on to represent Villeneuve at senior level, including scrum-half Jep Lacoste, who was to become one of France's finest coaches, at both club and international level, Jean Gironde, an outstanding stand-off for Villeneuve after the war, and René Verdier himself, who as a journalist would record and analyse the performances of the club for the best part of fifty years.

A natural leader and motivator, Galia was able to persuade others because they saw the strength of his own conviction. But a single-minded determination to succeed has to be based on talent. Unlike some whose ambition runs ahead of their ability, Galia was always able to set the example.

It was while calling at the offices of a Paris travel agency to make plans for his American venture that Galia met the woman who was to become his wife. "Jean was full of imagination and creativity," she said. "He was adventurous, but not an opportunist."[13]

It's true however that Ligue officials began to distance themselves from him - he lost his role as sole selector of the international team, no doubt because others felt he wielded too much power. But equally he had single-handedly set up Toulouse Olympique XIII, even coaching the side at times, and remained involved with the club until his death in 1949.

Galia had not only reached international standard in rugby league after doing the same in union. Boxing - at which he became a national amateur champion - and rowing both claimed his attention long enough for him to make his mark. To reach the highest level in at least three sports is beyond the means of most men. It shows an extraordinary diversity of sporting talent, bound together by an overwhelming will to win. Even those who dedicate their playing lives to a single sport sometimes turn their backs on what was once their overriding passion once their career is over. If Galia was not uniquely faithful to rugby league, he was never disloyal, always remaining close to the sport which he had been among the first to play in his native country.

From 1937 on, Galia's rugby league interest became focused on Toulouse, the city where he had made his home. One of the players recruited by Galia for his Toulouse club, the future international scrum-half, Sylvain Bès, would testify to Galia's influence both on that club and the individuals who played there. Born near Quillan, Bès was a former schoolboy rugby union international who, at the age of 18, could well have played for his home town club alongside Galia in the 1929 championship final against Lézignan - and was offered big money to do so until his elder brother, who was playing for the opposition, advised him against it. As a student in Toulouse, Bès played two seasons with Stade Toulousain in the UFRA set-up, before retiring prematurely with a serious knee injury. Three years later, the problem suddenly resolved itself and Bès returned to play rugby union with Carcassonne, showing the outstanding form which attracted Galia's attention.

"I didn't know what rugby league was," Bès admitted. "But with Galia I soon found out. There was no comparison at all between his methods and what I had been used to. In rugby union training sessions we just went along to amuse ourselves, but in rugby league we had to run and run, practising accelerations for twenty or thirty minutes at a time. At the beginning I was exhausted but Galia would say, 'You'll see, this is the right way. The harder it is, the better it is.' And of course he was right. He made us tremendously fit.

"I don't know where Galia learned his training methods - perhaps in England. But they were certainly effective. He was a good man, Galia. He built that club up from nothing. Rugby union players came and asked to play. There was no need to go looking for them."

That rigorous approach, characteristic both of the game and the man, was what Bès appreciated most. "Quality comes through when the game is hard," he added, "when the opposition is hard."[14]

As Galia's Toulouse team discovered, defeat can prove a better means to future triumphs than easy victories. France's international team had cause for a similar kind of reflection after they had faced a British Empire XIII in Paris. Against a strong side which not only included the likes of Jim Sullivan and Gus Risman but also the Australians Eric Harris and Vic Hey, France contributed fully towards making this match what RFL secretary John Wilson called "the best match I have ever seen in France".

In heavy conditions and despite the fact that Noguères and Rousse played while not fully fit, France held the Empire team to two Harris tries, one from Hey and three Sullivan goals in a 0-15 defeat. Rousié was not his usual self in attack, probably because he had had to use all his energy in defence. Jean Galia, the selector, said in a radio interview that his players were still in the early part of the season (it had only begun the previous month) and hadn't yet found their form.

The greatest success was the size of the crowd. Despite the dismal weather, over 25,000 spectators packed the Stade Buffalo to capacity, paying record receipts of 313,000 francs, which easily surpassed the previous best of 190,000 francs taken at the same ground three years before. It proved an excellent appetiser for the Australian tour.

On their British tour the Australians had lost the first two Tests and won the third. They now had the whole of January before them in France, where they were scheduled to play ten matches, including two Tests. The tour began on New Year's Day with the international match in Paris, which the tourists won easily enough by 35-6, before going on to beat Roanne, the South-West (at Bordeaux), Albi and XIII Catalan during the next fortnight.

The second Test, played at Marseille before 23,000 enthusiastic spectators, was a much more closely-fought match than the first, after the French had made several changes to their side, bringing in five new caps, among whom was the 18-year old Jean Dauger at stand-off. The youngster was a revelation as France almost got the better of the Australians, finally yielding at 16-11. But Dauger left a lasting impression on his more experienced opponents. The Australian captain told the story of one occasion when he was closing in to bring Dauger down, having got himself into exactly the right position to do so, when the young Frenchman simply drifted away from him, leaving his would-be tackler wrong-footed. "Dauger did something that I thought was impossible until I saw him do it," a baffled Wally Prigg said later. "He's one player we'll certainly hear a lot more about."

The tourists cruised through virtually all their remaining matches - against Côte Basque, Villeneuve and the South-East (played at Lyon). Charles Mathon was a spectator at the Lyon-Villeurbanne match and although, following the dispute with the chairman, he had turned his back on the club he had formed, he was still capable of giving an informed opinion. In a newspaper interview he analysed the differences between the Australian method of play and the French.

"The Australians' main advantage lies in their physical superiority," he commented. "They also play very much as a team. They are very fast but also very accurate in everything they do, keeping constant control of the ball.

"Their positioning on the field allows them to direct their attacks better and also to tire less easily than our players, who exhaust themselves attacking and defending.

"As far as selection is concerned, the Australians have a much easier task, considering that, along with the English, they have been playing this game for a long time. In France it's not the same situation."[15]

But the Australians didn't have it all their own way. A Midi-Pyrénées selection, captained by Sylvain Bès, played the hitherto all-conquering Aussies at the Stade des Minimes, Toulouse.

"I had been in the side which lost the first Test," Bès recalled. "I partnered Max Rousié at half-back. The full-back, Chaud, broke his collar-bone early in the match, we were down to twelve men and never managed to compete after that. I cried for a whole week.

"But the Midi-Pyrénées side was a strong one that knew how to play, though no-one expected us to win. As captain I was asked to negotiate the match bonus with the officials, who at first offered 200 francs a man. 'And what if we win?' I said. 'We'll give you a thousand each,' they replied, laughing because it seemed so unlikely."

The Australians had been playing the day before against Côte Basque, had picked up some injuries and had also suffered as a result of the Basque hospitality. These were the points offered in mitigation for their 15-0 defeat. But Sylvain Bès would hear none of it.

"That isn't a valid excuse," he answered. "It was an extraordinary match. We beat them fair and square and scored three converted tries to none. One of them, I believe, was the best I was involved with in my career. From a scrum I went blind, taking the Australians with me, then passed inside to the loose forward, Bruneteaud who ran open-side to score."[16]

Although the French could not be so jubilant about the other results of the Australian tour, in every other respect it was a huge success which allowed another wave of enthusiasm to unfold. The crowds had been overwhelmed by the quality of the play, which they turned up in large numbers to watch. If the Paris Test had been surprisingly disappointing, producing only half the receipts taken at the game against the British Empire, the Marseille match had been watched by 23,000, more than 20,000 had turned up at Lyon and only slightly fewer at Toulouse. The tour produced a healthy profit but just as significantly encouraged more and more people to play rugby league.

The Australians had caught the imagination. Several clubs were formed - in Paris and Perpignan, to name just two - with the name Kangourous Galia Club. Even the Army recognised the sport and was now prepared to allow rugby league to be played in its regiments. As a development initiative a championship match was taken to Nice, where a club was in the process of being formed. Marseille, which had hosted the second Test, was put forward as another expansion site while at the more northerly end of the country the Le Mans rugby union club was reported to be on the verge of converting to rugby league. Even if these plans did not all come to fruition, the Ligue was making rapid strides towards fostering the growth of the game in its target area, whose three extremities were now formed by Paris in the north, Bayonne in the south-west and Nice in the south-east.

In Provence clubs such as Carpentras, Le Pontet, Nîmes, Arles, Avignon, Orange and Cavaillon were busy laying the foundations of future development, while elsewhere other clubs which would find fame much later would form, including Saint-Gaudens and Pamiers. Of these, the founding of the Cavaillon club, born from the rugby union outfit which had been in conflict with the FFR over the qualification of players, was the most important because it would immediately join the professional division at the start of the following season.

The Provence club set the pattern which others would quickly follow. Carcassonne had also been in dispute with the Federation and under the direction of its chairman, Monsieur Ramond, who had already taken to rugby league, its members voted overwhelmingly to switch codes. It was a particularly important decision for rugby league in general, for the Carcassonne club would become one of the game's top names.

The even more important rugby union club, Narbonne, champions of France in 1935-36 (its third final in five years), found itself in similar bother with the sport's governing body. The owners of its home stadium had allowed a rugby league match between XIII Catalan and Bordeaux to be played there, with the usual result that the FFR put a ban on the ground, which also denied the Narbonne XV a place to play. Encouraged by the coach and former international Ribère, the club resoundingly passed a motion to join the rugby league ranks en bloc. But the defections did not stop there. Another top club, Brive, voted to break away from rugby union and also began preparations to join the professional division of the Ligue in the 1938-39 season.[17]

In the annual international with England, played in Paris, the Frenchmen showed the strides they had made by coming within a whisker of victory. Whether or not the promise of 1500 francs per man (about £10) for that win acted as the incentive, France showed plenty of commitment in coming back from 8-17 to finally go down by 15-17.

The amateurs did even better by winning their international at Odsal. Their 15-11 victory came, according to one report, as a result of their willingness "to take risks and to apply an enterprise and initiative which was so strange to English ways that the England team just didn't know what was coming next... They wouldn't go down for the ball, they wouldn't do the orthodox ... and from the scrum they would persist always in giving their backs the opportunities to do something with the ball and therefore provide the thrills." Clearly, if the French were closing the gap on their mentors they were intent on doing it their own way.

France's fifth international outing of the season came against Wales at Llanelli in front of a crowd which some estimates put as high as 40,000 spectators. It ended in a fifth defeat as the French, unable to gain much possession from the scrum, lost by 18-2. It prompted one journalist to write: "It is decidedly very difficult for our rugby players [of both codes] to raise themselves to the standard of the British and it will no doubt take many long years before our rugby league players can aspire to equal their opponents across the Channel."[18] The following season he would be proved wrong.

The Australian tour and the late start to the season of Toulouse Olympique put the championship into disarray. The Ligue therefore took the bold decision to stop all league matches at the end of March and go immediately into the play-offs, which would involve the top eight clubs, instead of the usual four. Lyon topped the table, but had played one match more than second-placed Roanne, while only Paris, Dax and Pau at the bottom of the table failed to make the play-offs. The outcome was that Albi met the much-fancied Villeneuve, semi-final winners by 3-2 over Roanne, in the final at Bordeaux. It was a superb match, in which Albi, with no real star players except the half-back Vignal, threw everything at Villeneuve in the last period of the match to become champions from seventh place. It was a disappointing end to the season for Villeneuve, who only the week before had seen Roanne reverse their championship semi-final form to take the Cup from them by 36-12.

That Cup final took place on the same day and in the same city - Toulouse - as the final of rugby union's championship and observers made the obvious comparisons between the crowds. The rugby union final brought gate receipts of 225,000 francs, while the rugby league cup final, which to this day carries less prestige than game's championship final, was a sell-out at the smaller Stade des Minimes though the takings only amounted to 88,000 francs. The presence of the former FFR president, Octave Léry, at the rugby league final was, however, regarded as a coup for the *treizistes*.[19]

But it was certainly another satisfactory season for the Ligue in general as match receipts, added to the Australian tour profits, kept its finances in a healthy state. There were now more than 150 clubs affiliated to the Ligue, putting out some 360 teams, 30 of them schoolboy sides, for whom the first organised competition was about to be introduced. In September the development of rugby league in the French colonies of Morocco and Algeria was announced. *Rugby à treize* was on the threshold of becoming a major sport for players and spectators alike.

Chapter Eleven
A GOLDEN SEASON

After satisfying the Ligue's criteria, all four rugby union clubs which had opted to switch to rugby league joined the professional division at the start of the 1938-39 season. Narbonne, Carcassonne and Brive had been among the cream of 15-a-side outfits and their departure was as much a blow to the FFR as a coup for the Ligue. The inclusion of the fourth club, Cavaillon, with significant wealth behind it, now meant that the Provence region was also represented at the top level of rugby league. With the success during the past year of the previous newcomer, Toulouse, this fifth season of the championship looked set to be the most strongly contested yet. "It was," said Sylvain Bès, "the era of the great teams. You could never be sure of winning because the competition was so even."[1]

The total number of open-age players now playing rugby league was put at 3,000 with a further 1500 at junior level. Union players continued to turn to league. At the top level, Aviron Bayonnais lost four of their best players in the close season, including the internationals Arotça, who left for Roanne (where he met up with fellow-internationals Servole and Chaud from Toulon) and Bergèse, who signed for Carcassonne. They were later joined by the international forward Delqué, captain of the prestigious Stade Toulousain. But the biggest sensation came when Jep Desclaux, Bergèse's international centre partner and captain of both France and USAP, joined Bordeaux for a reported fee of 80,000 francs. By coincidence it represented the same amount of money Jean Galia was said to have received from the Quillan rugby union club some ten years earlier. And yet, with exceptions such as Desclaux, the financial inducements offered to professional rugby league players appeared, in the main, no greater than what they might have received from their "amateur" rugby union clubs. As Marcel Laborde stated at a meeting of the Ligue before the start of the season, whatever players received was not to be regarded as wages but a payment for working time broken by training or travelling to matches. All players must have a job, he stated, echoing the principles of the Northern Union.[2]

Laborde himself was set to take over the chairmanship of the Ligue under an amendment to the constitution. François Cadoret would remain president but the administrative duties would be undertaken by a chairman who would change each year in August. Until August 1939 the role would be filled by Dr Simon Bompunt of Albi, who would be replaced by Laborde after that date.

But all *treizistes* were saddened to hear, as they looked forward to seeing their game reach new heights, that the strategically important Paris XIII had dropped out, finally succumbing to the capital's unique indifference to club rugby league. It should be said that Parisians showed probably less enthusiasm for watching rugby union. With an abundance of other attractions on their doorstep, the people of Paris seemed only interested in big events such as internationals, which they readily supported, but they turned out only in their hundreds, rather than thousands, to watch championship matches.

Further bad news came in November when Dax, which had lost nine out of nine matches - though often by only a small margin - decided not to continue their championship campaign. Their final match at Roanne resulted in a heavy defeat as Jean Dauger ripped through the Dax defence at will. Though gate receipts had held up reasonably well, the club's financial deficit was mounting, which led to a fatal split in the boardroom. The Ligue official, Monsieur Quéheillard, stated that both the Dax and Paris clubs would soon revive, but for Dax at least it proved to be the end of the road. They sold their stand and their players joined other clubs such as Côte Basque, Pau and Bordeaux.[3]

Elsewhere there were no such signs of financial difficulty, as gate receipts continued to increase. If the takings at Roanne for Dax's last match were the lowest in the league that day at 15,000 francs, Toulouse took 50,000 for the visit of Albi, while newcomers Carcassonne and Narbonne recorded 30,000 and 25,000 francs respectively. A fortnight earlier, the lowest receipts recorded on that weekend - 14,000 francs - were taken by Côte Basque, at home to Toulouse. By comparison, the rival rugby union club, Aviron Bayonnais, took exactly half that figure. On December 18th in Perpignan, XIII Catalan had gate receipts of 25,000 francs for the visit of Toulouse. Their rugby union counterparts, USAP, hosts to Aviron Bayonnais, took 17,000 francs.[4]

Was it purely by chance that the following Tuesday there were reports of a dispute between the Perpignan rivals? It was familiar territory, almost literally. The rugby union club, USAP, was in the process of buying a ground, which was used but not owned by XIII Catalan. The rugby league club, in conciliatory mood towards the *quinzistes*, agreed to the sale but at the eleventh hour USAP, still wounded by the loss only three weeks earlier of their captain and the outstanding player of his generation, Desclaux, to the *treizistes*, decided they must also keep their existing stadium, Stade Jean Laffon, claiming that they could not break the lease. XIII Catalan would consequently be left without a ground. Fortunately the local council stepped in and agreed to take over the Laffon stadium, where the rugby league club was finally able to move in.[5]

Nevertheless such was the popularity of rugby league that its development and expansion simply could not be held back. Several hundred fans braved the rain and cold to turn up at the Gare du Nord just to see the France team, accompanied by the Ligue president, Monsieur Cadoret, leave for England, where they would play the international match at St Helens on Saturday, 25th February, a date that would be one of the landmarks of French rugby league history.

The team was captained by Rousié (Roanne) at full-back. That decision alone showed the selectors' confidence in picking Noguères (XIII Catalan) and Desclaux (Bordeaux) in the centre, with Sarris (Toulouse) and Cougnenc (Villeneuve) on the wings, while stand-off Dauger (Roanne) would partner Brinsolles (Villeneuve) at half-back. In the forwards a very good back three of Bruneteaud (Villeneuve), Brané (Toulouse) and Blain (Côte Basque) combined with a front row of Gibert (Roanne), Durand (Villeneuve) and Bruzy (XIII Catalan). The England team, which might have lacked one or two stars but was still considered a good enough side, was as follows: Belshaw (Warrington); Batten (Hunslet), Morrell (Hunslet), Croston (Castleford), Brogden (Hull); Tracey (St Helens), Adams (Castleford); Thacker (Hull), Brooks (Oldham), Higgins (Widnes), Exley (Wakefield), McDowell (Widnes), Ellerington (Hull).

England took an early lead through tries by Brogden and Morrell. France, on the other hand, despite an array of talent, seemed unable to make the breakthrough until late in the first half when Rousié decided to change places with Noguères, who took up his regular position at full back. Desclaux moved to stand-off with Dauger partnering his clubmate Rousié in the centre. With that move everything fell into place. Desclaux, making his international debut, snuffed out England's potential attacks while sparking France's creativity. The first French try came from a burst from the scrum by Brinsolles and a pass inside to second-rower Brané, who charged over to make the half-time score 6-3.

France, with more possession from the scrums, began to make telling use of the ball. Early in the second half Dauger, who only the day before had not trained because of an ankle injury, mesmerised the opposition to add a second try which levelled the scores. After winger Cougnenc had dived in at the corner to put France ahead 9-6, Bruneteaud, a model of intelligence and consistency at loose forward, created the opening for Desclaux to cross for France's fourth try. Thacker's late touchdown for England was almost an irrelevance. At 12-9 France's dominance was complete. When the referee's whistle went, the 9,000 English supporters applauded the Frenchmen wildly, recognising that by their inventiveness and verve they had put England to shame. Rousié was shouldered by his team-mates, the first man to lead a French team of either code to victory on English soil.

After only four full seasons the *treizistes* had achieved what the *quinzistes* had never managed since the beginning of international matches in 1906. "[French rugby league] won its international spurs with its victory in England," wrote one leading sports journalist. "Not all French sports federations could say the same."[6]

And this despite numerous changes in the French team, in which there were now no survivors from the first international in 1934 - not to mention the fact that Jean Galia had been replaced as sole selector by a committee. But there was such an abundance of talent in France that a second international side containing such top players as Guiral, Chaud, Bès, Cussac, Servole, Rousse, Bonamy, Griffard and Claudel - to name but a few - could also have been chosen.

The English were very impressed. John Wilson said he had never seen such a brilliant French team. Just as offers had earlier been made to persuade Max Rousié to play in England, this time Jean Dauger, with his effortless pace and class, became the focus of attention. The Basque centre, who was such an effective foil for Rousié's exuberant strength in the threequarter line at Roanne, was reported to have been offered £1,000 to join an English club, but turned it down.

After France's amateur team had beaten their English counterparts by 13-3 at Bordeaux in front of more than 14,000 spectators, the professional side took on Wales in the same city for the international championship. Naturally enough the same side which finished triumphant at St Helens - with Noguères at full-back, Desclaux at stand-off and Rousié and Dauger in the centre - lined up to face the Welsh. With all those players in outstanding form, the 30,000 spectators who had turned up in anticipation of another French victory were not disappointed. Tries from Bruzy, Cougnenc, Blain and Desclaux and two goals from Rousié saw France deservedly win by 16 points to 10, with the forwards Williams and Thomas scoring tries for Wales, to which Sullivan added two goals. France had won the triangular tournament strictly on merit.

As an example of the extent to which rugby league had taken hold of the French public's attention, Rousié and Dauger appeared on the front page of the leading sports daily, *L'Auto*, which was previewing the championship final.

The Roanne pair must count as one of the greatest centre partnerships of all time, not only because each was an outstanding player in his own right but also because they complemented each other's style of play so well.

Dauger, the younger of the two, all speed and flashing grace, with lightning reactions which exploited any defensive chink, was a prodigy whose career in rugby league was to be curtailed by events in the offing.

Not for nothing do those Frenchmen old enough to have known him describe Rousié as a phenomenon. "He was on a level above all the rest," said Sylvain Bès.[7] Even team photographs seem to endorse that view: ever alert, vital, his energy is apparent even in two-dimensional black-and-white. "Maxou was the undisputed star of the international side," wrote his former Villeneuve team-mate, Ernest Camo. "His name on the team-sheet was sufficient to guarantee a big crowd."[8] In fact, apart from the very first, Rousié played in every one of his country's pre-war internationals.

Camo pointed to the ease with which Rousié brought off whatever he attempted - surely the sign of the outstanding player - as well as his catlike agility, the speed of his movement, with his body stooped forwards, always ready to spring into action, his powerful legs, either of which he would use to kick long and accurately.

Not only could Rousié not be categorised. He was never limited to a single position in the team. Beginning his career as a half-back, where he was irresistible around the scrum base, he moved out into the centre but also played stand-off and full-back. His ability to play anywhere in the backs was an asset to his team though perhaps a personal disadvantage, since he never settled into one position. There was something of that in his personal life too.

René Verdier recalled the first time Rousié was back in town.[9] When sportsmen return to the scene of their triumphs they're welcomed by those who have been glad to witness those feats and are just as glad to recall them. As he shook hands all round in the bars and cafés of old Villeneuve that morning, Maxou of course had a few aperitifs thrust upon him. Not that he'd taken much persuading. But it wasn't the best preparation for the afternoon's game.

As half-time in the Villeneuve versus Roanne match approached, however, Rousié had scored 20 points out of his side's total. They went on to put 37 points past the home side. In the stand Verdier turned to his friend and said, "What would he have done to us if he'd been fit?" It didn't bear thinking about, but they knew that this had been yet another unquestionably great performance from a player that Verdier and many others came to regard as the greatest of all time.

In this fifth season of rugby league in France, so many fine players had come together to demonstrate their increasing aptitude for the game and to create a championship which was evenly contested and highly entertaining for a public which flocked to see it. It was both surprising and disappointing then that the pinnacle of the season, the championship final, turned out to be a comparatively dull affair. The contest between Rousié's present and former teams, Roanne and Villeneuve (who had finished first and second respectively in the league table), produced a much less open match than they had done in the final of the Cup the previous season. The poor weather was significant but also there was a growing awareness of what was at stake, which constricted the play of both teams. The only try of the match, sealing Roanne's 9-0 victory, was however a length-of-the-field effort, finished by the ever-dangerous Dauger.

The Cup final, played a week later, brought together XIII Catalan and Galia's Toulouse Olympique in quite a different kind of match. Only the rainy weather remained the same. The local team was in confident mood against a Perpignan side which was contesting its fifth final in either Cup or championship in as many years. It was also a match which put Galia and Laborde in opposition once again.

The Toulouse scrum-half Sylvain Bès recalled: "We were convinced we were going to win. But a problem arose before the match. The loose-forward, Brané, and myself were the linchpins of the side. Now Brané was a chef by profession and had to go on business to an exhibition in Liège. The rest of the players promised him their bonuses if he came back in time for the final, but to no avail. We had to play without him. We were convinced that Laborde had paid him off."[10]

Certainly Laborde's reputation outside Perpignan was quite different from within the Catalan stronghold. There they laughed it off. "He might have arranged it," they said with a wink, as if Monsieur Marcel was all-powerful, "but he would never have paid."[11] Nor of course does the story take Brané's integrity into account.

The loose-forward was much missed. In an intense, hard-fought match, Toulouse played with great fire and spirit, scoring first through a try by Bès. But the Catalans gradually took control, with full-back Noguères, who had earlier kicked a penalty goal, showing all his class to create the winning try which gave the Perpignan side victory and the Lord Derby Cup by 7-3. It was a fitting end to an outstanding season.

During the summer of 1939 the city of Toulouse once again played host to the Ligue's annual congress, where delegates would hear that the revenue from the professional game had increased from just over two million to almost three and a half million francs. A no less significant detail was reported at the annual conference organised by the amateur division of the game at Orange in Provence. The secretary, Monsieur Darmaillac of Bordeaux, gave figures which suggested that, in total, more than 200 amateur rugby league clubs were in existence - a huge achievement in the five years since the game had been introduced. A delegation from Morocco even attended the conference.

Although rugby union could still claim more than twice as many clubs as rugby league, the 15-a-side game was in a serious state of decline. At its own congress the FFR reported 471 clubs in existence - a figure which showed a considerable decrease from the peak of almost 900 clubs some fifteen years earlier. The advent of rugby league was not the only cause of union's fall in popularity - a disaffection with the widespread brutality in the game was another - but it had undoubtedly quickened its demise. More than one ex-player recalled: "By 1939, we'd killed them off! Rugby union was dead."

Rugby league had taken steps to ensure that interest in the new code should not be diminished by dirty play. Unlike the FFR, which had allowed violence to get out of hand, the Ligue and its clubs were prepared to impose suspensions or fines on any player who, by his behaviour on the field, was found guilty of bringing the game into disrepute. The committee of the Albi club, for example, reminded their team that the paying public had a right to expect sanctions to be taken against over-aggressive players. Foul play, they considered, represented "an indirect attack on the prestige of the rugby league cause".

The secretary of the Côte d'Argent disciplinary committee agreed. "We must not hesitate to exclude ... all players who infringe the rules of good conduct on the field," he urged. "Let us not forget that, if new rugby league teams are born with every day that passes, it is not only because the game itself appeals to our young people, but also because they know they can play it with peace of mind."

The 1938-39 season had seen rugby league continue to progress, with record receipts for an international match and for a final. Administrators, referees and top players had joined the one-way traffic heading in rugby league's direction. Galia's name now headed a list of former rugby union internationals that were among the best France had produced: Rousié, Dauger, Guiral, Rousse, Brané, Petit, Griffard, Claudel, Blain, Desclaux, Noguères, Brinsolles, Samatan, Servole, Cussac, Arotça and others of high quality. Counter-attacks by the FFR would ensure that not all these players would end their careers playing rugby league, but the vast majority were convinced of the superiority of the new code.

"Our game was based on creativity," said "Titi" Teychenné, full-back of Galia's Toulouse Olympique. "We knew we had obligations to fulfil and a public to win over. Our main concern was the quality of the entertainment."[12]

One of Galia's colleagues in the Villeneuve rugby union side which converted to rugby league, Jean Barrès, recalled: "I quickly found out that rugby league demanded something quite different from rugby union, including fitness, positioning, defence and tactical awareness.

"In my first match, against Albi, I thought the end would never come. Those last ten minutes were hard and with Galia there was no slackening of effort..."[13] Antonin Barbazanges added: "For rugby league you need athletes, that's the big difference. In rugby union, if you wanted a rest, you'd just tell your team-mate to kick and that would give you time to get your breath back. But in rugby league, it's all action, action, action. That's why you need athletes who are in top condition."[14]

The desire to entertain the fans paid off. Sylvain Bès, one of the stars of Toulouse Olympique, remembered: "We would play to full houses, particularly against attractive clubs like Roanne, whereas the Stade Toulousain might get about 200 turning up."[15] His comment may contain an element of exaggeration, but Bès, a former Stade Toulousain player, was speaking from personal experience of the city's two top clubs. And whereas rugby union could still attract big crowds for major events such as finals, rugby league's championship was far more attractive week by week to the sporting public of the south-west.

Not everyone was convinced. Many stuck rigidly to what they knew best, claiming that league was too simple and that union was the more subtle sport. The journalist Pierre About was one such champion of union's virtues. About maintained that those responsible for creating the essential characteristics of rugby league - abolition of line-outs, replacement of rucks and mauls by the play-the-ball, reduction in the number of players - had realised that rugby union was a game not within the grasp of all athletes and, even less, of all spectators. Rugby league, he argued, had simply got rid of union's difficult aspects. But in doing so, he claimed, with dubious logic, league had revealed its own weakness, by showing that it was not the master of union's difficulties.

That writer's contorted reasoning appeared in a little publication under the general heading of "Sporting Crusades". Although it claimed to report both sides in the "War of the Two Rugbys", as it was sub-titled, there was no disguising where its sympathies lay.[16] The most even-handed piece in this booklet came from the former rugby union international Marcel de Laborderie, who had reported impartially, and sometimes enthusiastically, on rugby league's development in France. In an article entitled "If I were ten years younger" de Laborderie reflects on the differences between the two games and gives as an example the first international match between France and Australia.

"They [the Australians] were magnificent and seemed to have come from another planet... Unfortunately intelligence played no part in the contest ...

"Rugby league is a series of flashes in which neither the mind nor the lungs can regain their breath. Speed is the law of the game. Thought is the enemy."

Unlike Barbazanges and many others who had played both games, de Laborderie, a former rugby union winger, claimed that some of those "difficult" aspects of union had more than one purpose: "Ascrum or line-out allowed us time for observation and allowed our judgement to exercise itself usefully."

If there was not much doubt about which side de Laborderie would come down on, even if he had been ten years younger, the personal preferences he was expressing are the sportsman's prerogative. Other *quinzistes* sought to deny individuals that right. In the same publication three prominent union players were asked to say why they had refused to be drawn to league. The common theme was club loyalty. They claimed that to leave their clubs would be a form of betrayal - a word which shows the depth of feeling which the great rugby divide inspired. One of the three players, Jep Desclaux, who said he would never join the *treizistes*, despite having admittedly received an offer of 30,000 francs from Galia, claimed that he would be ashamed to succumb. Later in that year of 1938 Desclaux joined Bordeaux XIII, doubtless wringing his hands with guilt.

The partisans of rugby union, whether in the press-box or the directors' box, made much of rugby league's recruiting methods, regularly referring to the pillaging of their players. From the outset in 1934 Galia and his men had been branded as self-interested outlaws. The game of rugby league itself was disdained as the child of spite and revenge. Supporters of the status quo - in effect the FFR - never failed to associate Galia and his pioneers with the suspensions which most of them had received from rugby union's governing body. Consequently there was a strong feeling among the union standard-bearers that the rugby league rebels were profiting by their crimes as well as leading others down the same path.

Stealing players from rugby union was a charge often levelled against rugby league, whose bosses, it was argued, were only concerned with making money out of sporting entertainment and were prepared to pay the price for the stars who would attract the paying public.

"The truth is that they concern themselves with the people who fill the terraces to the detriment of the players on the field," wrote Alain du Manoir, the brother of Yves, a Racing Club de France player in whose memory the Challenge du Manoir tournament was instituted. "Out of this anti-sporting, anti-educational, anti-moral attitude was professionalism born."[17]

Such arguments ignored the fact that professionals made up just a dozen out of more than two hundred rugby league clubs which had sprung up in five seasons. Regardless of the professionals' motives, the players who joined all those amateur clubs could only have done so because they simply felt they would enjoy playing rugby league, and probably more than rugby union.

But it was the professional aspect of rugby league, its *sine qua non* in the eyes of many, that caused all the furore. No matter that rugby union was professional in all but name.

"To be a sham amateur is a serious mistake," thundered one unnamed contributor to *La Guerre des deux Rugby*. "To be a professional is an even more serious mistake. One does not correct a vice by making it official."

Professionalism to some was not the honest exchange that lifted rugby's transactions out of the envelope passed silently from director to player. It was a taint, a corrupting influence, a threat to the pure ideal of sport for its own sake. Even the administrators of the Ligue recognised the problematic connotations of the term professional. It was proposed that the word should be dropped from the title of the championship, which was to be amended to the "national" division, while the lower levels of the game would also lose their "amateur" denomination, to be called "regional" divisions. It was not until 1940, however, that the change was due to be adopted - too late to help alter fixed perceptions of the game.

Not all rugby league officials had understood the relationship between the sport which they administered and professionalism. The statement which had been issued following the meeting of the Ligue in August 1938 had, however, shown a welcome realism about the meaning of professionalism in rugby league. The stipulation that players should have a job and that what they received from playing was to be seen as an allowance for time spent in training or travelling to matches was an idea that found its origin in the history of the English Northern Union.

The statement derived from an exposé given by Dr Georges Déjeant, chairman of Côte Basque XIII, at the general meeting twelve months before. Déjeant's explanation of the broken time principle, to which rugby league's history is so tightly bound, opened up a new understanding of what the game was based on.

Déjeant also presented the historical divisions in rugby as being of social origin. The Rugby Union, he put forward, conceived the game of rugby as the prerogative of the higher classes. As a consequence the working-class players of the clubs of the North of England and then those of France were ostracised by their social superiors. The privileged ranks, having no need of broken-time payments, held fast to the amateur principle, from which it followed that their matches could only ever be friendly matches.

When players from the Northern working classes were allowed payments for time lost at work and were also encouraged to play for bonuses, Déjeant explained, the spirit of competition increased, resulting in cups and championships. The game of rugby as it was played then, however, was not much of a spectacle for the paying spectator.

"It was proved ... that rugby union was incompatible with competition," said Déjeant, adding in an aside, "something which has not yet been understood in France, in spite of the breakdown of relations with the British and the breakaway by UFRA."[18]

The transformation in rules, which allowed rugby league to evolve, Déjeant continued, had a remarkable effect: "The spirit of rugby was safeguarded and amazingly could be reconciled with the spirit of competition," he asserted. It was this competitiveness which the public, enthralled by the outcome of the match as much as by the exciting play, found attractive and turned up in great numbers to watch. "Spectators hate the casualness and snobbishness which are peculiar to the amateur player," argued Déjeant, referring to rugby union's stance in favour of "friendly" matches as opposed to organised competition. "Rather than the amateur who puts his hands in his pockets, spectators prefer the players who make it a point of honour to do without pockets in their shorts."[19]

Déjeant made further telling distinctions between the codes in an attempt to define rugby league's concept of professionalism, still not fully grasped in France. He quoted an observation he had picked up from the English: "There is one difference between the amateur rugby union player and the professional rugby league player: the latter receives his money in his hand; the rugby union player finds it in his boots."[20]

Déjeant further explained that rugby league's version of professionalism was in reality only semi-professionalism. Quoting the bye-laws of the Rugby Football League, he pointed out that players should have an occupation outside the game. It was never intended that the game itself should provide a living for its players. This was the basis on which the Ligue Française de Rugby à XIII would proceed. It was, he insisted, the system best suited to the attitude of French players, the most appropriate for spectators who appreciated the competitiveness of professional sport, and the most worthy of the sport's backers, who had set the themselves the task of triumphing over the hostility that faced them.

The Ligue's officials put forward plans for further development in the 1939-40 season. In the re-named "national" division the thirteen professional clubs would comprise all those teams which had played during the previous season but would leave out Brive, Cavaillon and Pau and would welcome two big rugby union clubs, one of which was thought to be Grenoble - a club which failed to make the starting line-up in 1934. The three former "professional" division clubs would drop down into the top flight of a re-formed amateur league consisting of several divisions. The amateur clubs had expanded to such an extent that reorganisation was necessary to make the competition more evenly balanced.

In fact, Grenoble again failed to start. Two months after the plans were put forward, the Ligue reverted to the line-up of clubs which had finished the previous season. But in spite of their decision to retain the status quo, the Ligue's officials would realise before very long that rugby league in France would never be the same again.

Their counterparts at the FFR, however, were panic-stricken at the new rugby's relentless march. The only solution left open to rugby union officials as they attempted to revive their own game was to turn to the British in a bid to persuade them to lift the sanctions imposed in 1931 in order to "restore vitality to [French] rugby, which had been abandoned by the public, attacked by rugby league and which was, all in all, at the point of death."[21] For their part the British demanded that the championship, which they considered to be the cause of many of the doubtful practices in French rugby union, should be abandoned in return for the reinstatement of international fixtures. It was not a great demand, considering the lifeline that was being offered. Other malpractices would continue as before. The French had not cleansed themselves of the professionalism which had also been at the basis of the RFU's original objections. Maurice Blein accurately assessed the situation in an English newspaper article, written in March 1939.

"Frankly, there is, so far as I can see, no more reason to resume relations than there was to break them in 1931," he wrote. "At that time everybody in France knew that most players of quality were being paid and it is said that the only reason some are not well paid now is that the men who pay them have not as much money as they used to have.

"But they do continue to pay. I know; and I also know that there are many men playing Rugby Union football in France now who have played Rugby League football in France. I have the receipts - the signed evidence."

The French rugby union authorities, having seen the number of their clubs halved in little more than a decade, jumped at the opportunity which their British counterparts had laid before them. The championship was dropped and in July 1939 Franco-British fixtures were restored to the international calendar.

But with the outbreak of war on September 3rd, 1939, French sport came to an immediate halt. Two months later, however, with military operations barely affecting life in France, which continued without the kind of disruption it would know some months later, the Ligue set about drawing up a war-time competition. It consisted of two pools: Pool A took in the clubs situated in Languedoc-Roussillon and Midi-Pyrénées (XIII Catalan, Toulouse, Albi, Carcassonne, Narbonne, joined by newcomers Lézignan and Millau); Pool B was made up of clubs situated along the Atlantic coast and its hinterland (Bordeaux, Côte Basque, Pau and Villeneuve, with the addition of Agen Sportif and Tonneins). The teams drew on players who had not been mobilised and juniors. Because of the distances involved, clubs farthest away from the south-west axis - Roanne, Lyon, Cavaillon and Brive - did not participate.

A season of some five months was eventually played and in the semi-finals of the championship play-offs, Pau beat Albi 19-8, while in the other semi-final XIII Catalan knocked out Villeneuve 22-7. The final was played on April 21st 1940 before a capacity 10,000 crowd in Toulouse, who saw the Catalans beat Pau 20-16 in a tight match.

In the Cup, the Catalans lost their semi-final 14-5 to Côte Basque, who were due to meet the winners of the second semi-final, to be contested by Carcassonne and Pau on May 12th. Two days before that date German tanks began massing along France's border. The match was never played.

Chapter Twelve
BY GOVERNMENT DECREE

France's startlingly swift military defeat in May-June 1940 put the whole country into an unprecedented state of turmoil. Following in the footsteps of their government, which had decamped from Paris, millions of French people left their homes and used whatever means they could to flee the advancing German armies, in effect becoming refugees in their own country. Families were split up, just as France was split up, divided by the enemy into occupied and unoccupied zones.

When Prime Minister Reynaud resigned in mid-June, 84-year old Marshal Philippe Pétain, hero of the First World War, took over at the head of a humbled nation and sought an immediate armistice with its German occupiers. The new government set itself up at the spa town of Vichy, where, on July 10th, members of the all but defunct democratic parliament gave full political powers to Pétain.

The shock of the *débâcle* had shattered the self-esteem of a nation which had always counted itself among the world's most powerful, not to say the most civilized. It was an unthinkable disaster.

But unlike other defeated countries France retained its sovereignty and therefore at least some element of self-determination. The overwhelming support given to Pétain by parliamentary deputies reflected the approval of the bewildered French public, who, if they had any conception at all of what the future might hold in these unique circumstances, shared the idea that the Marshal would help to save France's honour and might ultimately put the nation back on its feet. Pétain's policy of collaboration with the Germans - regarded as a means of reducing the risk of further catastrophes at the hands of the occupiers - had not yet taken on a pejorative interpretation.

Not all Frenchmen, however, had been plunged into despair by their country's military humiliation. Deep political divisions had existed in France throughout the thirties, the tensions culminating with the rise to power of Léon Blum's *Front Populaire*. In 1936 this socialist movement formed a government which lasted only briefly but long enough to reform working conditions, introducing the 40-hour week and paid holidays. Blum and his party were much despised by right-wingers who held them responsible for the decadence which, they contended, led to the *débâcle* of the defeat. That collapse now provided an opportunity for a return to "traditional" values. As Deprat, a character in Jean Dutourd's satirical novel *Au Bon Beurre*, put it: "When you think about it, you can say that we've been lucky to be beaten. It's God's will. I shudder to think what it would have been like if we'd won. If the Germans are in Paris, so be it. This little lesson will do France a considerable amount of good."[1] Pétain, venerated and venerable, symbol of a more glorious past, was the embodiment of the new-old philosophy which could now be put into practice, sweeping aside the aberrations of the previous régime which had left France in such a lamentable state.

The scope of the Vichy government's powers, in geographical terms, extended to virtually the whole of France. But with the northern half - which was also the more prosperous part - under German occupation, the French government's influence there was very limited. The rigorous enforcement of the demarcation line between the two zones severely hindered communication between government departments in Vichy and administrators in the north. In addition local authorities there were subject to German control. In the unoccupied southern zone - the poorer, less populated half of the country - the government was at greater liberty to act, though pressure was regularly brought to bear so that ministries were continually looking over their shoulders for possible German censure.

Despite all the restraints, material and otherwise, of a defeated country in the midst of a world war, Pétain and his ministers set about implementing new policies stemming from a particular vision of France's future. In the area of social policy Vichy was allowed a relatively free rein.

Since moral decadence was held to have contributed to the greatest blow France had ever been dealt, a social revolution was what was called for to put the country back on the right track. Revolution, though, is hardly the word for it. Served largely by men whose values were set by a previous era, the Vichy government turned its back on the new. Instead this nostalgically-inspired régime sought to recreate some hypothetical golden age where the traditional values of duty and self-sacrifice had pride of place and where individualism and modernity were shunned.

The Marshal, as ageing political leaders tend to do, looked to his country's bright-eyed, if physically unfit youth as the eventual provider of France's better future. In order to prepare the country's young people for that responsibility a department was created to re-structure and oversee "general and sporting education". Jean Borotra, the 41-year-old former Wimbledon tennis champion and international businessman, was appointed to run this department, known as the Commissariat Général à l'Education Générale et

Sportive, a section of the Ministry of Family and Youth which was headed by Borotra's friend and fellow-Basque, Jean Ybarnégaray.

Ostensibly non-political like other bureaucrats who now began to wield the power within the administration, Borotra had all the credentials to run the CGEGS. Like many high-ranking officials in other ministries, he had a military background and had previously seen active service in the First World War. After joining up at the age of 18, and later receiving the *croix de guerre*, Borotra, like so many of his fellow-combattants, had shown an unquestionable loyalty to Pétain, the Commander-in-Chief of the French Army who had successfully dealt with the mutinies of 1917 and who had become a national hero after the miracle of France's victory over Germany at Verdun in 1916. After studying engineering at the highly competitive Ecole Polytechnique and law at the Sorbonne, Borotra became a successful executive, developing his company's petrol pump business on an international scale. But it was his sporting exploits which gave Borotra such a high profile at Vichy. "The Bounding Basque", as he was known on tennis courts all over the world, won numerous titles, including the singles at Wimbledon twice, and was a member of the French Davis Cup team which was unbeaten between 1927 and 1932. Borotra and his fellow-countrymen, Brugnon, Cochet and Lacoste, the "Four Musketeers", took French tennis to heights which it has never since matched. Known not so much for his technical skill on the court as his overwhelming will to win, Borotra was a formidable and dynamic opponent as well as a highly popular champion.

In June 1940, a month before his appointment by Pétain, Borotra, then an Army captain, had made his mind up to leave France for England, where he had many friends and connections, in order to continue the fight against the Germans, as de Gaulle had done. But the events of July 3rd, when the British Navy scuttled the French fleet at Mers-el-Kébir to prevent it from falling into German hands, caused him to alter his plans and he decided instead to remain in his native country. Shortly afterwards he was nominated by General Weygand, the Commander-in-chief of the French forces whom he also knew through tennis, and Jean Ybarnégaray for the cabinet post in charge of general education and sport. "From that moment," Borotra stated, "I lived only for that mission; and the spirit of dedication to France, which was so nobly embodied by Marshal Pétain, soon permeated the Commissariat Général à l'Education Générale et Sportive."[7]

Borotra applied himself with his customary vigour to a task that had wide-ranging responsibilities. A commonly held view in the France of 1940 was that the Germans had been able to defeat the French because they were fitter and more disciplined. It was a reaction noticeable previously in French history in the wake of other defeats and was expressed most famously by the contention that the Battle of Waterloo had been won on the playing-fields of Eton. In the specific case of France's Second World War defeat, it was widely considered that pre-war laxism - too little discipline and too much individual freedom - had enfeebled the population. Those who were now responsible for leading the country out of this trough also believed that in the schools there had been too much emphasis on intellectual education to the detriment of physical pursuits. Participation in sport - as opposed to merely watching it - was to be strongly encouraged and would become part of Vichy's crusade to prepare a nation that would be physically better-equipped to deal with whatever the future held.

Sport and other outdoor activities would make an important contribution towards creating the society which Vichy wished to nurture. The Athlete's Oath - "I promise on my honour to practise sport selflessly, with discipline and fairness in order to become better and to serve my country better" - which was to be sworn by participants at sports rallies and competitions, illustrates the serious moral tone adopted by the government, under whose control all sport increasingly fell.

Though Borotra, who escaped arrest by the Germans more than once and was to be deported in 1942, was far different from the kind of political collaborator often associated with Vichy, he had little difficulty in coming to terms with the general educational aims professed by the government. Indeed he played a large part in shaping them.

Something of the Vichy philosophy finds an echo in his own background. Although there were few pro-British voices to be heard at Vichy, particularly after the Mers-el-Kébir incident, Borotra never lost his affinity with England. His first wife was English, as was his grandmother, and his sister also married into an English family. As a schoolboy, he spent holidays in Surrey, where he learnt the language and first took up the sport which was to make him famous.

Borotra soon developed an attitude towards sport which is typically associated with the public school-educated classes of the Home Counties. The honour of participating and the glory of winning were, he claimed, sufficient motivation for him throughout his long sporting career. Such principles hardly differed from those famously expressed by Baron Pierre de Coubertin, the founder of the modern Olympics and an Anglophile himself, who played a significant role in establishing rugby union in France and in fact refereed France's first rugby championship final in 1892. But Borotra's attitude at the head of his government department was not one of amateur élitism. The perfectly laudable aim was to encourage as many people as possible to take up sport or some physical activity - and there was nothing essentially new in that, since it followed on from work begun during the pre-war administration. There was, however, a significant difference. Borotra, like other Vichy officials who were no longer constrained by the parliamentary process which had died in June-July 1940, enjoyed considerably more power to act as he saw fit than his pre-war predecessors.

Nor did the Germans, at least at this early stage of the administration, seem particularly interested in what was for them a non-controversial area. Borotra and the officers of his department had a free hand in directing the country's physical and sporting education.

Borotra's Commissariat set about promoting many types of outdoor physical activity. Among them team sports were particularly encouraged since they taught co-operation and because - and this was a major Vichy theme - the interest of the individual was secondary to the collective will. Rugby was one of those sports identified as being specially valuable, since it fostered team spirit, respect for oneself as well as opponents and the need to confront difficult situations - all of which, it was supposed, would transfer from the playing-field to everyday life.

Sport was to become a kind of moral tonic and was not to be compromised. Amateurism was essential and now indivisible from the basic principle. As for the kind of underhand professionalism which had bedevilled certain sports in France and rugby in particular, Borotra made no bones about his views. "I consider shamateurism to be the main cause of the moral weakness which has appeared in certain sectors of sport in recent years and of the discredit which certain sports have brought upon themselves."[3]

Only three days after Pétain had been voted full powers, government ministers were making pronouncements about the directions their departments would take. Ybarnégaray's department saw its mission as the retraining of French youth. But even before announcing a programme of reform, Ybarnégaray was making statements about an area which did not appear immediately relevant to his declared aims. "No more professional sport in France" ran the newspaper headline summarising the minister's first decision, announced in a communiqué from Clermont-Ferrand dated July 13th.[4] The sports to which the ban would apply were football, wrestling and rugby. Cycling and boxing were under consideration.

It was obvious what Ybarnégaray meant by "rugby". The FFR had maintained its "amateur" stance even in the face of compelling evidence to the contrary, while rugby league was presented merely as the professional version of the same game. That news report, which came just three days after Pétain's confirmation as head of state, also gave the first official announcement of the appointment, as head of the sports service within Ybarnégaray's department, of Jean Borotra, who, it goes without saying, could be expected to share the same view. In addition there would be a "secretary-general" to look after each branch of sport. The minister added that he would be joined in his mission by people who shared the same "broadminded and disinterested" attitude.[5]

One of Borotra's first decisions was to set up a committee, constituted on August 15th 1940, to study the whole question of amateurism and professionalism. The committee members were Robert Foulon, Borotra's personal representative, who would become president of the French Tennis Federation; Armand Massard, president of the French Olympic Committee and of the French Fencing Federation; Paul Méricamp, president of the French Athletics Federation; Charles Denis, secretary of the Olympic Committee; and Jules Rimet, president of the French Football Federation, president of FIFA, and the only member of the group to have experience of administering a professional sport, soccer having officially embraced the idea of paying players in 1932. The Football Federation had earlier withdrawn, in 1937, from the agreement on use of stadiums which the FFR had instigated against rugby league. As president of the CNS, though, Rimet had also previously acted to ostracise the "professional" sport of rugby league.

Borotra wrote to Rimet before the committee met to outline some of the questions to which he would like answers. He began by stating his own feelings about professionalism: quite simply, he would have liked to see it banned altogether. But in the case of football Borotra wanted to know whether there was a case for continuing to remunerate the top players, particularly since France's prestige in international competition depended on maintaining a well-trained élite. "If professionalism [in football] is to continue," Borotra wrote, offering paid footballers a possible escape route, "I think I should inform you that I could not accept that the playing of football should be the players' sole occupation. Indeed I would insist that each of the possible professionals should in the future have a job ... so as not to risk setting a bad example ... to hundreds of thousands of young players ..."[6]

Wasn't this precisely the stipulation that rugby league, from its earliest days in the North of England, had enforced among its own top players, making them in fact semi-professional? And wasn't there equally a case therefore for allowing rugby league players to continue to play as semi-professionals - these players who had already brought international prestige to France?

Committees normally set out to enquire and report back. In this instance efforts appeared to revolve around justifying conclusions which had been already reached and which were in keeping with Borotra's own sporting philosophy.

"[Sport] must be and must remain disinterested," the committee found, when it gave its findings some six weeks later. "Youth must seek in the practice of sport only a noble, absorbing means of improvement and not the opportunity for a career which is ephemeral, at times brilliant, but sooner or later disappointing."[7]

The committee's first recommendation took no-one by surprise: professional sport should disappear and only amateur sport should remain. The amateur was defined as "one who practises sport or participates in competitions out of love for sport, without receiving for his participation a monetary prize or remuneration and without deriving or seeking to derive a means of making a living from it." But so that the present élite of international athletes could in time be replaced, a period of grace of three years was to be extended to football, boxing, cycling and pelota. At least one member of the committee, then, and one other high-ranking official had seen his sport accommodated by the findings.

The committee's thesis ended on a particularly high-sounding note. "The young athlete," it contended, "should become imbued with the sense of honour, of respect for one's word, of the principles of decency which will allow him to acquire the sense of uprightness and in the sporting life that of 'fair play' which has tended to become an empty word."

This worthy if idealistic view of sport was encapsulated not only by such conclusions but also by a phrase which was adopted as emblematic by Vichy. Sport, it asserted, was "a modern form of chivalry". Sport should not simply be pleasurable and healthy, it was to be esteemed for its indissociable moral values as well.

As Borotra's government agency began to clarify its aims in taking increasing control over the nation's sporting life, professionalism rapidly became an enemy of state. The amateur ethos was the ideal; earning money from sport was a base, contemptible practice. In particular Borotra found the transfer of players between clubs repugnant, seeing the buying and selling of players as degrading. The committee's recommendations were accepted and plans were duly drawn up to phase out professional sport over the stated period of three years. Despite protests from certain federations that, by denying the country's top sportsmen the right to carry out their profession, France's place in the world sports arena would be put in jeopardy, such highly popular spectator sports as boxing, football and cycling - at least in their present, professional form - were living on borrowed time.

The administration within which Borotra worked from 1940 until his German-inspired resignation in 1942 was, like the authoritarian, if not totalitarian state which it engendered, bound by ideologies. But although seeking to bring about national renewal, Vichy's policies - and not only with regard to sport - were based on notions which, if they had ever had any currency at all, belonged to a time forever lost. The association of sport with "chivalry", for example, was a chimera which might have arisen from some medieval mist. Family values, the ennobling experience of work, the return to the land worked by peasants with their simple dignity - these things spoke of a utopian concept dreamed up by old men at odds with modern-day reality. But, in the southern unoccupied zone at least, the Vichy government had a power to implement its policies which was unalloyed by the requirements of the democratic process. Those kings who, centuries earlier, had ruled by divine right had less power, it was said, than the man who took pleasure in pointing out that fact, Vichy's prime minister, Pierre Laval.[8] The authority of ministers, and the opportunity to exploit such power, was as potentially dangerous as it was new.

The minister for Family and Youth, Jean Ybarnégaray, under whose control Borotra's own department initially came, had fought with honour in the First World War, like numerous other Vichy notables. Outside politics, in which he had been involved as a parliamentary member for almost thirty years, Ybarnégary's main interest was in the Basque sport of pelota, to the extent that he had become president of its federation. In the Basque country there were close ties between pelota and rugby, the two sports sharing the same headquarters in Bayonne, a joint weekly publication and even some of the same officials.[9] If he himself was less interested in rugby than in pelota, the minister had friends and acquaintances for whom rugby was a passion. Ybarnégaray's close friend Georges Darhan, for example, would become president of Aviron Bayonnais, a club which had lost a large number of its best players to rugby league. Ybarnégaray himself particularly admired the outstanding former Bayonne player, Jean Dauger, who had been playing rugby league with Roanne. Interestingly, the Aviron Bayonnais club was where Borotra himself, as a schoolboy, had played rugby.[10] As far as sporting ethics were concerned, Ybarnégaray was less of a strict amateur than Borotra, or at least protested less strongly in its favour, since his favourite sport of pelota was, like rugby, shot through with professionalism, overt or not. The contradiction becomes transformed into hypocrisy when officials such as Darhan, who were involved in the administration of both sports, accepted on the one hand that pelota had embraced professionalism while at the same time consistently refuting the idea that rugby could have anything to do with the exchange of money. It was a question which Ybarnégaray always tried to evade. The only justification for allowing pelota players to be paid that the minister would ever give - and only in private - was that "they were professionals because they were the best."[11]

Ybarnégaray's pronouncement on sport and rugby league in particular therefore came as a bolt from the blue when he revealed seemingly official plans to local journalists in Pau. His remarks were reported in various newspapers on August 21st and 22nd - only six weeks after the setting up of the government at Vichy and just one week after Borotra's enquiry into amateurism and professionalism had been opened.

"The fate of rugby league is clear," announced Ybarnégaray. "Its life is over and it will be quite simply deleted from French sport."[12]

The minister had nothing else to say about the game, only mentioning it in response to a question raised by the journalist Jean Plaa because in Pau the matter was obviously of great local interest. But Ybarnégaray had plenty to say about professionalism in sport - of which he implicitly held up rugby league as an example.

"Professionalism must disappear totally," he declared. "Professionalism, whether open or covert, has done much harm: I have seen it in the sport I know very well, pelota. It is professionalism which, in most of France, has turned the public away from rugby matches and which has corrupted certain teams.

"Rugby was no longer being played for the sake of playing, but to win, sometimes for reasons which had nothing to do with sport...

" No more rugby league!"[13]

These intentions were widely reproduced in the press of the Basque region and in other areas of the south-west. Along with the decision to do away with professional sport, it was reported: "Rugby league is abolished."[14]

Ybarnégaray's mouthing of unconvincing arguments which had no doubt originated elsewhere nevertheless carried ministerial weight, even if he was only to remain in that position for another two weeks. They also implied that decisions had already been taken within a very short period of time - well before Borotra's committee of enquiry had had time to present its report. But it is not so surprising that such views on professionalism should be expressed. After all, Borotra himself had said, on accepting the post of commissioner in mid-July, that his own feelings about professionalism were already fixed and that he would have liked to see it outlawed.[15]

Representations concerning the fate of rugby league were made, either to Borotra or Ybarnégaray or both, by individuals whose motives were - to use a favourite Vichy adjective again - far from selfless. Though neither of them was sufficiently partisan in rugby matters to initiate a move against rugby league themselves, both were sufficiently acquainted with the game and its practitioners to be receptive to the opinions of others who had a deeper interest in the sport's fortunes than they.

Further government announcements showed the authority which Vichy ministers had at their disposal. It was announced that only one club for each sport would be allowed in towns of less than 50,000 inhabitants in order to end the rivalry which a profusion of smaller clubs could give rise to. The officials of sports federations would no longer be elected but nominated by the minister. And in order to protect athletes of international level, some of whom would be professionals, the state would undertake to look after their material needs within an establishment set up to allow them to train and develop as sportsmen - a concept which found an echo in communist states of the post-war era.

If the Vichy government was attempting to trace a line, however crooked or tenuous, from professional sport to defeat by France's neighbours in war, it was not the only one to be drawn. There was another, sketched with tremulous hand across this disastrous page in French history. The consumption of alcohol was another evil. The cumulative effects of too much drink, it was reckoned, had been evident in the ill-matched army which had been dispatched by the Germans. And so drinks with an alcoholic content of more than 16 degrees - aperitifs were the specific target - would be banned. Consequently Pernod and Cinzano were among those destined to join rugby league in Vichy's moral dustbin.[16]

However stringent or misguided the execution of it, the fundamental desire to re-establish the nation's moral and physical health, in the aftermath of defeat, is understandable. The same arguments put forward by Vichy were to be found being pushed around certain sporting circles by pre-war Cassandras.

The leading article of the pro-union booklet, *La Guerre des deux rugby*, published in 1938, is remarkably prescient, forecasting what would happen two years later. France is the last bastion of liberal culture beyond the Channel, it declares, but those few who man the ramparts count among their number a high proportion of "alcoholics, sick men and degenerates". The only proven remedy for this desperate state of affairs, the unnamed writer claims, is sport. Except that the government refuses to prescribe it and overburdened individuals cannot alone ensure the treatment of the "patient". And in the absence of *state intervention* [17], French sport is beset by the most disabling disputes and rivalry.

"The main quarrel is the one which divides France into two opposing camps: the professionals and the amateurs," the writer goes on.

"We would not care whether top sportsmen profited from their ability if the nation ... was capable of supporting ... this form of parasitism. But it is not so. France, which does not have [the means] to educate, look after and save its young people, sees all her attention, ... all her resources given over to the profit of a few professionals.

"It is not a question, as has been claimed, of whether an open professional is more virtuous than a 'shamateur'. It is a question of whether professional sport can fulfil an educational role."[18]

The writer sweeps aside the dishonesty which had run right through rugby union and to which its officials had for so long turned a blind eye. He appears to claim that only amateur sport can or would wish to train and educate young people. Then, towards the end of the piece, the writer comes clean, referring to the administrative divisions between amateurs and professionals in boxing and football before holding up the example of rugby which "sees growing on its weakened body the monstrous cyst of professionalism."

If the pre-war government had been lobbied in vain to "cauterise these wounds", the Vichy government, wielding its new broom, showed itself particularly sympathetic to such pleas. An undated report by a certain Dr Récamier, probably produced at the same time as the findings of the committee on amateurism and professionalism, presents additional reasons for acting to put rugby's house in order, or perhaps to rebuild it altogether.

Entitled "How to create a new attitude", the report asserts: "Rugby provides a typical example: at a time when, as a result of worthy efforts, our players reached a position where they had the physical fitness and technical knowledge to be able to compete with the best English [sic] teams, this magnificent game was entirely spoilt, in spite of the efforts of the Federation's officials, by acts of brutality and dishonesty. All critics have agreed that this was caused by a lack of education ..."[19]

But the organisation which had done most to clean up dishonesty in the shape of shamateurism and foul play, which had once again set standards on a level with the British and had presented a model for young people to aspire to - the Ligue Française de Rugby à XIII - was in danger of being discredited not for what it had or had not achieved, but for daring to rival the establishment game.

In spite of clear warnings such as those contained in Ybarnégaray's statement, however, rugby league's leaders remained optimistic that they could prevent the game from becoming a target for Vichy's crusaders. Marcel Laborde, who had been elected chairman of the Ligue in succession to Dr Bompunt, commented that he was not unduly worried about the implications for rugby league if professionalism were to be abolished because the great majority of rugby league players were amateurs.[20] At the annual congress, held on September 1st in Toulouse, where the Ligue's offices had now been transferred from Bordeaux, which was in the occupied zone, Laborde reiterated his belief, despite Ybarnégaray's apparent proclamation of a death sentence a week earlier, that rugby league would continue unaffected apart from the status of a minority of players. There would be no professional division, all players would now in fact become amateurs, playing in a competition which resembled the old rugby union structure, in that teams would contest first a competition organised in *départements*, with the best going on to a provincial championship, and then the top two in each region would play for the national title. Everything was put in place - at least for those clubs in the southern unoccupied zone - to start the season on October 13th. Mindful of the emphasis the government placed on the sporting education of young people, the Ligue made a formal requirement that each club should develop a junior section, as many had already done. To give further evidence of its moral scrupulousness, the Ligue decided to abolish the system of "goal average" to decide which team should have the advantage if two or more were level on points in the table. At each match the referee would go further than simply adjudicating in matters of forward passes and knock-ons and would keep notes on the "moral behaviour" of teams so that those with the best record would be placed higher.

On September 7th government reshuffles at Vichy resulted in the Ministry for the Family, Youth and Sport being subsumed within the Ministry of

Education and Ybarnégary losing his post. But the changes were more practical than ideological. Policies had already been put in place and were merely confirmed by the publication by Borotra's department on September 18th of a document which would be the forerunner of the "Sports Charter", which was to appear in its full form in December. It contained an affirmation of the principle that all professional sport must be banned. Furthermore, each sports governing body would require government consent, without which that sport could no longer exist.

In the meantime Borotra or his representatives were in close consultation with major sporting bodies, including, naturally enough, the FFR. The French Rugby Union's new chairman, Dr Ginesty, had been required, for example, to present a report summarising the current state of French rugby in its totality. It doesn't take much imagination to suppose what one of its major themes would be. The *quinzistes* would waste no time telling Borotra that rugby league was no more than a professional version of the orthodox game, that it was played by those who had been banned from union for professionalism, that it was run by those who sought only financial profit and that its effect on "rugby" had been simply divisive. It was not Dr Ginesty who drew up the report but another medical man, Dr Paul Voivenel, the honorary president of the FFR and the same man who had, some years earlier, taken up his pen to protest against the influence of thinly disguised professionalism in rugby union which had led to what he called *rugby de muerte*.

Voivenel reproduced his report in his book *Mon beau rugby*, published two years later in 1942.[21] In introducing what he had recommended to Borotra, Voivenel refers to France's general situation immediately after the defeat by Germany. "We have been awakened from our illusions," he begins, as if to echo Jean Dutourd's fictional reactionary Deprat. "The 'parties' in Rugby have disappeared as they have done in our national life," he continues, piously. "Without bitterness or spite, in a new Faith."

Borotra had written to Voivenel on September 18th to request a plan for the reorganisation of French rugby, which he wanted to see regain "its former brilliance". In making his recommendations, Voivenel was asked to make contact with Marcel Laborde, whose own findings are sadly not made available, except by minor references. A good deal of preliminary work had also been going on in the background. Borotra advised Voivenel that his office would be sending on to him copies of reports which they had either received or drawn up.

In his reply Voivenel first outlined a brief history of rugby, emphasising how the game had begun among students and pupils, who enjoyed playing for its own sake. But as money came in to rugby, so it lost its educational value, passing through a state of shamateurism to end up cynically flaunting its professionalism. Further proof of this "moral decadence" - another well-used term from the Vichy dictionary - came when a hat-making firm bought up the best players and had the temerity to win the championship of France. Then, with some confusion of the sequence of events, Voivenel recorded that rugby union, being deprived of its international matches for reasons that the British (now regarded with some revulsion at Vichy) took delight in exaggerating, witnessed its top clubs break away to form an independent body.

Rugby league is referred to not as an independent sport but as a schism, created by the player Gallia (sic), who had been expelled from the Federation and who was a very shrewd businessman. The openness of the professionals' situation was not in doubt but, added Voivenel, "'the fervour of the disciples', as M Laborde calls it in his report, was at least equal to their material interest."

Voivenel showed himself to be completely in tune with Vichy's principles - and why should he not be? He came from the same background and moved in the same circles as those now in positions of power and influence. The idea of unity in pursuit of a common goal - however hollow-sounding - and the condemnation of the corrupting effect of money in sport were the constant themes the doctor expounded while showing a fine contempt both for the facts and Laborde's own report. The semi-professional status of certain rugby league players, alluded to by Laborde, and raised by Borotra in connection with football, was dismissed as a euphemism. No matter that these were a minority of gifted individuals who might supplement their regular wages by playing rugby league. For Voivenel they were professionals who trained all week and travelled all over France to take part in "battles" in which their earnings were at least as important as the result. This was just one example of the lack of "moral education" in sport which France's military defeat had highlighted, Voivenel remarked, forgetting that money had entered sport in France, rugby included, even before the First World War, in which France had incidentally been on the winning side. Above all, though, rugby league was not to be regarded as a sport in its own right. Its existence could not be justified by "a modification in the rules and a slight reduction in the number of players". But in a Christian society, Voivenel pompously and condescendingly added, everyone should have the right of repentance. The prodigal child should be allowed to return to the family.

What Voivenel by this report and other union conspirators by their intrigues were now doing was to give the Federation, which was on its uppers both morally and financially, a quite undeserved second chance to reform, wiping out the memory of all those events of the past twenty years which had shown that this body was incapable of fulfilling its responsibilities and quite out of touch with developments in both sport and society in general. At the same time Federation officials and sympathisers were preparing to destroy the rival who had won both the moral battle and popular support.

Voivenel presented his report on the same day that the official announcement was made that all professional sport was to be banned. Just as Borotra's committee had recommended, in football, boxing, cycling and pelota, professionalism would be phased out - but within three years, despite earlier signs that it would be immediately suppressed. But a ban on professionalism would come into effect immediately for tennis, wrestling and rugby league, or as soon as the Commissariat had advised the federations concerned. Professional tennis players - the small number who played exhibition matches - and wrestlers only had to get used to the idea of not getting paid. Rugby league players, whether professional or amateur, would suddenly find that their game had been taken away altogether.

It was only a week later that Marcel Laborde and Simon Bompunt were summoned - separately - to Borotra's office at Vichy. Laborde saw the Commissioner on October 10th. It was reported in *L'Auto* that after Borotra had received Laborde and had studied the Voivenel report, he had decided, in the interest of French sport, to "re-establish the unity of rugby". That could only take place under the aegis of the FFR, which conformed to government requirements because it was an accredited amateur organisation. Laborde was asked to facilitate the integration of rugby league within the rugby union and acquiesced.

Meanwhile, unaware of their impending fate, rugby league clubs went ahead with their first fixture of the season on Sunday, 13th October. Because clubs had been reorganised in regions, rather than in divisions, there were some uneven results, such as Toulouse Olympique's defeat of Villefranche de Lauragais by 62 points to 5. There was a shock result, too, as US Providence Toulouse beat the former professionals, Albi, 7-3.

But there was a much bigger shock in store for rugby league players and supporters as they tuned in to the national radio service later that same evening. An announcement by Commandant Pascot, assistant to the Commissioner for Sport, Jean Borotra, was broadcast in which it was stated that, as a result of consultations with the FFR chairman, Dr Ginesty, and following a report drawn up by Dr Voivenel, president of the Pyrenees Rugby Union Committee, the Ligue Française de Rugby à XIII had agreed henceforth to join the FFR.

Pascot would chair a committee, consisting of Ginesty, Voivenel and Laborde, which would expedite the amalgamation as quickly as possible. Pascot's nomination as chairman of the committee, it was noted in the Toulouse newspaper with unintentional irony, "has met with unanimous approval among sportsmen and players of the oval ball game.... His fine career as a player is both proof of his authority and a guarantee of impartiality."[22]

It had already been announced that it would still be permissible for schoolboys and students to continue to play rugby league - as a preparation for playing rugby union, or as the same report put it, "for the stricter disciplines of the classic game."

In another article Marcel Laborde was questioned about his interview with Borotra which had taken place before the official announcement.

"We will be playing rugby union from now on," answered Laborde, "starting next Sunday with Carcassonne against Perpignan. Monsieur Borotra, who has recognised our work, has appealed for the co-operation of the Ligue. I have offered it fully. The Commissioner-General for Sport does not condemn our sport, since he proposes that it should be played by schoolboys, but he wants unification in order to reform rugby and re-establish the prestige of French sport. We are being rallied, rather than repudiated. Rugby league clubs will become rugby union clubs, with moral and material guarantees which I shall announce this week. All the clubs of the Ligue will have to implement these decisions, which will be done within the week.

"It might be appropriate to recall the famous words 'Let them be thus or not at all'. I have preferred to remain reasonably similar to what we were and carry on. My standpoint will, I am sure, serve sport in general and rugby in the south in particular."[23]

For his part, Borotra expressed publicly his gratitude to Ginesty, Voivenel and Laborde for the valuable contribution they had made towards restoring the unity of French rugby. But by being bracketed with Ginesty and Voivenel, two top *quinzistes*, Marcel Laborde became implicated in the surrender of rugby league. Further evidence, in the eyes of some, came when Ginesty, president of the FFR, offered Laborde the post of vice-president within the Federation, which was accepted.

As a defender of rugby league - in fact, the only man in a position to defend the game in these particular circumstances - Laborde's stance appears at best ambiguous. No one knows exactly what went on during that meeting in Borotra's office at Vichy. It is virtually certain, however, that Laborde would have been presented with a *fait accompli* and that he had no choice but to accept the "reintegration" of rugby league. What remains in doubt is how much the Ligue's president protested.

Laborde, with his legal training, had a reputation as a tough negotiator capable of using all the means at his disposal to defend his cause. As the head of the governing body which suddenly found itself being taken over by the rival sport, Laborde's agreement to the principle of merger seemed singularly meek. Could it be because - as he had been accused of doing before - Laborde saw within the situation a means to an end, an end which suited the cause of Perpignan rugby with all its history of division and dissension? Had Laborde's own position as secretary of the Chamber of Commerce in that region been threatened? Whatever had gone through Marcel Laborde's mind, his assertion that the abolition of rugby league was a rallying cry rather than a rejection of the sport was hard to take, even in an era of notable political doublespeak.

The reaction from *treizistes* was one of outrage, combined with an intention to fight a rearguard action, futile though it might be. First, François Cadoret, the official president of the Ligue but domiciled in the occupied zone and therefore unable to keep in close contact with events in the south, resigned in protest at not having been consulted. Cadoret, who would have had some justification in normal circumstances, claimed that Laborde, as chairman of the Ligue's executive committee, was overstepping his authority in agreeing to merge with the *quinzistes*.[24]

In the Basque country - now also separated from most of the rest of French rugby league by being in the occupied zone - reactions to the decision deriving from the assertions of their fellow-countrymen, Borotra and Ybarnégaray, were particularly strong. "Laborde has killed rugby league for purely local reasons" was the headline quote attributed to Monsieur Miremont, secretary of Côte Basque XIII, in response to questioning from none other than Maurice Blein, now working for *L'Auto*.[25] A second heading suggested that the Ligue's chairman had acted only in the interest of Catalan rugby.

"Rugby league was and remains a magnificent game," Miremont declared, "which has only done good for French sport. It should have been allowed to exist alongside rugby union, which it had forced to become more amateur and less brutal.

"As far as I am concerned, I shall to continue to train our youngsters in rugby league as long as I live. That doesn't contradict M Borotra's instructions."

The Côte Basque chairman, Dr Georges Déjeant, was more diplomatic, though no less staunch in his views. Laborde had written to him saying that he had taken responsibility for a "particularly painful" decision, Déjeant told the local newspaper.[26]

"It is hard to believe," Déjeant continued, "that the chairman of the Ligue was not forced into a merger with the [rugby union] Federation.

"M Borotra thought it necessary to demand the disappearance of rugby league ... The present times gave him the authority to act without ceremony. I believe that all discussion is misplaced if the banning of rugby league is an order which one must simply obey.

"But we are disturbed by two new facts. First, in the very week following the appointment of M Laborde as vice-president of the Rugby Federation, certain members of this new Federation met without his knowledge. Next, the majority of rugby union officials in the occupied zone are on record as having stated their opposition to the Commissioner's decision and refuse to accept both rugby league players and officials.

"Would rugby league now be justified in making an appeal?"

"... M Borotra has made a decision impartially but he has been misled by his information.

"M Laborde ... did not have the necessary competence to champion the cause of rugby league. He pleaded dissidence when what was required was to justify reform." Déjeant went on to give an exposé, as he had done on previous occasions, of what "professionalism" actually meant, what it derived from historically and how rugby league had become a socially valuable sport of a quite different nature from the game from which it originally sprang.

"But now, in France, it is condemned," he concluded, "because it was thought that it was merely an anarchic form of dissidence from rugby union!" He ended by making an analogy with another sport, horse-racing. Some racehorses run on the flat, others over the jumps, he contested, without anyone suggesting that one form of race should be banned for the benefit of the other.

Two days later Déjeant replied in the same newspaper to those who thought he had been simpling advocating professionalism. He ended with an unambiguous response: "Rugby union has worn itself out within a generation.... Rugby league belongs to the generations to come and to which I belong."[27]

The secretary of the amateur section of the Ligue, Monsieur Darmaillac, isolated from what had been going on by his situation in Bordeaux, in the occupied zone, and having been informed of recent events only through the newspapers, told Maurice Blein by letter: "Everyone is glorifying the unification of rugby which has now been achieved ... But will the 'normal' rugby be able to recapture its former vogue? I fear it is only an illusion. The decline of rugby union did not begin with the birth of rugby league, but well before. It is a crisis among its officials which has led the Federation to where it is now... At the moment we in rugby league are the ones who are held responsible. We shall see later..."[28]

In the same issue of *L'Auto*, the Roanne forward and ex-union international René Arotça who had only recently become a rugby league player after leaving Aviron Bayonnais, was asked his opinion of the recent moves.

"In my heart and soul, I remain faithfully attached to Aviron Bayonnais. Even playing rugby league at Roanne I never forgot my native land and my club," he admitted.

"Now that I am practically *hors de combat* [29], I am better placed to judge the situation impartially.

"In my opinion they have acted in a way which doesn't correspond to the wishes expressed by everyone. They were wrong to sacrifice rugby league, which, let's not forget, is an excellent sport for the development of young people and, being much less brutal, suits young players infinitely better.

"The two codes of rugby could live together - and complement each other."

Another former union international who had switched codes, Roger Claudel, spoke of what he owed to rugby league: "I used to think of myself ... as being quite competent in rugby matters," he said. "But I didn't think so for long. From the first training session [I attended], even before that session, in the dressing-room, Lance Todd showed me ... that I was no better than a little boy. To start with I didn't even know how to lace my boots properly ...

"With the ball in my hands it was even worse. I had to confess, as an international back-row forward specialising in creating gaps, that I didn't even have the technique to pass the ball properly.

"I wasn't the only one. Everybody, without exception, the Galias, the Rousiés, had to learn the same way ... Nothing can replace [rugby league] for the development of skill and stamina ..."[30] Claudel naturally envisaged that, because of the superior training that rugby league players had received, the standard of play in rugby union was now set to rise as a result of the amalgamation of the two games.

But when, for example, Côte Basque XIII obeyed instructions by merging with their union counterparts, AS Bayonnaise, the ex-league players, said Monsieur Miremont, found re-adapting to the 15-a-side code "laborious".

One of Galia's original pioneers, Gaston Amila, was also among those forced to return to the union fold. He might have spoken for many as he recalled: "I took up playing rugby union again, but without any real pleasure or enthusiasm."[31]

Another of the pioneers, Laurent Lambert, was a prisoner in Germany when the abolition of rugby league was announced, although he escaped the following year. "I was very sad to hear about the ban," he said. "We really thought that rugby league had had it, that it was all over."[32]

The former Villeneuve player and friend of Galia, Jean Barrès, went further: "It was a scandalous and completely unjustified decision," he commented. "And we were supposed to be living in a democracy!"[33]

The reasoning, the appeals all failed. The Commissioner could not go back on decisions already taken, came the formal riposte. In any case a double barrier against rugby league was set up when the Sports Charter was introduced two months later. All sports clubs from now on would require official authorisation and would have to belong to a federation. The federation itself would have to be recognised by the CNS, that same body which had held out for so long against giving the Ligue official status.

Some, notably Darmaillac and Déjeant, continued to campaign for the restoration of rugby league. But if the new rugby federation could not even keep the promises it had made as a result of the "agreement" between Ginesty and Laborde, what chance was there of the return of *rugby à treize*?

Those promises of reimbursement of funds, of no discrimination against rugby league players, of the opportunity to play the game at junior level (a committee was formed, which included the rugby league international Sylvain Bès, but it never met) all fell flat. Marcel Laborde resigned from the Federation on December 2nd in protest at this signal failure to honour its collective word. Another reason for his dissatisfaction was the flouting of the rule formulated in discussions between himself, Ginesty, Voivenel and Pascot, at which it had been agreed that the former rugby league clubs, now members of the French Rugby Union Federation, would participate in the regional championships and that players previously registered with them as rugby league players would have to rejoin the same clubs.

An interesting case is that of Jean Dauger, the 19-year-old prodigy who had been signed by Roanne XIII, but who had returned to his native Bayonne at the outbreak of war and played for Côte Basque XIII in the 1939-40 wartime championship. However, it was not for AS Côte Basque XV that he was now playing rugby union, but for Aviron Bayonnais, the club where he had played as a junior and which had been so stricken to see him leave for Roanne to play rugby league.

An equally high-profile player, the former rugby union international captain, Jep Desclaux, who had been a rugby league player with Bordeaux, should have joined the nearest former rugby league club to his home, which would have seen him play with the former XIII Catalan side, now renamed XV Catalan. Instead he was allowed to turn out for the rugby union club of his birthplace, Collioure.[34]

There was no question of continuing to play rugby league illegally, in defiance of the ban. Individuals may have wanted to continue playing on an informal basis, but organising and playing even a friendly game is a very public thing and would have been certain to be brought to the attention of the authorities. "It was unthinkable to play a sport which had been banned by Pétain's government," said the Lyon-Villeurbanne player, René Barnoud.[35]

It was left again to Dr Déjeant to take up the cause of the former rugby league clubs. On behalf of AS Côte Basque he had protested to Dr Ginesty that this former rugby league club was being systematically denied the opportunity to compete in the Federation's competitions as well as seeing some of its players drain away to other clubs in spite of the agreements in force. But when Déjeant received no response he wrote directly to Borotra to make a further generalised protest about the banning of rugby league by means of the "forced and unacceptable merger".[36] Déjeant alluded in his letter to previous discussions between the two men but told Borotra he regretted that "these conversations were not sufficient to make you want to find out what rugby league was to become, as organised under your authority." He went on to note misunderstandings when they last met, with Borotra having asked questions of Déjeant which the latter regarded as irrelevant ("Have you been a top sportsman yourself?", etc).

Bravely, Déjeant, more outspoken than the erstwhile rugby union officials who had now rejoined their former game in relative silence, made his views and his own position quite clear to the Commissioner. "I told you that I had come fresh to the game, that I was an independent and not a dissident and that it was others who bore the indelible mark of the old, parochial Rugby Union Federation. You ought to have realised that I was a revolutionary, in the same way that English rugby league was a reform; that rugby union belongs to a generation that is dead and that the new generation ... should find its own rugby in the tried and tested form of the Rugby League.

"Why go backwards? Why listen to these old men who want to see the lost rugby of their rediscovered adolescence? Why follow these utopians who make the vain claim to revive a game which they themselves have killed, several times over? Why think like these blind yet obstinate men who, in 45 years of experience, have only witnessed the 15-a-side code degenerate fatally like a plant which cannot adapt to its terrain?"

If Déjeant ever received a reply, none of his wishes came close to being heard. Many others had similar complaints, which also went without response.

"As a protest against being excluded from the Challenge de l'Amitié, the former rugby league clubs, Celtic de St-Denis, Girondins ASP, Nantes and Poitiers, have asked for rugby league to be revived," it was noted in the Presse du Sud-Ouest.[37]

Now that the threat of rugby league had been safely contained, the authorities made no effort to ensure, despite their agreement, that it was played by juniors and schoolboys. It was on their own initiative that the students of La Rochelle organised two matches in December 1940, as had been permitted, beating their counterparts from Saintes by 39-3 on December 1st and Royan Students 26-0 on December 15th - the last recorded time that rugby league was played in France before the Liberation.

The official pronouncement of the suppression of rugby league was signed by Pétain and would appear a year later, on December 19th 1941.

"We, Marshal of France, Head of the French State,

"By the law of 20 December 1940 relating to the organisation of sport;

"On the proposal of the Secretary of State for National Education and Youth,

"Decree:

"Art. 1: The association known as the French Rugby League, whose headquarters are at 24, rue Drouot, Paris, is dissolved, authorisation having been refused.

"Art. 2: The property of the dissolved association, in accordance with the preceding article, is transferred in its entirety to the National Sports Committee, which assumes all responsibility for it and which will be represented in the liquidation proceedings by its secretary-general, M

Charles Denis, officer of the Legion of Honour.

"Art. 3: The Secretary of State for National Education and Youth is charged with the execution of the present decree, which will be published in the Official Journal."

"Made at Vichy, 19 December 1941.

Ph. Pétain."

Chapter Thirteen
THE GERMAN QUESTION

Sport has always been abused by politicians and often the more extreme the régime the more the role of sport has been subverted to serve its rulers. The rise of fascism in the 1930s saw sportsmen accompanied into the arena by acutely nationalistic fervour. Mussolini's staging of football's World Cup in 1934, from which the host country emerged gratifyingly triumphant, was bettered only by Hitler's narcissistic Berlin Olympics two years later. Borotra's sportsmen and women likewise gave the straight-arm salute as they swore the Athlete's Oath.

Despite their professed differences, the Vichy régime's attitude towards sport had a good deal else in common with that of Nazi Germany. When, in 1940, the French bemoaned the lack of physical fitness of their young men and women, they were echoing the cry of the Germans, who, following their defeat in 1918, had blamed inappropriate education - in its widest sense - for the nation's military collapse. Hitler had identified a preoccupation with intellectual exercise to the detriment of physical education as a cause of the nation's defeat in the First World War. "Physical training ... is not an affair of the individual," he declared, "... it is a requirement for the self-preservation of the nationality, represented and protected by the state."[1] Instead of over-burdening the young with mental training, the future Führer proposed, schools must place more emphasis in their curriculum on physical exercise. Hitler's own preference was that German boys should learn boxing, because, he believed, it was a sport which promoted the "spirit of attack" as well as teaching young bodies to suffer blows. But sport in general was to be encouraged because it made the individual strong and bold and taught him to bear hardships.

The harnessing of sport to nationalistic ends continued in Germany through the 1930s. On the occasion of the rugby union match between Germany and France in Hanover in 1934 - almost the only international fixture still open to the ostracised French - a German administrator declared:

"A great nation like ours must direct its youth towards a sport which will give it self-discipline, courage and team spirit. Of all games, rugby is the one which encourages in the highest degree the finest qualities of the young citizen."[2] In a similar way to Vichy, the Germans - though with little success in rugby's case - sought to use sport as a means of directing the country's youth along a defined path and, as many a state has done since, as a vehicle for nationalism. Still, national differences were highlighted by the reaction of the French team to the ceremony that the Germans had staged before their 13-9 defeat. "Some of the French players admitted," continued the same report, "that the atmosphere was a little trying, with the flags, the singing and a Nazi procession before the match."[3]

The relationship between the French and German Rugby Unions took on special significance in that year. With the French having been denied their traditional fixtures against the four Home Unions since 1931, Germany was the only international partner left with whom matches had been played annually. Not that that counted a great deal. Although France and Germany had played against each other since 1927, the Germans had won just once - by a single point in Frankfurt - and these matches carried none of the prestige or public interest associated with the Five Nations calendar. In fact Jean Galia, before being banned by the FFR, is said to have been so unenthusiastic about playing against Germany that he refused selection on at least one occasion. Nor did the FFR regard Germany, or any other European nation, as a credible substitute for the British. But the events - more specifically the event - of the latter part of 1933 cast Germany and other potential European partners in a new light.

The first rugby league match ever to be staged in France had posed a major threat to rugby union's attempts to win back its public, who had become disaffected with the game, particularly since the breaking-off of international relations by the RFU. The England-Australia rugby league match of December 31st, 1933 had not only entranced those who had gone to see it but had created massive interest generally. It must have seemed to the FFR that any international moves on its part would go some way to stemming the rugby league tide. Is it purely coincidental then that France should play Germany in Paris the day after that first exhibition of rugby league and that an alternative international governing body, the Fédération Internationale de Rugby Amateur, should call its first meeting the day after that?

France became the most important member of the new organisation (the others, apart from Germany, being Belgium, Holland, Italy, Portugal, Romania, Spain and Catalonia). Its creation has been widely held to have been a French initiative, apparently confirmed by the federation's French name. It has been plausibly suggested, however, that FIRA, which is still in existence today, was a German innovation.[4] Though the origins of this organisation are of peripheral interest here, the moves which led to its establishment show the privileged relationship between rugby union's masters and a certain type of political régime. Of the founder members of FIRA, not only Germany and Italy were in thrall to fascism but similar political tendencies were or would be evident in most of the other countries too.

There remains the question of why Germany, a relatively minor rugby-playing country, should want to push itself to the forefront of international competition. Regardless of what has happened on the field of play, rugby union has always proved excellent ground for fostering relations between people with influence and sometimes similarly regressive views. Just as in the Vichy era, the heads of sports federations in Nazi Germany were designated by the government and not by election, as sport became a tool of Nazi propaganda. Links formed through rugby would be exploited by Germany, in an atmosphere of growing political unease in Europe, as part of a wider scheme to create stronger ties with France, while at the same time serving Hitler's aim of driving a wedge between France and Great Britain, these two countries being probable opponents of the Nazis' expansionist policy.[5]

When in 1939 the political situation in Europe became critical, another unexpected development took place. Out of the blue the British Unions re-opened negotiations with the French, which was surprising given that no purging of French rugby union had taken place to appease the RFU. On March 17th, in an unusual initiative, the secretary of the Board wrote offering to re-start international fixtures if the French would drop their championship. The matter was put before the annual congress on June 24th, was accepted by a voting ratio of two to one and a fortnight later the British replied announcing the resumption of international relations. Was a Franco-British rapprochement in political terms reflected in this thaw on the rugby field?

"Contrary to what would be claimed," one rugby historian has written, "it was not the Franco-British alliance in the forthcoming world conflict which would dictate the resumption but in fact the French clubs' sacrifice."[6] But how to account for the apparently unprompted proposal of the Board?

Written while war loomed, the letter was despatched on the first day of the Board's annual assembly and thus earned the distinction of being the only correspondence ever expedited by that body while the meeting was still in progress.[7] That reason alone suggests that political pressure, direct or otherwise, was brought to bear in order to sweeten relations between Britain and France. What all of this shows is the likelihood of diplomatic manoeuvring to achieve the agreement, only made possible by the exalted position enjoyed by the fifteen-a-side game.

By contrast the level of support which rugby league could count on was always offset by the significantly greater proportion of opposition ranged against it. There remains only the question of whether rugby league's enemies included the might of the German occupying forces.

In matters of domestic policy such as sport the Vichy government was allowed a more or less free hand, particularly so during the early stages of the Occupation. Ybarnégaray's declaration that there would be no more professional sport, with its clear implications for the future of rugby league, was made within days of the establishment of the régime, allowing little possibility of German intervention. Since also that statement of intent came out of internal rivalry mingled with a long-held concept of the nature of sport itself, there appears to have been no part in the matter for the Germans to play. During the three months which passed between Ybarnégaray's announcement and the official declaration there would, however, have been ample time for modification of those plans. Indeed, a period of grace - indefinite, as it turned out - was eventually extended to professionalism in some sports. As for the declared intention to ban rugby league, a guiding hand was needed to ensure that what had been plotted was in fact done. There was no lack of willing accomplices. But were there Germans among them?

It would have fitted with German policy to see rugby league banned. Although it appears at first sight that the Germans would not have been happy to see French rugby union benefit from the integration of *treizistes*, because that would strengthen the French national side who were opponents of the Germans, the attitude of the Reich towards France was to divide the nation internally while isolating the French from their allies. For this policy to be successful all avenues would be explored and all means would be used, including the traditional areas of sporting contact between France and Britain. France enjoyed good relations with Britain in rugby league and, since the resumption of relations in 1939, was back on speaking terms in rugby union. But the so-called reunification of French rugby, by which "professional" rugby league players would join forces with "amateur" union players, would once again force France out of the international establishment because the Board's rules on amateurism would be broken, and no doubt stir up the ill feeling which had existed between Britain and France throughout most of the decade. Furthermore there appears to have been the opportunity for the Germans to play this particular card, with the presence of at least one prominent Nazi sympathiser and ex-rugby union player at Vichy, namely Fernand de Brinon, the régime's ambassador to the occupying authorities who would be condemned to death in 1947. De Brinon, who was put on trial for treason and specifically his efforts in setting France against her allies, could not have failed to know about the machinations going on in rugby circles at the time and indeed to be involved in discussions leading to the suppression of rugby league.[8]

Documentary evidence has, however, not been found, although it is not in the nature of régimes to leave handy trails leading back to their ignominious deeds. The cupboards of the state archives are apparently bare. German involvement in rugby league's demise cannot be thought impossible, but if the occupying forces had been concerned enough to help get rid of the game, a later apparent *volte-face* would be hard to explain.

Maurice Blein, who had been present at the birth of rugby league in France, was now working at *L'Auto* in Paris, where he was in contact with the German authorities. Blein had received a letter from Monsieur Darmaillac, the untiring secretary of the amateur section of the Ligue, who had apparently read that the Germans were interested in rugby league. Blein's reply, in a letter dated 15th September 1941, is both illuminating and tantalisingly insubstantial.

"You might have read," Blein wrote, "that rugby league was a subject of interest in circles responsible for German sport, but any further information would be, to the say the least, premature.

"In fact I am very frequently in contact here with Lieutenant Keser, who is the official representative in Paris of Monsieur von Tschammer und Osten, who confirms that no decision has yet been taken in Germany concerning the organisation of the sport, and even less concerning the possibility of a match between France and Germany.

"This is the very latest information which I am passing on to you since it was provided this morning by Lieutenant Keser."[9]

Nothing materialised to support Darmaillac's hopes for the revival of rugby league in mainland Europe in - of all places - Germany, but the fact that a glimmer of interest had been shown by a person as influential as the Minister for Sport, von Tschammer und Osten, makes it unlikely that Germans could have played a part in the game's abolition in France only to consider reviving it later. In the absence of further relevant documentation, therefore, we can only conclude that Vichy, as in other matters concerning basic human rights, had no need to take lessons from the Nazis. In purely ideological terms, however, the ban was an act typical of the negativism of both Vichy and the Nazis, whose thinking defined itself as much by what it was against as what it was in favour of. The destruction of rugby league was the perfect example of how a right-wing political régime of the time might express its "reactionary, vengeful and essentially petty nature".[10]

Chapter Fourteen
COLLABORATION AND CONSPIRACY

It was in Paris on one cold, grey afternoon in late October, that I met Jean Borotra. I had already received a reply from his personal assistant which answered the vital question.

"[Monsieur Borotra] remembers that the banning of rugby league was decided, in 1941, by the Director of Sports, who was himself a rugby union player, and who was convinced that the disappearance of rugby league would favour the development of rugby." Borotra later confirmed that the Director of Sports was Colonel Pascot.

His assistant had told me on the phone that she hoped I would be able to meet this *"immense personnalité"*, even if only for a short while. He was much in demand, even at the age of ninety-five.

Borotra's apartment on the Avenue Foch is one of the smartest addresses in Paris. This vast boulevard, a football pitch length from one side to the other, radiates from the Arc de Triomphe and is lined with banks and embassies. The Germans also established their headquarters here during the Occupation.

Through this same entrance lobby - all marble, mirrors and red carpet - leading to Borotra's top-floor apartment the hundreds of guests, including ambassadors, international businessmen, members of the All-England Tennis Club and others with high connections, used to come to take up the ex-champion's invitation to cocktails on the evening of the last day of the French Championships at Roland Garros.

Shown in by the housekeeper, welcomed by the personal assistant, I took a seat in a pannelled drawing-room off the vast hall and waited for the former Commissioner for General Education and Sports.

"So sorry to keep you waiting," he said, extending a hand, pointing out the Davis Cup on the coffee table, before leading me off into his study, where we sat at either side of his desk.

"He looks forward to speaking English," said his assistant, placing my letter before him. "We don't often get the opportunity nowadays." We began in English, he telling me about how rugby had begun in England. I soon gained a similar impression to the one Dr Déjeant had remarked on fifty years before. Monsieur Borotra was welcoming and charming and skilled in making the kind of conversation he thought appropriate (he had spoken casually to Déjeant about the practice of medicine in Biarritz, for example, which was not what the doctor wanted to discuss), but eager to move on when he felt the conversation was steering into areas where he didn't wish to proceed.

Borotra was also evidently hard of hearing and even in French the conversation was desultory as he, keeping the subject merely at a polite level, insisted on asking me the questions. I explained the circumstances of the banning of rugby league and then asked what the official motives had been.

"Was I responsible for that?" he asked.

You said Pascot was responsible.

"Was it before I was deported?"

It was.

"But Pascot couldn't have done that without my authority."

Put together with what Borotra had earlier stated by letter, despite the reference to 1941 instead of 1940, this was about as close as it was possible to get to confirmation of the *treiziste* legend that Borotra had signed rugby league's death warrant, but Pascot had supplied the incriminating evidence.

And were there other *rugbymen* at Vichy too?

"Oh yes."

We talked also about the role of yet other rugby players, in the Resistance.

"I also took risks," he noted.

He did. Borotra was forced out of his position at the Commissariat in the spring of 1942, after eighteen months of worsening relations with the Germans, who found his less than compliant attitude unacceptable, even going so far as to suspect that the real aim of his department - physical regeneration of the population through sport - was not a civil, but a military one.

His attempt, later the same year, to make for North Africa was foiled when he was intercepted by the Gestapo. After the ordeal of interrogation he was taken to the notorious Fresnes prison before being transferred to Sachsenhausen concentration camp. Had it not been for the intervention of the King of Sweden, a former tennis partner, Borotra might never have seen the outside of Sachsenhausen again. He was kept in special confinement in Austria and remained there for the rest of the war in the company of other notables among whom were former heads of state and generals. He tried more than once to escape, and finally succeeded, helping the Allied liberation of the castle where he and the others had been held.

Borotra's survival owed something to his own courage, his connections and his former position at the head of the Commissariat at Vichy, the post which, on his resignation, was to be taken over by Colonel Pascot.

"Now, have you any further questions for me?" he concluded. "I have a board meeting to attend."

After the interview, taking my arm for support, he showed me out on to the landing outside the apartment and called up the lift. It was unfortunate his memory hadn't been able to call up those essential details as easily.

The scale of Borotra's brief as Commissioner necessarily involved delegation to those with specialist responsibilities or interests - to Colonel Pascot, for example. Vichy was a time of opportunism - where the ambitious could succeed beyond their limitations and, in the absence of a proper democratic framework, could act with impunity. Similarly those with friends in high places could exert a disproportionate influence. It was a time for knowing the right people. Such networks are part of the rugby union set-up. The old school tie system is not only an English phenomenon.

Borotra's testimony was the clearest proof I had yet had that Colonel Joseph (Jep) Pascot had been the focus of rugby union pressure to get rid of rugby league. More than that, in fact. Borotra was suggesting that the Director of Sports had shown a good deal of personal initiative in the matter.

Few direct accusations have been made in print but the finger has always pointed at Pascot as the individual culprit. Henri Garcia asked "Who played the role of Lady Macbeth?"[1] Those who had been around long enough had the answer.

"Everyone knows," said Noël Altèze, a former union player himself, "that Pascot and his services were responsible for the abolition of rugby league."[2]

"We knew through friends who were army people and players themselves that it was Pascot who banned the game," Antonin Barbazanges confirmed.[3]

That is what rugby league people who experienced this shameful period at first hand have always believed. Pascot has long been the demon at whom their wrath has been directed.

Joseph Pascot joined Borotra's government department in September 1940, the month after Ybarnégaray's declaration that professional sport was finished.[4] A career soldier, he was also a former rugby union international who had represented France six times between 1923 and 1927. Born in 1897 at Port Vendres, a fishing village between Perpignan and the Spanish border, Pascot played his first rugby there before moving to Roussillon's capital, playing first for the Green Devils and then US Perpignanaise. Although he later played for Narbonne and Auch, it was with USP, between 1920 and 1926, that his career was at its height, when he played in the championship finals of 1921, 1925 and 1926, ending up on the winning side in the first two. He was reckoned to be a good stand-off who benefited from playing alongside a scrum-half with an excellent pass, Jean Carbonne, but was not of the same class as his Perpignan team-mates Roger Ramis or Marcel Baillette. It has been suggested that his international selection was possibly prompted by his coach, Gilbert Brutus, who was a selector of the France XV.

The 1925-26 season was a key year for USP. Pascot returned from his army posting in Morocco to be selected, ahead of Amédée Cutzach, a future international who had played stand-off most of the season, for the championship final against Stade Toulousain. Cutzach had good reason to be dismayed. He had played brilliantly, only to lose his place to Pascot, who, it was said, had been brought back into the side so that he could then reclaim his international place. The 11-0 defeat in the championship final brought about the crisis within the club which resulted in the departure of Gilbert Brutus and half the team, including Cutzach, to Quillan. Pascot, who had the financial security of an army officer, was not one of them. The departure of Brutus also had the effect of ending the rivalry - at least within the club - with Marcel Laborde.

When Laborde, as the Ligue's chairman, was forced to accept the ban on rugby league in 1940, he and Pascot, as former members of USP, had known each other for a long time. It is a remarkable coincidence that a former player and a former official of the very same Perpignan club should come together at a meeting which seals rugby league's fate and that they should then form half of the committee which sets about uniting the two codes. Compelling evidence then for Laborde's apparent unwillingness to fight, were it not for the fact that in Perpignan it would be entirely wrong to equate membership of the same club with like-mindedness.

Hardly anything of Pascot's involvement leading up to the announcement of the ban was reported. But one reference to Pascot's work behind the scenes came from Dr Ginesty, the FFR president who had, with Pascot, met in Toulouse in October 1940 to decide how best to dismember the Ligue Française de Rugby à XIII. After a match involving Pascot's old club at Perpignan, Ginesty went so far as to say, choosing his words carefully, "Rugby has had the good fortune to see Commandant Pascot [as he then was] take charge as Director of Sports where he has played a role which his modesty prevents him from expanding upon ..."[5]

Later events were more revealing. When Pascot took over from Borotra as head of the Commissariat in April 1942, he began to show himself in a clearer light.

It came as something of a surprise when Pascot declared that professionalism, which Borotra had wanted to see disappear, would be allowed to continue in certain sports. "Professionalism in sport must no longer be considered as some shameful disease," Pascot affirmed.[6] The statement confounded those who believed that the former rugby union player was totally opposed to professional sport, for that was the basis, repeatedly emphasised, on which rugby league had been banned. His contradiction of his department's previous view not only revealed how much influence an individual could wield at Vichy but also underlined the charge that professionalism had been a handy excuse to get rid of the troublesome rival.

Professionalism, then, survived under Pascot despite the time-limit fixed by Borotra. It sometimes took on a curious form, imposed by the autocratic methods of the Colonel. In football, for example, the 1943-44 season saw the formation of regional teams composed of professional players taken from the top clubs.[7] The experiment was a disaster and benefited no one.

Sports associations, and consequently their member clubs, were subject to the Pascot's summary interruptions and injunctions. They were not well received. Motions of no confidence were widely expressed.

"There is great discontent in certain sporting circles ... concerning the administrative methods of Colonel Pascot," it was noted in government files. "He has not lacked volunteers but they have been discouraged by a lofty indifference and promises which have not been kept."[8]

Pascot's administration differed from Borotra's in more than one way. Borotra, for example, kept the Germans at arm's length as much as possible. Eventually they lost patience with him, forced his resignation and then deported him. Pascot, however, seems to have admired the occupiers. At least that was the impression given when he congratulated and applauded them at public events.[9] As a result, both by such actions as these and by his position at the head of a Vichy department, Pascot was to become a target of the clandestine *Sport-Libre* movement, in which the two former Lyon-Villeurbanne players, Charles Mathon and René Barnoud, had become involved. One of the tasks which this resistance movement set itself was to hinder Pascot in his official functions, succeeding on at least one occasion in preventing him from giving a public address.[10]

In contrast to Pascot's compliance towards the occupying forces, Mathon and Barnoud played important roles in resisting the enemy after the Germans had taken control of the southern, so-called "free" zone in November 1942. Two months earlier an increasingly collaborationist Vichy government had taken the first steps towards conscription of French labour for factories in Germany, where French workers were sent to help the occupiers' war effort. Originally begun as a means of securing the release of French prisoners-of-war, the scheme soon evolved to entail the compulsory deportation to Germany of young Frenchmen at ever-growing rates. This programme, known as the Service du Travail Obligatoire, instigated in February 1943, caused many young French people to rethink their position towards their country's predicament.

Through their sporting contacts, Mathon and Barnoud aimed to subvert the forces of occupation and repression, a factor recognised in their movement's name, *Sport-Libre*. "It was Mathon who first had the idea," said

Barnoud. "The intention was to have in every sports club an official who was able to give young people the chance to join the *maquis* and avoid being sent to Germany on the STO."[11] The two ex-players provided sports clubs with information which would allow young sportsmen who faced deportation to escape that fate by directing them via Grenoble, Barnoud's home town, to the *maquis* of the Vercors region.

Sport-Libre consisted of numerous cells, each of which comprised three men. Each man had the duty of creating another cell by recruiting two others known only to him. The two others then each had to create another cell by introducing two more members to form another cell of three, and so on. Because of the essential element of secrecy it is not known how widespread the network became, but Barnoud managed - ironically - to found one cell by recruiting fellow-sportsmen who, like himself, had been enlisted as physical education instructors by Vichy's Commissariat des Sports.

François Récaborde, one of Galia's pioneers and prime mover of the Pau XIII club, was another former player who joined the resistance movement. Deported to Buchenwald concentration camp in 1943 for his activities, he had been involved in the resistance organisation *Combat* and had organised the protection and safe passage of British and American pilots before his capture by the Gestapo and subsequent torture. He was eventually liberated from Buchenwald and received several decorations, both British and French, including the *légion d'honneur* and *croix de guerre*.

Max Rousié had already been awarded the *croix de guerre* with bronze star for his courageous actions in halting a German advance in 1940. Roger Claudel, the international forward, was killed by the Germans in action in the Vosges in 1944.

As for Jean Galia, at the outbreak of war he owned most of the cinemas in Toulouse and others in towns such as St-Gaudens and Castres. After the Germans occupied the free zone in November 1942, Galia came under pressure from the Gestapo to show the anti-Jewish propaganda film *"Juif Süss"* in his cinemas. He refused, preferring to close down his most centrally-situated cinema, the Plaza on Place Wilson, rather than bow to the Germans' demands. The Gestapo believed that Galia's refusal stemmed from the fact that his wife was Jewish (in fact Madame Galia is of half-Jewish, half-Catholic descent and therefore not within the ethnic parameters laid down by the Nazis). Galia resisted their threats and furthermore assisted a number of those Jews whom he knew through the cinematographic industry to escape, via the area in which he had been brought up, into Spain.[12]

The involvement of these and other ex-players suggests a possible link between the sportsman and the resistant. Borotra perceived sport as a pathway towards the nation's physical renewal, even perhaps as preparation for military counter-attack against the Germans, who quickly became suspicious of his motives. Borotra's notion of the transferability of behaviour on the pitch to life's less even surface was an attractive, if unoriginal idea. Much later he expressed the view that sportsmen would be more naturally inclined towards resistance than others.

"Sportsmen are perhaps more impassioned," this most self-motivated of tennis champions said. "As far as rugby is concerned, it is a combative sport and those who are attracted to it may be more willing to engage in physical combat in war."[13]

Teams and clubs also engender a familiarity and trust between similarly-minded members. A person involved in the subversive and potentially very dangerous activity of resisting a merciless enemy needs to be able to have confidence in his colleagues. As Borotra recognised, "You would not betray your team-mates."[14] The step from the rugby team to the resistance group could therefore be but a short one, as the partnership between Mathon and Barnoud showed.

Barnoud himself, however, would not be persuaded of the link, nor by the easy categorisation of resistance workers. "They came from all sections of society," he said. He went on to explain: "In the unoccupied zone we were relatively free. This freedom was expressed in terms of leanings towards Vichy or towards de Gaulle. But who knew anything of de Gaulle at the beginning? Nobody. But it was through resistance movements and their clandestine newspapers that he became known. When the appearance of these newspapers coincided with the presence of the Germans in the unoccupied zone, with the persecution of Jews and of the resistance, the compulsory service in Germany, then inevitably people took an increasingly anti-German position. But it's a long way from that to say that sportsmen were more inclined towards resistance than they were towards Vichy. There were some great resistants among sportsmen, just as there were Pétainists among sportsmen."[15]

As if to prove Barnoud's point, it was evident that Colonel Pascot's concept of duty and service to others was quite different. An authoritarian who demanded close observance of the procedures he had laid down, he was a representative of a régime that had adopted moral rigour as a major element of its reforms. One of the main pillars of Vichy's bastion of righteousness was the family unit and the values it was meant to encapsulate. Pascot's personal - and not so private - behaviour sometimes ran counter to the ideals which his government held to and the values which it tried to promulgate.

The father of at least one illegitimate child, Pascot had various mistresses, one of whom was also his assistant and with whom he became involved in an embarrassing scene which was reported back to Vichy.

The report alleged that Pascot and his mistress, arriving at Perpignan station by the express from Paris, were seen by Pascot's wife, who was waiting for him with his driver. Madame Pascot, distraught at seeing her husband again in the company of the woman with whom he had promised to break off his relationship, had to be restrained as she threatened to kill his mistress and then kill herself. She then made her way to her hotel, where shortly afterwards the driver found her leaving her room with a gun in her bag.

"These facts and a certain number of others," the report concluded, "have been known not only to the staff of the Commission but were the talk of Vichy."[16]

As the Allies started to gain the advantage during the course of the war, attitudes towards Vichy and the Germans not only started to shift, but those which had often had to remain silent were now able to be given voice. On May 7th 1944, Racing Catalan (formerly XIII Catalan), played a match at Vichy in the presence of Marshal Pétain. Noël Altèze and Paul Déjean both played in that game and, like the rest of the players, shook hands with the Head of State, though some showed a marked reluctance to do so. Colonel Pascot was expected to be there. In the event someone else turned up in his place. Marcel Laborde, accompanying the Catalan team, alluded in ironic terms to Pascot's absence in his speech at the reception. It was believed that Pascot had deliberately stayed away, afraid of coming face to face with Laborde again.

"Monsieur Marcel Laborde, in the name of Racing Catalan and in front of a host of directors and officials, took it upon himself, with some well-chosen but unequivocal words, to remind those assembled of certain truths," commented Altèze.[17]

The most convincing testimony to Pascot's role in the suppression of rugby league and Laborde's exoneration came soon after the Liberation, for it was only then that significant details began to emerge. On September 22nd 1944 a conference took place at the Municipal Theatre, Albi, in order to assess what had happened to rugby league during the war period and what the next steps would be. The question of the role of Marcel Laborde in the dissolution of rugby league in 1940 was discussed. Whether or not Laborde's famous oratory skill played a part in convincing the audience is now impossible to say, but the outcome of the conference was unanimously in his favour.

The secretary of the Albi club, Maurice Metgé, later reported: "It was obvious that Mr Laborde had never betrayed the cause of rugby league for the sake of a vice-presidency of the French Rugby Federation. His exposé was remarkable. I would even go as far as to say that I have never known Laborde as brilliant, to the extent that, when he had finished, no one had any questions to ask of him and rounds of applause broke out from all parts of the theatre."[18]

There was immediate approval of the motion that Laborde be absolved from responsibility for the fateful events of 1940 and an expression of future confidence in him was passed. In the absence of formal documents, the evidence provided by Metgé, a journalist by profession, is the most important testimony to what actually took place in Vichy. As secretary of the club whose chairman was Dr Simon Bompunt, who had been called to Borotra's office at the same time as Laborde, Metgé's account remains the definitive one. Although Metgé himself had been in captivity in Germany at the time of the ban, he claimed to have made a serious investigation of the whole matter on his return.

"The movement against rugby league started in the Basque country," he stated. "Rugby union was behind it, with Ybarnégaray speaking on their behalf to Borotra. The one who carried it out, unquestionably, was the representative from the other end of the Pyrenees, then head of Borotra's cabinet, namely Pascot. Certainly, it was Borotra who signed, but Pascot held his hand ...

"Through his friends and his pen, Mr Laborde did not cease to resist the hidden manoeuvrings of the opposition camp. Borotra wrote to him saying that he would do nothing without having seen him. He was summoned to Vichy after addressing a memo to the Minister. Dr Bompunt joined him by plane to defend rugby league.

"Both had been drawn into a trap. They had been called to be told: 'You must disband or I will force you to disband with the consequence of greater sanctions against the Executive Committee of the League.'

"They [the Vichy officials] knew all the tricks. Mr Borotra received Mr Laborde alone and then, some time later, Dr Bompunt alone. He did not speak at all to Dr Bompunt about rugby league, but only about his views on multisports clubs. Bompunt was unable to direct the Minister towards the main aim of his visit to Vichy.

"Mr Laborde accepted [the fusion of the two codes of rugby] on condition that guarantees were given to the former rugby league clubs.

"Our rugby league colleagues asked Mr Laborde to accept a vice-presidency of the Rugby Union Federation in order to defend rugby league...

"Mr Laborde [eventually] resigned. He protested to Pétain, informed him of the shameful past of this Pascot, the most cynical professional. Nothing was done. Once more, lies and immorality won the day."[19]

Chapter Fifteen
THE HERETICAL TRADITION

On a misty day the castle of Montségur can be reached only by climbing up through clouds. Like other fortresses at Peyrepertuse, Puilaurens or Quéribus, it defies its site, straddling a spiny dome that rises to a height of 1200 metres amid the Pyrenean foothills. Once inside its sheltering walls, open to the sky, the visitor may have the impression, since there's a sheer drop on all sides, of floating in mid-air as if on the back of some giant bird.

Perched midway between heaven and earth, Montségur provided, in early medieval times, a proper setting for those who aimed for a kind of terrestrial perfection, the Cathars. Taking its name from the Greek word meaning "pure", this dissident form of Christianity, though it originated outside France, flourished in the tolerant atmosphere of twelfth-century Languedoc, after taking root in an area which stretched from Toulouse and beyond in the west, down towards the Pyrenees almost as far as Perpignan and up the Mediterranean coast and its hinterland, with particular strongholds around Carcassonne and the Aude valley.

The Cathars replaced the laxism and moral ambiguities of the official Catholic Church with a far more rigorous religious and moral code. Their asceticism and search for purity contrasted starkly with the dissolute way of life of the representatives of the more orthodox faith. The Cathars' alternative version of Christianity was, however, perceived as heresy by the established Church. And the Church struck back with its considerable might, beginning with a Papal decree which outlawed the heretics.

From Paris and the North the political wing of the establishment went into action, determined to crush the Cathars' continued defiance. Archbishops and noblemen from the North descended on defiant Languedoc, determined to enforce Papal law. By both physical force and inquisition, these crusaders, as they regarded themselves, gradually re-asserted their dominance, laying siege to the Cathar strongholds. Any land or property inhabited by the Cathars was considered to have been defiled and had to be laid waste. The bloody, so-called Albigensian crusades gradually exerted a grip on the south, with towns and villages sacked and Cathars burnt at the stake. A combination of religious intransigence and political opportunism proved a powerful force, as the heretics discovered to their loss. The Cathars retreated to the fortresses at Montségur, Puilaurens, Peyrepertuse and Quéribus to resist their opponents' zealous hounding. They would all eventually fall to their pursuers.

Montségur was not the last of these to surrender but its fall symbolises the defeat of the Cathar movement. Apparently impregnable - as its name, meaning "safe mountain", suggests - it withstood siege for almost a year until its defences were penetrated in March, 1244 by an advance party of Basques, led up the rockface by a local guide. Montségur fell and its 200 Cathar occupants were burned at the stake in the field below the castle walls. A treasure hoard, which according to legend was kept within the castle, has never been found to this day.

There is in all this a kind of historical allegory of the fate which befell rugby league almost 700 years later. The facts might not match exactly - nor is there much common ground between the Cathar ascetics, who renounced materialism, and paid sportsmen - but the essential elements of both stories have much in common. In both cases a culture flowered in the south and south-west and found the support of the people because it offered an honest alternative to the decadence and excesses of the existing Paris-based hegemony until, by various forms of deceit, the status quo reasserted its dominance. Just as French rugby league's founders, from the beginning, were at pains to underline that their game was an alternative and not a dissident movement, so the Cathars did not see themselves as heretics until the Albigensian crusade marked them out as such.

Nowadays it isn't just the *treizistes* who wear the Cathar mantle. The whole of the population of a certain area of the south-west, with its epicentre around Carcassonne, sees itself as part of the Cathar tradition. In some cases the name is taken simply for commercial reasons, as the various businesses connected to the tourist industry of the area will testify. But at another level it's a means of establishing an identity which proclaims separateness from the rest of France - especially from the north and Paris. It reveals an individuality which is bold enough to stand up for its own particular values and which from time to time defies the prevailing tone set by the capital.

Rugby league follows in the Cathar tradition because it demonstrates a similar mentality, which began as an alternative to the abuses of the ruling authority, the FFR, with its headquarters in Paris. Rugby union people of Languedoc will also claim to represent the Cathar tradition. But for them its meaning is restricted to a regional identity. At best theirs is a shallower kind of separateness based on cultural differences between the people of the south-west and those of the rest of France. There is nothing of the ideological differences, based on attitudes to rugby and sport in general, which mark rugby league people out from those who follow the other code.

Honesty in sport has long ceased to be an absolute if indeed it ever was. Yet it is this characteristic - this openness of intent - which most strikingly marks the difference between the two codes of rugby, both on and off the field.

It's remarkable how profound an effect was produced when the founders of rugby league, not long after the 1895 split, decided to remove four players from the pitch as well as those untidy heaps of bodies which obscure both the ball and assorted thuggery. The intention was to make the game better to watch and better to play, but at the same time it gave the sport a clarity - a lucidity, as the French themselves say - which not only threw individual brilliance into the spotlight, but also turned the glare on individual errors. Rugby league is a game where weaknesses - technical, physical and psychological - are soon clinically revealed. It is more confrontational than the older form, because the defender faces the attacker front on, man on man. As is so often said, there is nowhere to hide. Galia himself perceptively pointed out, after that first England-Australia match, that it's a game that will not tolerate mediocrity.

But that is not the same thing as saying that the game can only be played by an élite, which was an early conclusion reached by many observers after watching their first rugby league match.[1] The levels of fitness, speed and skill shown by the Yorkshire tourists in May 1934 left spectators incredulous. How could performances like this be achieved by working men?[2] These players had to be professionals. The fallacy became widespread.

Despite the fact that thousands took to rugby league with only the thought of enjoying themselves, the professional tag was one which stuck - or which was made to stick - to the exclusion of any other perception of the sport. Yet of the 200-plus rugby league teams operating during the final full season before the game was prohibited, only fourteen were professional. Even then, the so-called professional players were only semi-professional and relied on a full-time job for their main income.

The amateur-professional dilemma in France was in some ways a replication of what had happened in England a little more than a generation earlier. The north of England and south-west of France were gripped by rugby. Money entered the sport because public demand allowed it. By contrast, for the rugby-playing classes of the capitals, with their concentration of power, authority and wealth, sport was simply recreational and the very idea of professionalism was disdained.

The difference in attitude towards professionalism in rugby is mirrored by a discussion of the 1895 split which appeared in an official RFU publication: "The two principal causes of the trouble were the growing popularity of the game in these two counties [Yorkshire and Lancashire], with a consequent increase in gate receipts, and the fact that northern players at that time were chiefly of the type which - in those counties at all events - was accustomed to valuing its activities, of whatever kind, in terms of cash when they could get it."[3]

Such arrogant remarks suggest the contempt in which the popularisation of the sport among other social classes was held by the public school and university types who had first formed rugby clubs, a contempt which was also nurtured by others who took their cue from them. This concept of sport as an essentially English upper-class occupation was not lost on the French. "The English do not consider sport as an international domain," wrote the playwright Jean Giraudoux, at the time when France was being ostracised by the Home Unions. "It is an English empire."[4]

But empires eventually crumble and, as Giraudoux went on to remark: "It is difficult to defend the theory of aristocratic rugby against a wildly enthusiastic south [of France] where they want it for the common man."[5] The resulting era of professionalisation in France around 1930 was therefore "a tribute to the democratisation and specialisation [of sport], which accelerated during this period."[6]

The major problem which arose from rugby's great upsurge in popularity in the period immediately following the First World War was not the professionalisation of the sport but the inability of its officials to keep pace with change and to take control of events. A perplexed FFR, like the RFU before it, could not stomach the fact that the majority of the people now playing the sport which it was supposed to administer did not share the same view of rugby's purpose. These officials, many of them still based in Paris and unrepresentative of attitudes in the provinces, had not altered their ideas since the early days of the gentleman amateur, for whom active participation in sport was an ennobling experience and above all one which was unrewarded. "Playing the game" was all. The notion of playing for money destroyed sport's essential purpose and virtue. The officials of the FFR were as unwilling to accept - publicly at least - that men should play for money as they were unable to understand the development of sport as a form of popular entertainment.

The English Rugby Union's attitude to France in the 1930s was as dismissive as it had been towards the north of England in the 1890s. They must either play the game, or not at all. The FFR's response was typically supine. When England broke off relations in 1931 France's only thought was how best to regain favour and be re-admitted to the inner international circle. That was uppermost in the FFR's collective mind when briefly considering whether to accept the RFL's offer to become involved in setting up rugby league in France.

Had the FFR chosen to become involved in the "neo-rugby", a whole new world would have opened. Instead this conservative-minded governing body chose not to leave the comfort of the old world, if the old world would have it. Given the nature of that body, that is understandable. But what is unacceptable is that the FFR should then use every method available from the much-consulted rugby union book of dirty tricks to obstruct and impede rugby league's existence.

The French Rugby Union could not understand, let alone embrace, the changes taking place. It was incapable of accommodating professionalism, this dominant feature which marks out the twentieth century from the nineteenth. And the keynote of professionalism - winning - was something that neither the RFU nor the FFR, unlike the RFLand the Ligue, could accept as the ultimate goal in sport.

It is significant that Galia and Laborde, two men who understood well the mood of the times, were both shunned by the FFR, with the consequences that we now know. The far-sighted Laborde seemed to be alone among top rugby officials in being able to assess the situation in sport in the mid-1930s. "Professionalism in sport has become a social fact," he said, before even seeing a game of rugby league. "In rugby in particular it is the direct consequence of unbridled development. It is no longer appropriate to deny the evidence. It is preferable to recognise openly this state of affairs, which has been all too readily concealed as if it was something shameful that cannot be spoken about."[7]

The attitude of the French Rugby Union towards rugby league was nothing if not consistent. Its intentions had been made clear from the first abortive attempt in 1921 to play rugby league in France. The same hostility was being encountered right up to the end of the twentieth century.

Villeneuve suffered just such belligerence when, in November 1998, club officials were making arrangements to stage a televised evening match at Agen rugby union club, with whom Villeneuve had hitherto enjoyed good relations. The game was set to go ahead when the news reached the ears of the former chairman of Agen and ex-president of the FFR, Albert Ferrasse. "Unthinkable," fumed the union fundamentalist. It would be a "sacrilege" if *treizistes* were to enter the "temple".[8] In a wonderfully oblique counter-thrust, René Verdier, a Villeneuve *treiziste de la première heure*, told Ferrasse and his men not to worry. The grass would grow back again.[9]

Old guard maybe, but Ferrasse and other *quinzistes* still had clout. Minutes before the Villeneuve and Agen officials were about to sign their agreement, a fax from FFR president Bernard Lapasset landed on the Agen chairman's desk. The FFR was "not favourable" to the arrangement, and added further insult by referring to rugby league by the old name of *jeu à treize* , with all its connotations of rugby apartheid. And so Villeneuve were refused permission to play on the Agen ground, despite its status as a municipal stadium. It was left to the Eurosport producer, Bruno Bensimon, to reflect: "There is terrible hatred. One has the impression that union lives in fear of league even slightly emerging into the spotlight. The political influences are very real..."[10]

Jacques Fouroux became another notable victim of rugby union's pressure tactics. Following his spectacular "defection" (also referred to as "treachery" and "treason") from union to league, the former international coach helped set up a regional competition, played in summer, to take his new sport to a wider audience than it had been enjoying. The final was to be played at the Stade de la Méditerranée, Béziers, on September 16th, 1995 and a verbal agreement had been made with the town's deputy mayor. Two weeks before the final, the municipal authority decided they could not host the match. Top rugby union officials had been in contact with the mayor's office, making it clear that the staging of a league match in Béziers was "unacceptable". They let it be known that if it went ahead an All Blacks tour match scheduled for the same stadium in November that year, and possibly other high-level matches, might end up being played elsewhere. In spite of the agreement in principle with Fouroux, and despite the fact that part of the stadium hire charge would benefit junior rugby union in the town, the mayor's office surrendered to the union bullies' demands.

"Prohibited in 1940," ran a *Treize-magazine* editorial, "rugby league is once again the victim of Vichy-style discrimination in 1995 - because it has committed the unforgivable crime of continuing to exist."[11]

Although he had made many claims for rugby league, believing that this game was the "rugby of tomorrow", Fouroux made a less spectacular return to union. Only Fouroux himself, a businessman as well as an official, knows what pressures he had been subjected to before giving up on rugby league, which, he finally admitted, was not his game. His attempts to leap across the divide proved finally what a chasm lies between the two games as he consigned himself to perdition in the eyes of one or the other.

Fouroux's conversion to rugby league was hailed by some, but derided by others, particularly *treizistes* who had been around a while. "He's a *quinziste*," they said dismissively, as if there was no coming back from that point, a trait as defining as a religious creed.

The intensity of feeling produced by an allegiance to one side or the other can be underestimated by outsiders. The league-union polemic has caused divisions within communities, even within families, in a way that the English rugby league follower, for all the prejudices he has had to suffer, has not experienced to quite the same degree. "You would have had to live through the years 1938-39, the period of our major expansion, just to have an idea of the hatred which the rivalry between *Treize* and *Quinze* inspired throughout France," said Jean Larronde. "It set father against son. Engaged couples separated. Friends no longer spoke to each other."[12]

The *treiziste* has a strong sense of injustice, accumulated over the many years of union's obstructionist tactics, among which the Vichy ban was their greatest achievement. Just as the underlying stresses and tensions in French political attitudes intensified during the Occupation almost to the point of civil war, so the conflict between the two codes of rugby reflected that general situation, as the pre-war divisions were heightened by the finality of Pétain's decree.

For French rugby union Vichy was the "divine surprise" which suddenly allowed *quinzistes* to regroup and re-establish themselves as they pleased. The outdated notions held by members of the FFR hierarchy now found new currency in the equally backward-looking administration at Vichy. Both the FFR and Vichy tried to reverse the tide of professionalism. The two bodies were united in their cause because they had individuals in common who cherished the same ideals, which they attempted to realise in less than open fashion. Ideals may not be the word for it. The banning of rugby league was not a question of morals or ethics. The only principle involved was that of removing opposition to rugby union's declining supremacy. Could there have been any other reason for making the playing of rugby league, even by amateurs, a civil offence?

French rugby union's present-day predominance can be traced back directly to that reprehensible régime. The fifteen-a-side game's stabilisation during the war years, halting an apparently irreversible decline, was due to the intervention of officers of that puppet government who gave the older game a crucial second chance while snuffing out the threat posed by league. It is to French rugby union's everlasting shame that it should have been linked so closely with that reviled administration.

What became of French Rugby League's considerable funds has never been established. According to the 1939 conference figures, gross receipts reached almost three and a half million francs that season. At the outbreak of war the Ligue's bank balance was believed to stand at 1,200 000 francs - around £300,000 at today's rates.[13] By contrast the popularity of rugby league as well as its own loss of international fixtures had put the FFR's finances in a precarious position, leading the secretary-general to report to the Federation's annual congress in 1938, "The fall in receipts has caused us considerable harm".[14] Under the terms of the Sports Charter an unauthorised federation - and rugby league was refused the right to exist by Pétain's decree - could have its funds confiscated and disposed of to other federations. Where, then, are we to imagine, in the absence of any official information, that rugby league's money ended up? The Ligue's accounts and files all disappeared, never to be found again. According to René Verdier, "They took the lot. Even our kit."[15]

It was hardly a consolation but rugby league could at least claim the moral high ground. At the end of the war *treizistes* looked to General de Gaulle's so-called Algiers edict of 7th October 1943, which promised to reverse those measures which had been enacted by Vichy. Importantly, de

Gaulle declared an intention to quash any dissolution or merger among sports oganisations which the Vichy régime had enforced. That put rugby league, a victim of Vichy and the collaborationists, firmly on the side of the resistance, to the extent that the game became identified as a *sport-résistant*.

At the Liberation *treizistes,* following in the Cathar tradition of revolt against corrupt authority, set about re-asserting their rights and attempting to win back what had been snatched from them. René Barnoud, acting with the *Sport-Libre* movement in Lyon, was among those who seized the opportunity to set up a new order, not just for rugby league but for sport in general. Guns in hand, Barnoud and his fellow *résistants* took part in the liberation of Lyon. One of their first targets was the government offices in Lyon, where they threw the Vichy officials out. Afterwards *Sport-Libre,* formally recognised by de Gaulle, began removing - though not physically this time - all the directors of clubs, committees and federations who had been designated by Vichy and replacing them through free democratic elections.

Representatives of *Sport-Libre* went up to Paris to speak to de Gaulle to ask for special consideration to be given to the administration of sport, which came under the aegis of the Ministry of Education. But the euphoria which had accompanied the Liberation and the expectation of creating a new order quickly evaporated.

"We didn't want sport to be the poor relation of education," Barnoud explained. "For eleven days we waited patiently to be seen by de Gaulle. Finally we were seen by his secretary, who asked us who we were and what we wanted. We told him we were the representatives of millions of sportsmen and sportswomen. 'If there are so many of you,' he said, 'you should organise a convention on sports issues and General de Gaulle, who is a great politician, will hear your voice. Goodbye.'"

Barnoud was forced to conclude: "Our resistance movement, after the war, served no purpose at all."

Barnoud was not the only one to feel let down by the new administration. Paul Barrière was another former *résistant* who had reason to be aggrieved when he came up against post-war officialdom. Barrière, the 24-year-old nephew of Jean Bourrel, the philanthropic ex-chairman of Quillan rugby union club, was a *maquis* leader in the *département* of Aude. His main sporting interest was not so much rugby as cycling, though he was soon to become active in another fight - to raise rugby league from the dead. The former chairman of the Ligue, Marcel Laborde, casting around for someone with the energy and tenacity to lead the potentially long struggle to resurrect rugby league, artfully persuaded Barrière that he was the man for the job. Barrière was not convinced but agreed to take rugby league's dossier up to Paris in order to begin the process of having the game reinstated. Once again the dead hand of officialdom blocked the way. A muttered remark from a civil servant was intended to finish off what a long wait in the Ministry corridors had not managed to do. There would be no return for rugby league, Barrière heard.

For the second time the game appeared to have been the victim of an unjust and undemocratic process. But Laborde had chosen well. A refusal was only likely to make Barrière, the resistance leader who had fought to clear France of the iniquities of the Vichy régime, more determined to succeed.

Barrière led the long struggle to re-establish rugby league first at Carcassonne, as a club official who was no older than most of the players, before becoming vice-chairman, then chairman of the French Rugby League. Other important pre-war figures returned to help resurrect the game: Marcel Laborde himself at Perpignan, Simon Bompunt at Albi, Claudius Devernois at Roanne for instance; without forgetting Jean Galia, who helped bring Toulouse Olympique back to life.

At amateur level, there was a clear need for rugby league to establish itself on a wider basis in order to ensure the flow of top players towards the professional élite. Great strides had been made before the war to expand the game although in many places the structures of club administration had been flimsy. The journalist Gaston Bénac outlined the task which lay ahead: "While maintaining this family spirit which was its strength and which still remains among its former officials, [rugby league] will need to push back the frontiers of its recruitment, both in terms of players and officials."[16] Proposing that two distinct sections be created - one to cater exclusively for the amateurs and one for the professionals - Bénac went on to stress the importance of increasing public participation in amateur rugby league, with special emphasis to be given to schoolboy level.

Bénac's recommendations had already been put into practice when war broke out, as the secretary of the amateur section, Monsieur Darmaillac, pointed out in a letter to him written in May 1944. Darmaillac reiterates amateur rugby league's pre-war success, including three victories out of four matches played at international level, and the gradual progress and development of the game throughout France, even though they had been still some way short of achieving their aims. Soon, Darmaillac asserted, they would again have their chance to achieve the "definitive success" longed for by "the little family which has never stopped meeting to discuss the past and plan for the future."[17]

A makeshift championship composed of two pools, south-east and south-west, had been under way since the autumn when a symbolic match took place in Paris - at the Parc des Princes, no less - on February 4th 1945 between Villeneuve and Carcassonne. Though the match was a charity event, in aid of the Forces Françaises Libres still fighting in Alsace, it gave a taste of what was to come. For the first time since 1939 Parisians could see for themselves those stars whose careers had been interrupted by the war - Marius Guiral, Maurice Bruneteaud and Félix Bergèse for instance - while witnessing the emerging brilliance of young players such as the extraordinary full-back Puig-Aubert, the superbly athletic second rower Edouard Ponsinet, and the big, skilful loose forward Gaston Calixte.

Not just in Paris but throughout the former league strongholds the massive sense of release that accompanied the end of the war brought France's sporting public out in their thousands. The players, directors and fans who had seen their game closed down during the war years came back with a vengeance. Rugby league quickly returned to the stadiums: Carcassonne kicked off their golden era by lifting the 1945 championship, narrowly defeating Toulouse, and were finalists in the cup. New clubs at Avignon and Marseille would join the top division.

Rugby league lost no time in reproducing the kind of spectacular sporting event which had been its hallmark before the war. But a return to the pre-war status quo had its negative side too. As a gesture of goodwill the French Rugby League had allowed free stand admission to all rugby union international players at that Paris charity match. By contrast Marius Guiral, who was Villeneuve's fullback on that day, and who had been a member of the Agen side in rugby union's 1943 championship after being forced to return to the code following the Vichy ban, told reporters that, even though he had presented his rugby union international's card, he had been refused entry to the Agen stadium for a championship match just a few weeks earlier.[18] The discrimination, the hypocrisy showed no change.

Certain players like Desclaux and Dauger, having returned to rugby union in 1940, decided to stay there, and even represented the national side, despite the odour of professionalism which the English RFU, in a new spirit of post-war camaraderie, obligingly failed to detect. Dauger, by temperament one of the least mercenary of players, had been torn between returning to play rugby league with Roanne, who were keen to have him back, and continuing to play union with Aviron Bayonnais in his home area. The union club practised a "strict, very strict amateurism"[19] and would not stoop to using cash even to sign up such an outstanding player as Dauger. What clinched the deal for them, though, was that Dauger, together with his wife (who had actually wanted Jean to return to rugby league with Roanne), was offered the job of manager of a members' club owned by Aviron Bayonnais, on the assumption that he would stay with the union team. When Dauger was finally recalled to the international XV at the age of 33 to face Scotland in 1953, the Scots, mindful of his pre-war rugby league experience, objected to his selection and threatened to call the match off. The French Federation called their bluff, claiming that they were acting in accordance with the legislation of the International Board and that the Scots had no right to question their policy. The essentials of the French Federation's defence were expressed in an error-strewn newspaper account: "From a reliable source one learns that Jean Dauger went to the League before he was 17 years old in 1939, was unpaid, and gladly returned to the Rugby Union in 1940. After being suspended for a year he rejoined his old club Aviron Bayonnais, which in France enjoys a high reputation for its amateur spirit ..."[20] What the French were claiming was that Dauger, having signed for Roanne as a 17-year old, was exempt from the rules on amateurism because he was still a minor. In any event the Scots backed down, the match went ahead and arguably France's greatest-ever centre added a third union cap to the two he had won in 1945 against the British Empire and the British Army, where, incidentally, he had played against Bradford Northern's Ernest Ward and Trevor Foster and Salford's Gus Risman - the wartime spirit had temporarily erased the distinction between professional and amateur - and alongside Jep Desclaux.

On resuming relations with France in 1939 the Home Unions had specifically reminded the French Federation that "no player who has been proved guilty of receiving payment, other than actual out-of-pocket travelling and hotel expenses, is ever allowed to play Rugby Football again or to act in any official capacity in connection with any Rugby Football Club." On behalf of the French Rugby League, the RFL raised with the RFU the matter of former rugby league professionals reverting to "amateur" status in rugby union. The Rugby League's secretary, Bill Fallowfield, who had taken over from John Wilson, told the press: "While I was in France recently I saw a contract, signed by the player and countersigned by his father in which the player was to receive money for his services with a Rugby Union club."[21] Fallowfield went on to complain to the Home Unions, demanding that the French Rugby Union should come clean on professionalism so that an agreement could be made between the two organisations. Asked to respond, the RFU secretary blithely claimed to have no information on the matter. And the fifteen-a-side game carried on in much the same way as before, slipping sealed envelopes into pockets or ensuring undemanding jobs for its star players. Better to tolerate covert professionalism than to leave the field open to rugby league. Furthermore, the suppression of rugby union's championship, which the British had "advised" as a prelude to renewing international relations with the French, had lasted less than four years, having restarted in 1943 with numerous ex-rugby league players playing key roles. Not only that but the FFR had instituted the kind of knock-out cup competition which the Ligue had been running since its first season.

But despite its close links with the agencies of an authoritarian state the FFR proved no more capable than before of promoting fair play. The southern zone championship final between Agen and Montferrand, marred by violence, proved the point. In an attempt to appear stern, the Federation carpeted two Montferrand players, banning one of them for life, but took no action against Agen for leaving two other Montferrand forwards with a broken nose and arm. After several ultimatums had been volleyed off in various directions, including one from the Montferrand chairman, an Agen player was also suspended, which only resulted in Agen threatening to pull out of the final against the northern zone champions a fortnight later. Once again the State was forced to intervene to put the FFR house in order when Colonel Pascot stepped in to ensure cooperation from Agen by threatening the club with sanctions.

As in other aspects of life in France, the hoped-for revolution in sporting ethics never happened. Official recognition for rugby league was proving as difficult to obtain as it had been before the war. If the outcome of the war had confirmed rugby league's moral victory, Vichy had also re-asserted rugby union as the official, state-recognised form of rugby. Far from suffering during the war period, the union code had greatly benefited and would find its post-war progress, aided by a well-developed infrastructure and network of influence, so much easier as a result. Would rugby league be able to resist the secret lobbying of its tormentor, the FFR? The CNS, that association of sports federations that had black-balled rugby league's application so often before the war, was proving as impregnable as ever. The FFR played on its usual cartel to maintain the exclusion zone. But the Ligue's president, Paul Barrière, having won over the officials of the sport he had known best, cycling, found support among two minor sports, archery and real tennis, to gain the three votes necessary for admission.

Rugby union had lost the argument but remained determined to maintain its stranglehold, which was facilitated when the chair of the CNS was taken by none other than the FFR president, Alfred Eluère, who was closely connected with Aviron Bayonnais, having set up the members' club which the ex-rugby league player Jean Dauger was to be found managing when not playing rugby union.

The FFR argued that, since one federation could only administer one sport, and because there were two sports called rugby, one of them would have to change its name. And so rugby league was forced to be known by the nondescript title of *jeu à treize*, the thirteen-a-side game, in contravention of the law allowing a federation a free choice of name. Not until 1993 did French rugby league finally earn the right to call itself the Fédération Française de Rugby à XIII. A neat twist to this already convoluted story - a reinvention of history worthy of certain former communist régimes - was that the newly-named Fédération Française de Jeu à XIII could not now claim any reparation for the funds and property taken by Vichy because it had not existed at that time.[22]

Five years on, the French Rugby League had no capital resources and fewer players than it had had at the time of the ban. The game had now seen almost as many years' inactivity as there had been championship seasons.

Five years is a considerable period in a player's career and a number of those in their prime in 1939 had now retired. Others, having been forced into reunification, as it was euphemistically designated, decided not to rejoin their former rugby league clubs now that the British had obligingly re-opened international competition and removed the threat of sanctions against shamateurism.

If rugby league had been played in the schools during the war years, as the 1940 edict had allowed, then young players would have started to come through to the top level. But the shortfall was now serious and the game had to find new players capable of adapting quickly to their code. In a situation like this rugby league officials had no qualms about plundering rugby union clubs. There was nothing illegal in that and it was the players' free choice to accept or decline. The Perpignan rugby union club, USAP, alone lost more than half of its 1944 championship-winning side.

It was not one-way traffic. As early as 1939, when rugby league was at its height and union at its lowest ebb, the Ligue had proposed a war-time protocol so that neither code would take players from the other body without consent. In 1944 Paul Barrière repeated the Ligue's wish to live in peace with the Federation and suggested a further non-aggression pact. When, some three years later, a formal document was drawn up, the union clubs refused to be reined in, bleating that personal choice was being threatened, demanding total freedom and turning down flat any agreement with rugby league. Pure hypocrisy, of course, as a member of the Pyrenees Committee pointed out. "We all know here that the Federation's clubs pay their players and some of them more than league. Whether the FFR gives us permission to sign certain rugby league players or not, they play for us anyway." Not only first-team rugby league players were being recruited by union clubs, but juniors were being signed up too, further depleting league's resources. As a writer in the Albi yearly review put it: "The freedom which the rugby union clubs were demanding was the freedom to destroy rugby league by strangulation." Antoine Blain, the former international who became secretary of the French Rugby League, also suggested that if rugby league really had pillaged rugby union, then the FFR would not have refused the official agreement which would have protected union from its rival.

The *quinzistes* however were able to demonstrate that they had lost none of their old touch in string-pulling and political manoeuvring. The cultivation of the media, politicians and civil servants - anyone, in fact, likely to be able to put pressure on rugby league - all were means by which to grind the enemy down. Meanwhile they insisted on their own blamelessness, never admitting to numerous accusations of shamateurism which they knew, because of the complicity of those involved, could never be proved. Half a century later, when the game of rugby union was at last girding itself to enter the world of twentieth-century sport with just five years to spare, and allow professionalism into their bastion, the FFR was to be found still dithering over uttering that unspeakable word. Like the taxman, but for different reasons, the union men were suspicious of the word "professional". They preferred the term "non-amateur".

Despite all the obstacles, rugby league managed to regain a foothold. There were some spectacular results, the most remarkable of which was the immense achievement of the 1951 international side, who took on the Australians in their own backyard and left them shaking their heads in disbelief. Upsetting all the odds, the French didn't just beat the Aussies, they did so in a style that left the opposition looking clueless. Inspired, always inventive, France piled up 35 points to 14 in the Third Test in Sydney to humiliate the Australians with a 2-1 victory in the series. Thousands lined the streets of Marseille as the team returned home to an American-style ticker-tape welcome. The inimitable Puig-Aubert, who had been offered a massive contract to play in Sydney, was voted France's sportsman of the year. The Federation's bank balance was swelled by the unprecedented success of the tour and rugby league was back in the big time.

But not for long. For every club that joined the French Rugby League, such as Avignon or Marseille, another dropped out - Brive or Narbonne, for example, both of which reverted to union. Though the top clubs attracted both big crowds and young players keen to play the game, it was a different matter elsewhere. Rugby league no longer had the player base that it had had before the war. Equally important, there were fewer officials willing to run clubs. The loss of even a single individual could have important repercussions - for example, the death of the Côte Basque XIII chairman, Dr Déjeant, drowned in 1942, resulted in that club lacking the impetus to achieve the same level of success as before the war. Despite the best plans of Darmaillac and his colleagues, there was a similar decline generally in the number of amateur clubs, which were now concentrated in a smaller area. Nor was there any rugby league played in the schools, or very little, owing to a total absence of PE teachers qualified to teach it. All in all it became a players' market, with the inevitable consequence for the game's finances.

Rugby union's strike was to have effects that lasted long after the war had ended. The war years had seen an unprecedented rise, thanks to the efforts of Vichy's Commissariat Général aux Sports, in the French public's participation in sport. If rugby league had still been played during that period it would almost certainly have outpaced its union rival. Instead union was given the further inestimable advantage of being made compulsory in schools, with the new FFR president crowing: "I agree with Pascot. Rugby [union] is a manly sport which will regenerate the people."[23] Vichy had not only stripped rugby league bare. It had land-mined the game's post-war future, with the result that French rugby league, less than a generation after it had begun, would enter a period of slow decline.

Numerous rugby league players and officials had been actively involved on their own account in the resistance, playing significant roles in the eventual liberation of France and the overthrow of the collaborationist Vichy régime. Rugby union players were of course equally well represented in the ranks of the *résistants*. If the game of union as an entity had become aligned with Vichy, while league was identified with the resistance, individual players and officials were left with individual choices. There is a poignant comparison to be made in the cases of two rugby union men. Joseph Pascot, the former US Perpignan and French international, who acted so iniquitously on behalf of rugby union at Vichy, was put on trial after the war like so many of his government colleagues, was sentenced and then reprieved. Gilbert Brutus, the former Perpignan player, coach and international selector, born like Pascot at Port Vendres, was captured by the Gestapo and tortured before being found hanged in his prison cell in the Citadel of Perpignan.

Each man had reacted to the Occupation according to his own will. It was an absurdity that no such freedom of choice could be exercised in rugby. That injustice, born out of jealousy, is recognised by fair-minded observers. "Rugby league should have been, and could have been regarded as a game in its own right, without analogy to orthodox rugby," wrote Gaston Bénac.[24] Henri Garcia's comment on the refusal of the CNS to recognise rugby league - a precedent of the Vichy decision - is equally telling. "Whatever the excuses of self-defence, it remains an abuse of power," he wrote. "Every sport has the right to exist and only players and spectators can decide to adopt or reject it."[25]

Those thousands of players and spectators who had taken to rugby league between 1934 and 1939 had embraced not only a different set of rules but a different mentality as well. When, in November 1940, Monsieur Darmaillac suggested - erroneously as it turned out - that the spirit of rugby league no longer existed, he was alluding to something that went beyond the touchlines.[26]

Asked to name the essential qualities of the game, any *treiziste* will begin by talking of the necessity to *faire le spectacle*, to put on a show, to entertain the public. That in turn means that more is required of the players. "The game places great demands on its players both in terms of physical condition and individual technique," said André Passamar. "The player is therefore forced - and this isn't necessarily true of rugby union - to push himself to the limit."[27]

Tintin Saltraille recalled the immediacy with which Frenchmen adapted to the game: "A new mentality, new knowledge were required so that a new spirit (of play and of conduct) would be appreciated and embraced by both public and players, with the result that France and the south in particular came to love the new form of rugby.

"The spectators were thrilled by the simplicity, speed and variety of continually renewed attacks and for the players it was their happy fortune to be able to comply with the demands of this great game."[28]

The originality of the game of rugby league, its evolution both as a sport and as a cultural entity was and remains a source of pride. The writer Jean Roques, evoking the origins of the Racing Club d'Albi, the very town which gave its name to the Albigensian crusade, recalled the deep satisfaction among the local people at the creation of a rugby league club in their midst. With the distinction of having a unique cathedral and museum[29] on their doorstep, they would also, as founder members of the Ligue, have a sport of their own.

"Just as we had been Cathars, we were *treizistes*, men apart," he wrote, before going on to recall the words of Stendhal.[30] "*Cultive ta différence*," advised the great 19th century novelist.

Despite the intolerance shown towards their form of dissidence, *treizistes* have unknowingly followed that recommendation, cultivating what makes them stand out from others and daring, like heretics, to play their own game their own way.

AFTERWORD

French rugby league remains defiant and, if all things were equal, would flourish. Antoine Blain, the dual international who became secretary of the French Rugby League Federation after the war, was one of many who saw how well the 13-a-side game suited the French temperament. "If there hadn't been rugby league, there would only be rugby league," he maintained, enigmatically. What he meant was that rugby league, in reforming the game of rugby, principally by reducing the number of players and thus making the game more entertaining, had prevented rugby union from ever making those changes. If the rugby league movement had not existed, rugby union would happily have taken the same route. But, as *treizistes* the world over know, there is more to the success of a sport than its attractiveness either to play or to watch. How else to explain the fact that for every rugby league player in France there is two-thirds of a union team?

Those same comments made by French players and observers in the 1930s still apply today: rugby league was then and is now a highly demanding, intense sport which is spectacular to watch. But with the passage of time it becomes more and more difficult for a given sport - soccer being the obvious exception - to increase its audience or the number of its participants. Rugby league's startling rise in France in the 1930s will never happen again anywhere.

French rugby league has had some notable successes in its seventy-odd years' existence, but those triumphs have often been against the run of play. The full pattern of development from junior and schoolboy level through the professional ranks towards international status has never been complete because parts of the jigsaw have always been missing.

The importance of establishing rugby league's right to exist on an equal footing with other sports is therefore of fundamental importance to the game's future. For that reason the national commission of enquiry into the events of the Vichy years was an important step forward. But there is a second reason why it is important to officially establish at the highest level what happened to rugby league in the name of the Vichy régime.

In October 1997 the Minister of Sport, Mme Marie-George Buffet, announced that the government-backed enquiry would be constituted to make a "rigorous evaluation of sports policy in France under the Vichy régime."[1] The announcement came after the Minister had addressed the Union of Jewish Students of France, when she spoke of the "crimes against humanity committed by those who governed France between 1940 and 1944."[2] At a time when the Papon trial was at the forefront of people's minds, Mme Buffet's comments were welcomed by the students, who, through their chairman, demanded to know the whole truth concerning the crimes committed in the name of the French State. "We will not allow our past to be hidden from us," said the student leader.[3]

The banning of rugby league may seem, alongside a long list of war-time atrocities, unimportant by comparison. Except that freedom of choice and thus freedom in sport is a basic democratic right and that it is axiomatic that the treatment of its minorities is one measure of a country's civilisation.

The commission of enquiry into sport in France during the Occupation produced its findings in March 2002. Out of 180 pages of text, approximately one page relates to rugby league, with two other minor references. But at last there is official confirmation of what *treizistes* have always believed.

The report states: "The action against rugby league was the result of steps taken by the French Rugby (Union) Federation which saw an opportunity to get rid of a dangerous rival. Rugby league ... had been introduced into France in 1934 during a difficult period for rugby union. The latter had been deprived, since 1931, of international competition following the breaking-off of relations with the British, who objected to its 'touting' [of players], which was incompatible with amateurism, and its extremes of rough play. Rugby league quickly flourished, recruiting top players even from the 'enemy', creating clubs and acquiring a large following who were attracted by the novelty and by play which was often more entertaining than that of the '*quinzistes*', whose quality had declined. 'The war of the two rugbys' was merciless and Union was on the defensive. When the Commissariat Général was set up, influential officials of the French Rugby Federation endeavoured to eliminate the rival code, which they portrayed as a dangerous aberration... Dr Paul Voivenel, a leading Pétainist and honorary president of the FFR, presented to Borotra a report which advocated the abolition of rugby league, both professional ... and amateur...

"The decree of 19 December 1941 dissolvedthe Ligue de Rugby à XIII and, refusing to allow a period of adaptation which was granted to other professional federations (cycling, boxing, football...), even went so far as to prohibit the playing of the sport by amateurs! Thus was the fate of rugby league sealed, its players being invited to return to the fold of the [Rugby

Union] Federation, where, according to its president, Dr Ginesty, 'their moral and technical re-education would take place.'"[4]

However, following a change of government, the report was not made widely available. The matter of possible compensation remains unbroached. As the founder of the lobby group XIII Actif, Robert Fassolette, pointed out to the Minister, it is unacceptable that rugby league should have been banned by government decree without a word of apology from its instigators during the intervening period, nor even a suggestion of reparation for the damage done to the sport at a time when it was at its height and was flying the French flag with distinction at international level.[5] We should not therefore be in a hurry to say the past is best forgotten. In fact, in the best democratic interests, we have a duty to remember.

FOOTNOTES

Chapter One:
The French Perspective

1 Conversation with Paul Déjean and Augustin Saltraille, Perpignan, 23 August 1995
2 Ibid.
3 Ibid.
4 Ibid.

Chapter Two:
The State of the Union

1 Richard Holt, *Sport and Society in Modern France*, pp.66-7
2 Evidence provided by Noël Altèze in letter to author, 5 July 1995
3 *Les Deux Rugbys dans l'Aude*, p.40, quoting from *Le Livre d'or de Lézignan XIII*, 1975
4 *Les Deux Rugbys dans l'Aude*, p.42
5 Paul Voivenel, *Mon beau rugby* (Toulouse, 1962), p.120
6 *Les Deux Rugbys dans l'Aude*, p.46
7 *Rugby*, 16 December 1916, quoted in *Les Deux Rugbys dans l'Aude*, p.46
8 Henri Garcia, *La Fabuleuse Histoire du Rugby* (Paris, 1973), p.254
9 J-P Bodis, *Histoire mondiale du rugby* (Toulouse, 1987), p.200
10 Holt, op. cit., p.68
11 Bodis, op.cit., pp.150-1
12 *La Dépêche*, 6 May 1925
13 Voivenel, op. cit., pp.108-111. The Spanish word *muerte*, meaning "death", has an association with bullfighting.
14 *La Dépêche*, 13 May 1929
15 Ibid.
16 P-J Bergès, *Le Rugby à Carcassonne*, quoted in *Les Deux Rugbys dans l'Aude*, p.52
17 *La Dépêche*, 20 May 1929
18 Gaston Bénac, *Champions dans la coulisse* (Toulouse, 1944), p.186
19 Quoted in *La Dépêche*, 20 May 1929
20 *La Dépêche*, 26 April 1931
21 Marcel de Laborderie, *L'Almanach du Miroir des Sports*, 1936, p.178
22 *The Times*, 2 January 1913
23 Letter, 27 January 1913
24 *Manchester Guardian*, 22 April 1930
25 *The Times*, 23 April 1930
26 Quoted in *Manchester Guardian*, 2 March 1931

Chapter Three:
The Playmakers

1 *Midi-Olympique*, 1 September 1930
2 Ibid., 8 September 1930
3 Ernest Camo, *Souvenirs de vingt ans de vie avec mon ami Jean Galia*, p.57
4 Ibid., pp.60-1
5 *Midi Olympique*, 29 August 1930
6 Camo, op. cit., p.71
7 *La Guerre des Deux Rugby* (Paris, 1938), p.8
8 Letter to author, 5 July 1995
9 Spelt Vaills in contemporary reports in the Perpignan newspaper, *L'Indépendant*.
10 Altèze, loc. cit.
11 Interview in *XIII Catalan: 50 ans d'épopée*, p.20
12 Letter from Mme Galia to author, 18 June 1996

13 Camo, op.cit., p. 93
14 *L'Indépendant*, 1 February 1933
15 Voivenel, *Mon beau rugby*, p.120
16 Council minutes, 27 October 1921
17 Ibid., 27 March 1922
18 Ibid., 12 November 1912
19 Ibid., 13 May 1931
20 Gaston Bénac, *Champions dans la coulisse*, p.186
21 Maurice Blein in *Sport-Digest*, January 1950, p.32
22 Serge Darboit in *Sport-Digest*
23 RFLarchives
24 *Daily Dispatch*, 4 January 1934
25 *L'Auto*, 1 January 1934
26 *L'Excelsior*, 1 January 1934
27 *L'Auto*, 1 January 1934
28 *L'Echo des Sports*, 3 January 1934. The need for a new name was taken up in other publications, e.g. *L'Auto*, which asked readers for suggestions (16 March 1934).
29 *L'Indépendant*, 1 January 1934
30 Camo, op. cit., p.97
31 *Daily Dispatch*, 3 January 1934
32 Camo, op. cit., p.98
33 *L'Indépendant*, 2 March 1934
34 Reprinted in *L'Indépendant*, 5 March 1934
35 Interview with Antonin Barbazanges conducted by Jérôme Cavalli, Toulouse, October-November, 1985
36 26 February 1934
37 Interview with Madame Mathon, Villeurbanne, 28 October 1993
38 *Treize* no.57, April 1984, pp.16-17
39 Bénac, op.cit., p.187
40 *L'Auto*, 28 February 1934

Chapter Four: Galia's Boys

1 *Yorkshire Post*, 6 March 1934
2 *Treize*, January 1982
3 *Yorkshire Post*, 6 March 1934
4 *L'Indépendant*, 18 February 1934
5 *Yorkshire Post*, 9 March 1934
6 Interview, Oct-Nov 1985
7 *Yorkshire Post*, 13 March 1934
8 *Treize*, January 1982
9 Ibid.
10 *Yorkshire Post*, 28 March 1934

Chapter Five: First Steps

1 According to the account given in *L'Auto*, 17 April 1934
2 Henri Garcia, *Rugby-Champagne* (Paris, 1961), pp.36-7
3 *Yorkshire Post*, 16 April 1934
4 *Yorkshire Post*, 17 April 1934
5 *L'Auto*, 17 April 1934
6 *La Petite Gironde*, 7 May 1934
7 *Yorkshire Post*, 15 May 1934
8 Ibid.
9 The letter does not appear to be among the RFLarchives. It is re-translated from an article in *L'Echo des Sports*, 20 March 1934
10 *Yorkshire Post*, 14 May 1934
11 *Paris-Soir*, 20 August 1934
12 *L'Indépendant*, 15 May 1934
13 *L'Auto*, 3 and 4 March 1934
14 Reported by *Yorkshire Post* and *Manchester Guardian*, among others, 18 May 1934

Chapter Six: The Villeneuve Initiative

1 Letter from Madame Galia to author, 18 June 1996
2 *Yorkshire Post*, 15 September 1934

Chapter Seven: The Catalan Connection

1 *Treize* no.57, April 1984, pp.28-31
2 Conversation with Paul Déjean and Jacques Jorda, Canet-Plage, 25 August 1994
3 *L'Indépendant*, 25 February 1933
4 *L'Auto*, 11 March 1934
5 *L'Indépendant*, 12 March 1934
6 *L'Indépendant*, 4 May 1934
7 *L'Auto*, 16 September 1934
8 *L'Indépendant*, 22 March 1934

Chapter Eight: Coup d'envoi

1 *L'Indépendant*, 2 October 1934
2 XIII Catalan: *Cinquante ans d'épopée*, pp.15-16
3 Like certain other players at the time, Vignal's name is recorded spelt in different ways, such as Vignals and Vignials. His first name is also sometimes recorded as Eugène - an inexplicable error; his middle name was Emile. Coincidentally, Vignal's brother, Gaston, a referee, did not share the same spelling of the family surname: through a mistake at the registrar's office his name was spelt Vignials. (Information provided by the daughter of Jean-Marie Vignal.)
4 *La Dépêche*, 15 October 1934
5 *La Petite Gironde*, reprinted in *Le Villeneuvois*, 24 November 1934
6 *Le Villeneuvois*, 15 December 1934
7 Evidence provided by Madame Mathon
8 Interview with René Barnoud, Villeurbanne, 28 October 1993
9 Ibid.
10 René Barnoud, *Quel drôle de ballon*, p.66
11 Ernest Camo, Max Rousié, *Le Dieu du Stade* (Villeneuve, n.d.)
12 *The Times*, 28 January 1931
13 Barnoud, loc. cit

Chapter Nine: Irreconcilable Differences

1 *Le Réveil*, 22 July 1934
2 Conversation with René Verdier, Villeneuve-sur-Lot, 18 August 1994
3 Information provided by Jean Larronde
4 *L'Indépendant des Pyrénées* (not to be confused with the Perpignan *Indépendant*), 31 August 1934
5 *L'Auto*, 16 September 1934
6 *Miroir des Sports*, 22 October 1935
7 *L'Auto*, 16 September 1934
8 Ibid.
9 *L'Auto*, 23 April 1936
10 *L'Auto*, 25 June 1937
11 *L'Auto*, 8 January 1937
12 *Paris-Soir*, reprinted in *L'Auto*, 15 January 1936
13 *News Chronicle*, February 1938

Chapter Ten: Breakthrough

1 The Saturday sports edition of the *Yorkshire Evening News*, 28 September 1935
2 *L'Auto*, 16 September 1936
3 Interview with René Barnoud, Villeurbanne, 28 October 1993
4 Interview with Jean Barrès conducted by René Verdier on the author's behalf, February 1995
5 Georges Pastre, *Histoire générale du rugby, vol.1* (Toulouse 1968), p.209
6 *La Petite Gironde*, 20 September 1937
7 *La Dépêche*, 10 July 1937
8 *La Dépêche*, 24 October 1937
9 Pastre, op. cit., p.223
10 Barnoud, loc. cit.
11 Interview with Dr Mourgues, *L'Auto*, 24 November 1937
12 Conversation with René Verdier, Villeneuve, 18 August 1994
13 Conversation with Madame Galia, Toulouse, 30 March 1998
14 Conversation with Sylvain Bès, Toulouse, 19 August 1995
15 *La Voix du Peuple*, 4 January 1938
16 Sylvain Bès, loc. cit.
17 Information provided by Jean Larronde
18 Marcel de Laborderie, *Miroir des Sports*, 3 April 1938
19 Pastre, op. cit., p.229

Chapter Eleven: A Golden Season

1 Conversation with Sylvain Bès, Toulouse, 19 August 1995
2 *L'Auto*, 14 August 1938
3 *L'Auto*, 11 January 1939
4 Information provided by Jean Larronde from various regional newspapers
5 *L'Auto*, 20 December 1938
6 *L'Auto*, 15 March 1939
7 Sylvain Bès, loc. cit.
8 Ernest Camo, Max Rousié, *le Dieu du stade*

9 Conversation with René Verdier, Villeneuve, 18 August 1994
10 Sylvain Bès, loc. cit.
11 Conversation with Paul Déjean and Noël Altèze, Canet, 23 August 1995
12 *Treize* no. 57, April 1984
13 Interview, February 1995
14 Interview, Oct-Nov 1985
15 Interview, March 1995
16 *La Guerre des deux rugby*, 1938
17 Ibid.
18 *La Gazette de Biarritz*, 30 September 1937
19 Ibid.
20 Ibid.
21 Garcia, *La Fabuleuse Histoire du rugby*, p.292

Chapter Twelve: By Government decree

1 Jean Dutourd, *Au Bon Beurre* (Paris 1952)
2 Sir John Smyth, Jean Borotra, *The Bounding Basque* (London 1974), p.125
3 Bibliothèque Nationale, AG II 459 CC XXXIV
4 *La Dépêche*, 15 July 1940
5 Ibid.
6 Quoted in J-LGay-Lescot, *Sport et Education sous Vichy* (Lyon 1991), pp32-3
7 Bibliothèque Nationale, AG II 459
8 HR Kedward, *Occupied France* (Oxford 1985), p22
9 Robert Fassolette, *Histoire politique du conflit des deux rugby en France* (unpubl. thesis 1996), p262
10 Letter to author, 16 March 1994.
11 Jean Larronde, who posed this question many times to Ybarnégaray, in letter to author, 7 September 1998
12 The interview was published in slightly differing forms in *La France*, *Le Patriote des Pyrénées* and *L'Indépendant des Pyrénées*, 22 August 1940
13 *Le Patriote*, 21 August 1940
14 *L'Indépendant des Pyrénées*, 21 August 1940
15 Speech, 13 July 1940
16 *L'Indépendant des Pyrénées*, loc. cit.
17 My italics
18 *La Guerre des deux rugby* (Paris 1938) p2
19 Bibliothèque Nationale AG II 459
20 *La Dépêche*, 28 August 1940
21 Paul Voivenel, *Mon beau rugby* (Toulouse 1942), pp 220 & ff. This section is deleted from the second edition, published in 1962
22 *La Dépêche*, 17 October 1940
23 *La Petite Gironde* (Toulouse edn.), 17 October 1940, quoted in Bonnery and Thomas, *Le Jeu à XIII* (Paris 1986), p 17
24 *L'Auto*, 19 October 1940
25 *L'Auto*, 1 November 1940
26 *La Gazette de Biarritz*, 4 November 1940
27 *La Gazette de Biarritz*, 6 November 1940
28 *L'Auto*, 1 November 1940
29 In more than one sense: Arotça was unable to play, having been seriously wounded during the German offensive
30 *L'Auto*, 30 October 1940
31 *Treize* no. 57, April 1984, p15
32 Interview with Laurent Lambert, Cannes, 6 August 1985
33 Interview conducted by René Verdier, February 1995
34 *La Presse du Sud-Ouest*, 19 November 1940
35 Interview, October 1993, Villeurbanne
36 Letter of 16 February 1941, reproduced in Bonnery, *Le Rugby à XIII*, pp118-9
37 25 July 1941

Chapter Thirteen: The German Question

1 *Mein Kampf* (transl. Ralph Manheim, Pimlico, 1992), pp372-5
2 *Manchester Guardian*, 29 March 1934
3 Ibid.
4 R Fassolette, *Histoire politique du conflit des deux rugby en France*, pp180-3
5 Ibid.
6 H Garcia, *La Fabuleuse Histoire du Rugby*, p292
7 Fassolette, p193
8 Fassolette, pp204-7
9 Reproduced in Bonnery,p113
10 David Smith, *Left and Right in Twentieth Century Europe* (London 1970), p12

Chapter Fourteen: Collaboration and Conspiracy

1 *Rugby-Champagne* (Paris 1961) p41
2 Conversation with author, Canet, 23 August 1995
3 Interview, Toulouse, Oct-Nov 1985
4 The date is confirmed by Pascot in a statement published in *La Vie de la France sous l'Occupation*, vol.II, p875. Jean Larronde dates Pascot's official appointment as 8th September, soon after which he was made a colonel.
5 *La Dépêche*, 30 December 1940
6 Pascot's views are presented at length in his *Politique et doctrines sportives* (Paris 1944)
7 J-L Gay-Lescot, *Sport et Education sous Vichy*, p167
8 Bibliothèque Nationale, AG II 459 cc XXXIV
9 J-T Fieschi, *Histoire du sport français de 1870 à nos jours* (Paris 1983), p 100
10 Ibid., p103
11 Interview, Villeurbanne, October 1993
12 Letter of Mme Galia to author, 18 June 1996, and subsequent conversation, Toulouse, 30 March 1998
13 Conversation with author, October 1993
14 Ibid
15 Conversation, Oct 1993
16 Bibliothèque Nationale, AG II 543 cc 142
17 Letter to author, 5 July 1995
18 Quoted in Bonnery, p115
19 Ibid., p105

Chapter Fifteen: The Heretical tradition

1 Among them Gaston Bénac (Paris-Soir, 2 January 1934)
2 Suggested, for example, in *L'Indépendant des Pyrénées*, 15 May 1934
3 UA Titley and R McWhirter, *Centenary History of the Rugby Football Union*, 1970, p112
4 Jean Giraudoux, *Le conflit international du rugby* in *Les annales politiques et litteraires*, 15 March 1931, pp249-50
5 Ibid.
6 J-T Fieschi, *Histoire du sport français de 1870 à nos jours* (Paris 1983), p78
7 *L'Indépendant*, 25 August 1934
8 *La Dépêche*, 3 November 1998
9 *La Dépêche*, 4 November 1998
10 *L'Equipe*, 12 November 1998
11 *Treize* no 171, September 1995
12 Letter to author, 5 March 1997
13 *News Chronicle*, 22 November 1945
14 *Rugby*, no 358, 30 July 1938, quoted in Fassolette, *Rugby à XIII ou Jeu à XIII*, September 1997
15 Conversation with author, Villeneuve-sur-Lot, 18 August 1994
16 *Champions dans la coulisse*, p190
17 Quoted in Bonnery, *Le Rugby à XIII le plus français du monde*, pp114-5
18 *Paris-Presse*, 4 February 1945
19 Jean Larronde, letter to author, 22 June 1998
20 *The Times*, 10 January 1953
21 *Morning Advertiser*, 31 December 1947
22 Fassolette, op. cit., p16
23 Quoted in Lucien Remplon, *Ombres noires et soleils rouges: histoire du rugby au Stade Toulousain*, p77
24 Bénac, op. cit., p190
25 *La fabuleuse histoire du rugby*, p286
26 *L'Auto*, 1 November 1940
27 Conversation with author
28 Letter to author, 8 September 1995
29 Dedicated to the work of Toulouse-Lautrec
30 Jean Roques, *Calendrier-revue du Racing-Club Albigeois*, 1958-59

Afterword:

1 AFP, Oct 1997
2 Ibid.
3 Ibid.
4 Letter to Minister, 17th February 1998
5 *La politique du sport et de l'éducation physique en France pendant l'occupation*, Report presented to Marie-George Buffet, the Minister for Youth and Sport, Paris, March 2002

SELECT BIBLIOGRAPHY

Barran, Robert,
Le Rugby des villages, Paris, Les Editeurs Français Réunis, 1974

Barnoud, René,
Quel drôle de ballon,
Lyon, A Rey, 1977

Bénac, Gaston,
Champions dans la coulisse, Toulouse, Editions de l'Actualité Sportive, 1944

Bodis, J-P,
Histoire mondiale du rugby, Toulouse, Editions Privat, 1987

Bodis, J-P and
Lafond, Pierre,
Encyclopédie du rugby français, Editions Dehedin, 1989

Bonnery, Louis,
Le Rugby à XIII le plus français du monde, Limoux, Cano & Franck, 1996

Bonnery, Louis and
Thomas, Raymond,
Le Jeu à XIII, Paris, PUF, 1986

Camo, Ernest, *Max Rousié, Le dieu du stade*, Villeneuve-sur-Lot, Imp. Louis Moulinié, n.d.

Camo, Ernest,
Souvenirs de vingt ans de vie avec mon ami Jean Galia, Villeneuve-sur-Lot, Imp. Louis Moulinié, n.d.

Delaney, Trevor,
The International Grounds of Rugby League, Delaney, 1995

Durand, Yves,
Vichy 1940-44, Paris, Bordas, 1972

Dutourd, Jean,
Au bon beurre, Paris, Gallimard, 1952

Fassolette, Robert,
Histoire politique du conflit des deux rugby en France, unpubl. thesis, INSEP, 1996

Fassolette, Robert,
Rugby à XIII ou Jeu à XIII, abstract from INSEP thesis, September 1997

Fieschi, J-T,
Histoire du sport français de 1870 à nos jours, Paris, PAC, 1983

Garcia, Henri,
La fabuleuse histoire du rugby, Editions ODIL, Paris, 1973

Garcia, Henri,
Rugby-Champagne, Paris, Editions de la table ronde, 1961

Gay-Lescot, Jean-Louis,
Sport et Education sous Vichy (1940-44), Lyon, PUL, 1991

Halls, WD,
The Youth of Vichy France, Oxford, OUP, 1981

Hitler, Adolf,
Mein Kampf,
translated by Ralph Manheim, London, Pimlico, 1992

Holt, Richard,
Sport and Society in Modern France, London, Macmillan, 1981

Horne, Alistair,
To Lose a Battle: France 1940, London, Macmillan, 1964

Kedward, HR,
Occupied France, Collaboration and Resistance 1940-44, Oxford, Basil Blackwell, 1985

Kedward, HR,
Resistance in Vichy France, Oxford, OUP, 1978

Lacouture, Jean,
Voyous et gentlemen: une histoire du rugby, Paris, Gallimard, 1993

Michel, Henri,
Histoire de la résistance en France, Paris, PUF, 1984

Michel, Henri,
Vichy Année 40, Paris, Laffont, 1966

Noguères, Henri,
Histoire de la Résistance en France, Paris, Laffont, 1969

Nolte, Ernst,
Three Faces of Fascism, Munich, R Piper & Co Verlag, 1969

Passamar, André,
L'Encyclopédie de Treize-magazine, Toulouse, Treize-magazine, 1984

Pastre, Georges,
Histoire générale du rugby, Toulouse, Editions Midi-Olympique, 1968

Paxton, RO,
Vichy France, Old Guard and New Order 1940-44, Knopf, 1972

Remplon, Lucien,
Ombres noires et soleils rouges: histoire du rugby au Stade Toulousain, Toulouse, Gazette Editions, 1998

Rioux, Jean-Pierre (ed.),
La Vie culturelle sous Vichy, Brussels, Editions Complexe, 1990

Ruby, Marcel,
La Résistance et la Contre-résistance à Lyon et en Rhône-Alpes, Lyon, Editions Horvath, 1995

Smith, David,
Left and Right in 20th Century Europe, Longman, 1970

Smyth, Sir John,
Jean Borotra, the Bounding Basque, His Life of Work and Play, London, Stanley Paul, 1974

Voivenel, Paul,
Mon beau rugby, Toulouse, L'Héraklès, 1942

Hoover Institute,
La Vie de la France sous l'Occupation, Paris, Plon, 1957

Le Calendrier-revue du Racing-Club Albigeois 13 1958-59

Le Livre d'or du Racing-Club de Roanne, 1948

Les Deux Rugbys dans l'Aude, Conseil Général de l'Aude (Service des Sports), 1998

Treize-magazine, no 57, April 1984; no 151, September 1993

XIII Catalan, Cinquante ans d'épopée, Perpignan, Editions du Castillet, 1984

MAPS AND TABLES

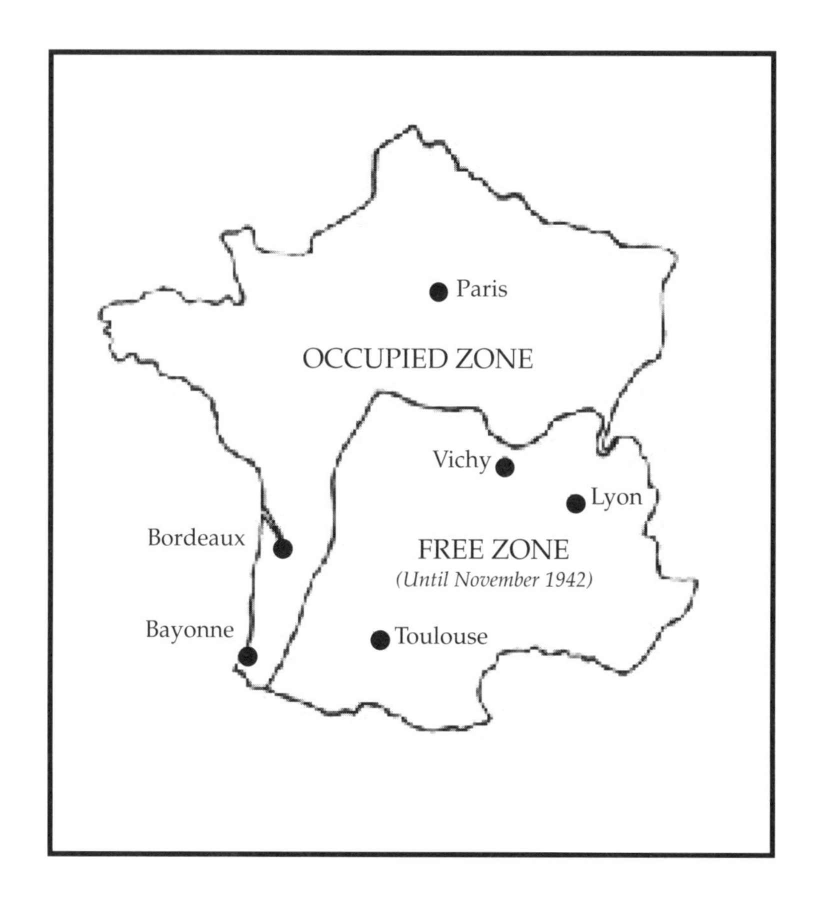

FRANCE 1940-42

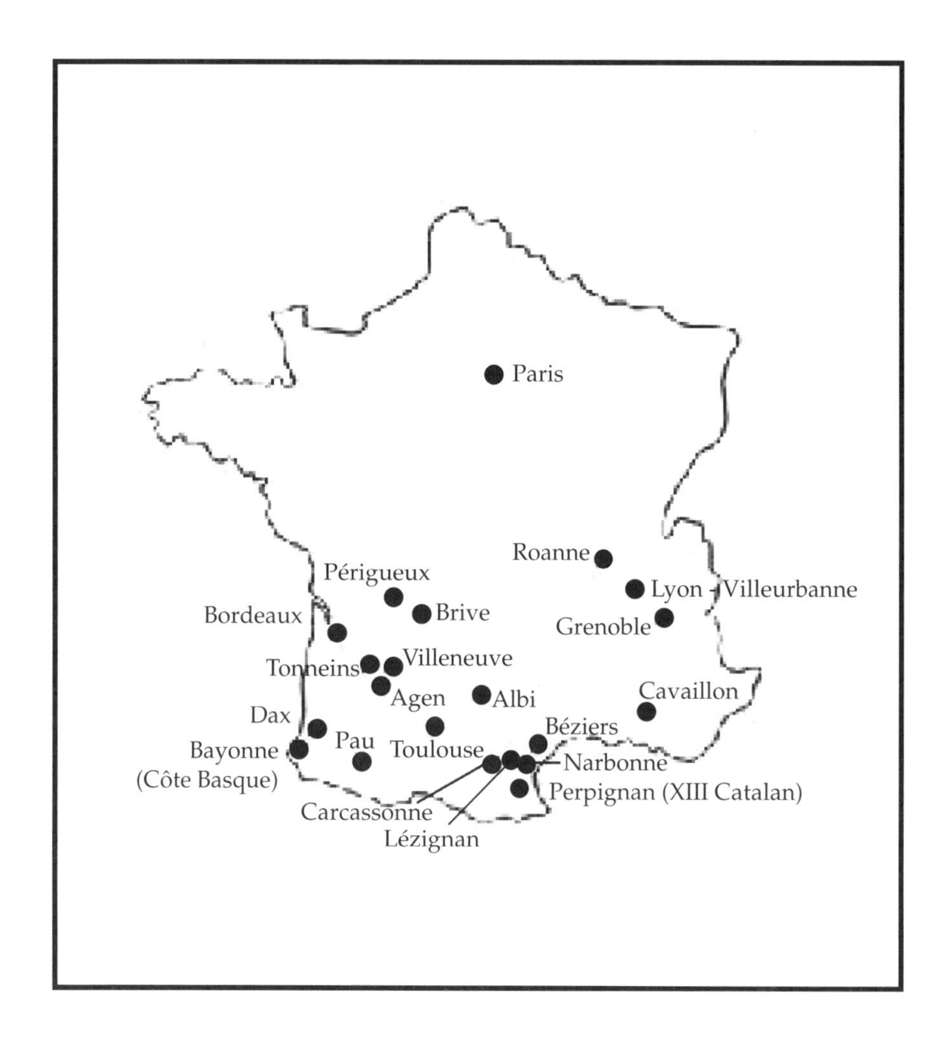

THE PROFESSIONAL CLUBS
WHICH BECAME ESTABLISHED 1934-40

SEASON 1934-35

	Played	Points
Villeneuve	18	49
Bordeaux	18	42
Lyon-Villeurbanne	16	40
Roanne	16	40
Pau	16	34
XIII Catalan	17	33
Albi	17	26
Paris	16	25
Côte Basque	15	21
Béziers	13	15

(Three points for a win, two for a draw, one for a loss)

For the first and only time in the history of French rugby league, the championship was decided on points, Villeneuve taking the inaugural title.

Each club should have played 18 matches, playing against all the others on a home-and-away basis, although because of the problems associated with grounds only Villeneuve and Bordeaux managed to complete their full set of fixtures.

SEASON 1935-36

The competition expanded to 14 clubs, divided into two pools of seven which finished the season in the following order:

POOL A	POOL B
Bordeaux	XIII Catalan
Villeneuve	Lyon-Villeurbanne
Côte Basque	Roanne
Paris XIII	Albi
Pau	Celtic de Paris
Dax	Périgueux
Agen *(withdrew after 3 matches)*	Gallia de Toulouse *(withdrew after 2 matches)*

A system of play-offs was introduced, the top four in each pool qualifying. In the semi-finals XIII Catalan beat Roanne and Bordeaux defeated Lyon-Villeurbanne.

XIII Catalan became champions after beating Bordeaux 25-14 at the Parc des Sports de Suzon, Bordeaux in front of 14,150 spectators. Referee: Mr Dobson (Featherstone).

SEASON 1936-37

The Ligue decided to revert to a single pool of ten teams, whose final standings were:

	Played	Points
XIII Catalan	18	50
Bordeaux	17	41
Roanne	18	40
Côte Basque	18	40
Lyon-Villeurbanne	18	38
Albi	18	37
Villeneuve	17	33
Dax	17	30
Paris	16	21
Pau	17	19

A top-four play-off resulted in XIII Catalan beating Côte Basque and Bordeaux defeating Roanne.

The final was won by Bordeaux on home ground at Parc Suzon when they defeated XIII Catalan by 23-10. The crowd figure was given as 14,300 with a further 4,000 locked out. The referee was Mr F Peel of Bradford.

SEASON 1937-38

The arrival of Toulouse Olympique increased the number of clubs to eleven, although Toulouse's late start to the season and the Australian tour disrupted the original programme of matches.

	Played	Points
Lyon-Villeurbanne	19	46
Roanne	18	43
Côte Basque	17	42
Bordeaux	19	42
XIII Catalan	18	41
Villeneuve	18	41
Albi	19	34
Toulouse	15	33
Paris	20	30
Dax	18	22
Pau	15	19

A top-eight play-off eventually resulted in a final between Albi and Villeneuve, who had beaten Bordeaux and Roanne respectively.

Albi became champions from seventh place when they defeated Villeneuve 8-3 at Parc Suzon, Bordeaux, watched by 14,880 spectators. Referee: Mr Howell.

SEASON 1938-39

The championship expanded to 14 clubs with the arrival of Narbonne, Carcassonne, Cavaillon and Brive. Paris, however, withdrew from the competition.

All matches were played in a single pool and each club, with the exception of Dax who withdrew after 9 matches, completed a full fixture list of matches home and away against every other club.

	Points	Difference
Roanne	65	+345
Villeneuve	58	+127
Carcassonne	58	+26
Bordeaux	56	+156
Toulouse	54	+125
XIII Catalan	48	+132
Lyon-Villeurbanne	47	-53
Albi	46	+96
Côte Basque	43	+3
Cavaillon	35	-130
Brive	34	-245
Narbonne	34	-320
Pau	26	-251
Dax	*(Withdrew after 9 matches)*	

In the semi-final play-offs Villeneuve defeated Carcassonne while Roanne knocked out Bordeaux.

Roanne became champions after defeating Villeneuve 9-0 at the Stade Vélodrome de Lescure, Bordeaux in front of 15,788 paying spectators, with approximately 4,000 others having complimentary tickets. Referee: Mr F Peel (Bradford).

SEASON 1939-40

A war-time championship of two pools, beginning in December 1939, was instituted as follows:

Pool A (7 teams): XIII Catalan, Lézignan, Narbonne, Toulouse, Albi, Carcassonne, Millau
Pool B (6 teams): Côte Basque, Pau, Villeneuve, Bordeaux, Agen Sportif, Tonneins

In the semi-final play-offs XIII Catalan defeated Villeneuve and Pau beat Albi. XIII Catalan and Pau met in the final at the Stade des Minimes, Toulouse, watched by 10,000 spectators. XIII Catalan won 20-16.

COUPE DE FRANCE 1934-40

1935 Lyon-Villeurbanne beat XIII Catalan 22-7 at Toulouse
1936 Côte Basque beat Villeneuve 15-8 at Bordeaux
1937 Villeneuve beat XIII Catalan 12-6 at Bordeaux
1938 Roanne beat Villeneuve 36-12 at Toulouse
1939 XIII Catalan beat Toulouse 7-3 at Toulouse
1940 Not played

INDEX

M. Benjamin (Maurice), agent technique de 1re classe de l'aéronautique, a été révoqué.

SECRÉTARIAT D'ÉTAT A L'ÉDUCATION NATIONALE ET A LA JEUNESSE

N° 5285. — Décret du 19 décembre 1941 portant dissolution de l'association dite Ligue française de rugby à treize.

Nous, Maréchal de France, chef de l'Etat français,

Vu la loi du 20 décembre 1940 relative à l'organisation sportive;

Sur la proposition du secrétaire d'Etat à l'éducation nationale et à la jeunesse,

Décrétons:

Art. 1er. — L'association dite Ligue française de rugby à treize, dont le siège social est à Paris, 24, rue Drouot, est dissoute, l'agrément lui ayant été refusé.

Art. 2. — Le patrimoine de l'association dissoute, en vertu du précédent article, est transféré sans modification au Comité national des sports, qui en assume toutes les charges, et qui sera représenté aux opérations de liquidation par son secrétaire général, M. Charles Denis, officier de la Légion d'honneur.

Art. 3. — Le secrétaire d'Etat à l'éducation nationale et à la jeunesse est chargé de l'exécution du présent décret, qui sera publié au *Journal officiel*.

Fait à Vichy, le 19 décembre 1941.

PH. PÉTAIN.

Par le Maréchal de France, chef de l'Etat français:

Le secrétaire d'Etat à l'éducation nationale et à la jeunesse,
JÉRÔME CARCOPINO.

The government decree banning rugby league in France, as published in the Official Journal